Hanging Out in the Virtual Pub

Hanging Out in the Virtual Pub

Masculinities and Relationships Online

Lori Kendall

UNIVERSITY OF CALIFORNIA PRESS

BERKELEY   LOS ANGELES   LONDON

Portions of this work previously appeared in slightly different form in the following sources and are reprinted here by permission of the publishers: "'Oh No! I'm a NERD!' White Masculinities Online," *Gender and Society* 14(2): 256–74. © 2000 Sage Publications. "'The Nerd Within': Mass Media and the Negotiation of Identity among Computer-Using Males," *Journal of Men's Studies* 7(3): 353–69, 1998; "Are You Male or Female? The Performance of Gender on Muds," in *Everyday Inequalities: Critical Inquiries,* ed. Judith Howard and Jody O'Brien (Malden, Mass.: Blackwell Publishers, 1998); "Meaning and Identity in 'Cyberspace': The Performance of Gender, Class, and Race Online," *Symbolic Interaction* 21(2): 129–53. © 1998 JAI Press.

University of California Press
Berkeley and Los Angeles, California

University of California Press, Ltd.
London, England

Library of Congress Cataloging-in-Publication Data

Kendall, Lori, 1958–
  Hanging out in the virtual pub : masculinities and relationships on-line / Lori Kendall.
      p.   cm.
  Includes bibliographical references and index.
  ISBN 0–520–23036–1 (cloth : alk. paper).—ISBN 0–520–23038–8 (pbk. : alk. paper)
    1. Internet—social aspects.   2. Multi-user dungeons—social aspects.   3. Social interaction.   4. Interpersonal relations.   5. Men—Identity.   6. Masculinity. I. Title.

HM851 .K46 2002
303.48'33—dc21   2001004246

Manufactured in the United States of America
10 09 08 07 06 05 04 03 02 01
10 9 8 7 6 5 4 3 2 1

Contents

Acknowledgments

I owe a great many debts of thanks to many people who contributed to my efforts on this project. This book began as my dissertation research, and I thank the Regents of the University of California for fellowship grant money that assisted in the completion of the dissertation. My dissertation committee members, Vicki Smith and Nina Wakeford, provided critiques, encouragement, and pointers to information and resources I might have missed. I was also fortunate to participate in a writing support group, which included Estee Neuwirth, Ellen Scott, and Bindi Shah, all of whom read many chapters (multiple times) and helped me achieve greater clarity of thought and expression. In addition, many other colleagues provided critical readings, commentary, and emotional support, including Fred Block, Cliff Cheng, Martha Copp, Jim Doyle, Michael Flaherty, Judy Howard, Steve Jones, Vernon Lee, Lyn Lofland, Nick Mamatas, Melinda Milligan, Peter Nardi, Judy Newton, Jodi O'Brien, Marc Smith, and Mary Virnoche. I give special thanks to Lynn Cherny and Eva Skuratowicz for their friendship and support, especially throughout the dissertation process.

I owe a special debt of thanks to Judy Stacey. She acted as a superlative dissertation chair and was also instrumental in helping me bring this work through the crucial transition from dissertation to publication. In addition to her incisive critiques and an uncanny ability to push my thinking further, she has provided me with ample advice and encouragement. In short, she has been everything one could wish for in a mentor and supportive colleague.

This book was also greatly improved by many people at the University of California Press. Among them, Naomi Schneider was instrumental in shepherding this project through many revisions. Erika Büky and Robin Whitaker very skillfully edited the manuscript and helped me clarify numerous passages. Any remaining errors are mine.

I also owe many thanks to the people of BlueSky, whom I unfortunately cannot name here. In addition to being open and honest, they were extremely generous throughout the research project, providing me with information, technical assistance, friendship, and in some cases, shelter and meals. They have been extraordinarily willing to tolerate my scrutiny and questions even when they sometimes disagreed with my conclusions and analysis. I hope they find something of value in my portrayal of them here.

Finally, thanks to Jerry McDonough for his strong and constant support of this work and its author. His specific contributions are far too numerous to list.

1 Blue Sky in the Morning

Late one morning in Berkeley in November 1994, I head off to my local pub. I'm hoping someone there will have heard from Rob, a friend currently en route to California from Colorado. I'm supposed to meet Rob later in the afternoon at UC Davis, seventy miles east of Berkeley, but don't want to make the trip if he's been held up by snows over the pass at Tahoe. Even if I do drive to Davis, I'll spend lunchtime here at the Falcon, where I can always find people I know, chatting and hanging out for a bit.

The Falcon is a small, out-of-the-way place, known mainly to its regulars, who tend to shun the occasional curious passersby. The utilitarian furnishings look a bit worn and include so many different styles that one patron says it looks "as though a used furniture store had exploded." A large schoolroom chalkboard hangs next to the bar. Today when I enter, the heading at the top of the chalkboard reads "Fave of the 50 Ways to Leave Your Lover." Various bar patrons have listed a phrase next to their name:

Fave of the 50 Ways to Leave Your Lover

OD on Crack, Jack
Sell the pics to the paper, Draper
Reveal that you're gay, Ray.
Give her the slip, Flip
Glue her to the wall, Paul
Slip Out The Back, Jack
hit her with a truck, buck
Don't like your new Teddy, Freddy
Be Seeing You, Lou
Change the locks, doc
move, no forwarding address, bess
Blow her away, Jay

As usual around lunchtime, the bar is crowded. A few people sit singly at tables, but most sit in small groups, often milling around from table to table to chat with others. As in many such local bars and pubs, most of the regulars here are male. Many of them work for a handful of computer companies in a nearby high-tech industry enclave. The atmosphere is loud, casual, and clubby, even raucous. Everybody knows each other too well here to expect privacy at any of the tables.

After exchanging greetings with several people, I ask if anyone has heard from Rob in the last twenty-four hours. "Does anyone know where he's staying in Reno?" Eric, a slight, pale, scholarly-looking young man with long hair pulled back into a ponytail, waves from one of the corner tables. People often retreat to the quieter corners when they've brought work to do into the bar. He calls, "I heard he departed Steve's [in Colorado], but nothing since." I reply, "Last I heard he was stuck in Reno due to snow, but he was supposed to call this morning, and I haven't heard from him. I wonder if he got chains?" Eric shrugs, shakes his head, and returns to his work.

At a table near the bar, Dave, a big, tall white man in a long leather coat, breaks into song, "Oh-a-wishing well will ya give me what ah want, will the prahce be no ob-ject?" Sam, a short, stocky Filipino, counters with, "That's the sound of the men working on the chain . . . ga-a-ang. That's the sound of the men working on the chain . . . g-a-a-ang." Adding to the cacophony, Rick grabs a microphone set into the wall near the bar and announces, "CHALKBOARD!" In response, Mike gets up and adds "Keel over dead, Fred" to the chalkboard.

Meanwhile John shows Sam an ad in the paper for an upcoming music store sale, and they discuss prices on guitar stands. Dave, finished with his singing, shouts out, "I HUNGER!" Chris stands up from the same table and calls out, "HUNGER ROLL CALL!" Chris, Sam, Dave, and I raise our hands; Rick shakes his head no and waves the Power Bar he's eating.

Andrea, a petite woman with lightly tanned skin and short brown hair, enters the bar. Mike, happy to see her, comes over and gives her a big hug, then picks her up and, pretending she's a football, starts running across the room with her as she laughs, a bit bewildered. Greg shouts out, "Don't spike her in the end zone!" then blushes wildly and insists he didn't intend the double entendre. "I just meant don't throw her down on her head!" Several others nearby roll their eyes, and Andrea smirks at Greg.

At the table where I've taken a seat, Mike, John, Sam, and Chris engage in a mock argument over the relative virtues of stringed instruments versus keyboards. When the argument dies down, I ask, "Should I assume

Rob bought chains and drive to Davis where he originally was supposed to meet me? Or should I assume he's stuck in Reno and wait in Berkeley to hear what he's doing?"

Chris smirks at me and says, "Chains! Kinky!"

John says, "I would just go with the original plan. It's up to him to call you if he does something weird."

Chris persists, "So what would you and Rob be doing with chains, hmmmm?"

I laugh and whap Chris lightly on the shoulder.

John glares at Chris. "That joke is getting old, boyeee."

Mike chimes in, "Chris, that dead horse, he ain't gonna move no matter how hard you kick."

In response, Chris pulls a large lever, and a trapdoor opens under John, who falls through the floor. Conversation continues normally, and a few minutes later John returns through a door at the back.

. . .

Well, it didn't quite happen like that. It's true that most bars don't have trapdoors conveniently located exactly beneath the patron you wish to chastise. You may have guessed by now that the Falcon's location is not a back street in Berkeley. The Falcon is a hangout on an online forum called BlueSky.[1] I've presented an approximation of a set of conversations that occurred online and entirely through text. I did visit the Falcon on that November morning and greet people who were already there. "John" did get annoyed with "Chris" for harping on a bad joke. Chris's retaliation involved a text command to the computer program that runs BlueSky, causing the character that John uses online to be shunted from the Falcon to another "room" on BlueSky.

By introducing BlueSky, the Falcon, and some of its patrons in this way, I risk implying that I and the other BlueSky participants spend our time online enacting an elaborate pantomime of bar behavior. Perhaps we even appear to take our virtual metaphors too seriously. But rather than present the above narrative as an example of what "really" happens online, I propose it as something akin to the *feel* of interactions on BlueSky (although the Falcon is usually much more chaotic than the above exchange conveys, as may become apparent later). True, sitting down at a computer and logging on to BlueSky differs significantly from walking down the street and into a neighborhood pub. For one thing, Eric would never be able to get work done in such a boisterous place were it not merely a window on his computer screen that he can ignore at will. But the bar metaphor encompasses the friendliness, random bursts of song lyrics, joshing, and mock (and occasionally more serious) arguments that occur on BlueSky. Also, the online textual description of the Falcon plays into the metaphor, describing the site as a bar "with myriad tables and chairs of every conceivable material, height, and design, as though a used furniture store had exploded," and BlueSky participants themselves use the local-pub metaphor to explain their relationships with each other and the appeal of hanging out on BlueSky.

In the ethnography of BlueSky that I present here, I use the pub metaphor to help interpret BlueSky's social world. Although participation on the Internet is increasing, probably more people are familiar with bars than with Internet chat spaces, if not from their own experience, then from media representations of bars, such as the television program *Cheers*. The bar or pub metaphor also conveys something of the character of the social space on BlueSky, the participants' relationships, and their use of the social space that BlueSky provides (Byrne 1978). Because the clientele is mostly male, the Falcon provides a space in which people enact and negotiate masculine identities within a particular class and race context (Cavan 1966; LeMasters 1975; Katovich and Reese 1987; Smith 1985; Communication Studies 298, 1997). The territoriality of BlueSky's distinct group of "regulars" also resembles that of the patrons of a neighborhood bar (Cavan 1966; Katovich and Reese 1987; Smith 1985).

TEXTUAL VIRTUAL REALITIES

BlueSky is a type of interactive, text-only online forum known as a *mud*. "Mud" originally stood for "Multi-User Dungeon," based on the original multiperson networked Dungeons & Dragons–type game called MUD. Muds are also sometimes referred to as Multi-User Domains or Dimensions. For a time, one could quickly start a "flame war" on one of the Usenet mudding newsgroups by making a statement about what the acronym MUD means.[2] To oversimplify the arguments greatly, some participants seek to deemphasize the historical connection between muds and earlier Dungeons & Dragons games, while others see this as an unrealistic "sanitizing" of the historical record. Although I am more sympathetic to those who seek to acknowledge muds' lineage, herein I take a third path, referring to muds in the lower case (except where I quote other written materials) to deemphasize the acronym and its origin. Participants use the term "mud" as both a noun and a verb. "Mud" can refer to a type of mud program or to a particular social space using such a program. "Mudding" refers to participation on muds, and a "mudder" is a mud participant. By using "mud" as a word rather than as an acronym, I reproduce mudders' own terminology and also reflect the increasing recognition of muds as a particular genre of online forum.[3]

As in other online chat programs, people use Internet accounts to connect to mud programs running on various remote computers. They can then communicate through typed text with other people currently connected to that mud. Muds also allow participants to create programmed "objects," which convey the feeling of being in a place, adding richness to the social environment. Hundreds of muds are available on the Internet. Many still operate as gaming spaces. Others are used for meetings, for pedagogical purposes, and as social spaces.

Muds can be considered a type of text-based "virtual reality" in that people have the feeling of being present together in a social space. Stone has suggested that in fact several types of text can constitute forms of virtual reality or at least have served as part of the continuum in the historical development of "cyberspace." She proposes as a starting point in this continuum the seventeenth-century exchange of written descriptions of experiments among scholars. "By means of such writing, a group of people were able to 'witness' an experiment without being physically present" (1991: 86). Anderson (1991) similarly describes the role of textual representation in the creation of a feeling of community among dispersed people in his analysis of newspapers as key to the formation of national identities in the New World.[4]

Other media may similarly connect geographically dispersed people and provide a sense of connection with people never encountered face-to-face. For instance, like the long-standing tradition of travel narratives (Pratt 1986), television's *You Are There* promises people a "visit" to other times and places so they can get to "know" people they may never meet. Adams suggests that television itself can also be viewed as a place, to the extent that it is "(1) a bounded system in which symbolic interaction among persons occurs (a social context), and (2) a nucleus around which ideas, values, and shared experiences are constructed (a center of meaning)" (1992: 118). As such, television provides viewers with the experience that they are interacting with others, either through vicarious identification with people and places viewed on it, or through the knowledge that large numbers of dispersed others are also viewing the same images.

By the same logic, online forums can also be viewed as places. World Wide Web pages provide experiences similar to television in that they often provide pictures (sometimes even motion pictures) of other people and places and can similarly be viewed by multiple, remote others. The term "surfing," ubiquitously used to describe browsing on the web, also derives from television experience, in which people "channel surf." The variety of material available on the web exceeds that found on television, and the experience of choosing links to follow may provide an even greater sense of going somewhere. The World Wide Web also enhances the possibilities of interconnection with others in that some web pages include links to chat spaces. Some also display the number of "hits" so far—that is, the number of times a page has been accessed. This statistic allows people to imagine the number of others who have shared their viewing experience and even allows them to compare popularity of websites.

More interactive forums—such as e-mail lists, newsgroups, and chat rooms—provide an even greater feeling of contact with remote others because they allow people to interact and respond to each other. Of these, "synchronous" forums—those that allow for near-instantaneous response (including the various chat programs and muds but not including e-mail lists and newsgroups)—can provide a particularly vivid sense of "place" and of gathering together with other people. Rather than merely viewing a space through the electronic window of television, many people feel that when they connect to an online forum, they in some sense enter a social, if not a physical, space. Conversation in such chat forums takes place at a pace similar to face-to-face conversation, the room description and most of the objects remain stable from visit to visit, and people's entrances and exits generate text messages that allow them to "see" each other come and go.

Researchers have also described bulletin boards systems (BBSs) as giving people a sense of group membership in a common place (Baym 1995; Correll 1995; Myers 1987). For instance, Correll (1995) indicates that participants on the Lesbian Cafe describe it as a space. BBSs enable participants to post messages and read what others have posted. These messages resemble e-mail more than synchronous conversation. Even if people are logged on to the computer system at the same time, with posts and responses occurring in fairly rapid succession, they have less of a feeling of sharing the same space and time than participants in synchronous forums have. On the Lesbian Cafe, participants frequently had to redescribe "objects" in order to maintain the spatial metaphor. Object descriptions changed depending on the messages people wanted to convey and because of their forgetfulness. Also, lag time between posts decreases the sense of copresence. Although gaps in conversational rhythm also occur on muds, often because of network slowdowns, they are usually brief. BlueSky participants almost always remark upon these instances of "lag," illustrating the extent to which time delays in communication disrupt the feeling of shared space and conversational competency.

"MULTITASKING" AND THE SELF

Meyrowitz, writing about television, suggests that "the information transmitted by electronic media is much more similar to face-to-face interaction than is the information conveyed by books or letters" (1985: 118). Although, superficially, muds and similar online forums bear a strong resemblance to texts, they may be closer to face-to-face interaction than television is. Muds are interactive and occur in "real time"; that is, participants are connected simultaneously, and communications are transferred back and forth nearly instantaneously. Rather than merely observe people with whom they cannot interact (as on television), participants on muds can engage in conversation with others, requesting more information, questioning representations, and redirecting topics of conversation. Thus, online interactions provide connections with other people who probably seem more "real" to most participants than people seen on a television screen.

Meyrowitz also argues that television "invades" the space of the viewer without completely displacing the reality of that physical space. Reading, on the other hand, requires fuller attention, such that "the reader tends to be removed from those physically present" (1985: 124). While Meyrowitz may overestimate the engrossment necessary for reading, his description of the dual reality created by television provides a useful perspective on mud participation. Like television, muds enter the participant's physical locale without completely redefining it. Online interactions can at times become intensely engrossing, and some participants report experiencing physical sensations that echo the experiences of the characters who serve as their online representatives, or analogues.[5] However, while participating in social interaction online, mud participants may also be participating in other online or offline activities. In any case, each participant has a physical body that remains involved in experiences separate from the interactions occurring online.

For instance, when mudding for long periods of time, I frequently leave the computer to get food, go to the bathroom, or respond to someone in the physical room in which I'm sitting. If the text appearing on my screen slows to a crawl or the conversation ceases to interest me, I may cast about for something else offline to engage me, picking up the day's mail or flipping through a magazine. Thus although the mud provides for me a feeling of being in a place, that place in some sense overlays the physical place in which my body resides. Both "places" constitute a type of reality, and either may engross my attention, but the mud place remains more ephemeral, transparent, and easily disrupted by events in the physical world. Muds are particularly vulnerable to events such as power loss or modem disconnection, which can abruptly destroy the conceptual space of the mud, dropping me back fully into experience of the physical world.

This split in attention between two experiential worlds or places introduces a problem with viewing cyberspace as a separate sovereign world. Nobody inhabits *only* cyberspace. Online participation requires the form of split attention I have described, as many media experiences do (reading, movies, radio, etc.).[6] Most BlueSky participants report a well-developed ability to "multitask." They use this term, derived from computer hardware operations,[7] to refer to engaging in several forms of online interaction and media use simultaneously. Many use computer windowing systems that allow them to view multiple online spaces, or they split their attention between the computer screen and television, radio, or other offline activities. BlueSky participants frequently mud while at work and use their ability to multitask to get work done while they socialize online. Indeed, many of my interviewees reported acquiring the ability to multitask specifically through their mud participation.

Some commentators have suggested that such attention splits result in understandings of the self as multiple (Stone 1995; Turkle 1995). To the extent that people make different presentations of self in different forums, multitasking does provide evidence of the multiplicity of the self. However, Goffman (1959, 1974) suggests that, despite the ability to adapt our presentation of self to accommodate different social situations, people resist viewing the self as performative. To some extent, our performances of identity acquire their meaning precisely from the belief that they are not performances. We organize social life to allow us to tell meaningful stories about ourselves, while accomplishing a "sleight-of-hand" concealment of the distance between the "I" that tells the story and the "I" about whom the story is told (Goffman 1974).[8]

Although people seek essentialized bases for themselves and the selves they encounter online, the performative nature of identity there seems almost unavoidably obvious. Tales abound of multiple and fluid identities and of online deceptions and revelations (McRae 1997; Reid 1994; Rheingold 1993; Stone 1995; Turkle 1995). Online participation enables the creation of multiple personae, facilitating varying presentations of self. However, people also engage in different presentations of self to different audiences in other arenas of everyday life and did so before online forums existed. Both Goffman (1959, 1963, 1974) and Gergen (1991) document numerous pre-Internet examples of this multiplicity of identity performance. But despite the mundaneness of such splits and fractures of identity, people (in U.S. and similar cultures, at any rate) still tend to perceive their identities and selves as integral and continuous. They persist in describing themselves in essential, unchanging terms. (For a discussion of a more relational experience of self, see Kondo 1990.)

SOCIOLOGICAL STUDY OF CYBERSPACE

As the use of online communication media has increased, so too have media and academic accounts of online life. These accounts have tended to treat cyberspace as a completely separate, isolated social world, "without taking into account how interactions on it fit with other aspects of people's lives" (Wellman 1997: 446).[9] A few works have begun to examine connections between online and offline interactions. While Baym's linguistic research on a Usenet newsgroup devoted to the discussion of soap operas does not specifically discuss the offline lives of the people she studied, she points out the importance of the "multiple external contexts" within which computer-mediated communications are situated (1995: 141). (See also Baym 1993, 1996, 2000.) Similarly, Turkle (1995) includes interview material from mud participants about their offline lives. However, her analysis focuses mostly on each individual's psychological profile and history, which she connects to the person's potential use of muds for personal growth and development. While she includes some discussion of the relationship of online socializing to changing political and economic realities, she relies mainly on interviews and participants' own descriptions of their experiences. This provides a view of online life that insufficiently distinguishes the very different social contexts of different forums and overemphasizes the degree of personal choice involved in online self-presentation.

Discussions that construct cyberspace as a distinctively different arena of social interaction emphasize the differences between online and offline interactions and suggest that offline "rules" concerning identity do not apply online. This stance is popular among both researchers and online participants. Turkle has proposed, for instance, that "technology is bringing a set of ideas associated with postmodernism . . . into everyday life" (1995: 18). Her interpretation of postmodernism specifically highlights multiplicity and fractured identity, and she suggests that a primary appeal of online interactions is the possibility for people to enact identities unavailable to them offline. "The Internet is another element of the computer culture that has contributed to thinking about identity as multiplicity. On it, people are able to build a self by cycling through many selves" (178).

Descriptions such as Turkle's characterize social effects as flowing mostly from cyberspace to the offline world, rather than the other way around. The identities people bring to their cyberspace interactions matter less in these stories than the new lessons of self they carry with them from their online interactions. This represents cyberspace as a separate but equivalent social arena, with its own rules and logic. It also suggests that the existence of online forums represents a distinct break from previous social life and implies that online interactions provide experiences unavailable offline, some of which have powerful effects on people's selves.

Such a portrayal finds favor with many online participants, for whom it offers the hope of a "postmodern" transformation of "modern" society. For instance, John Perry Barlow, a well-known net personality, commentator, and writer, wrote "A Declaration of the Independence of Cyberspace" in response to the signing of a United States law that would impose limits on online communications.[10] Barlow's manifesto addresses itself to "Governments of the Industrial World":

> I declare the global social space we are building to be naturally independent of the tyrannies you seek to impose on us. . . . [Cyberspace] is an act of nature and it grows itself through our collective actions. . . . We are creating a world that all may enter without privilege or prejudice accorded by race, economic power, military force, or station of birth. . . . Your legal concepts of property, expression, identity, movement, and context do not apply to us. . . . Our identities have no bodies, so, unlike you, we cannot obtain order by physical coercion. (Barlow 1996)

Barlow acknowledges that his declaration was written in "grandiose" terms. However, his assertion that cyberspace constitutes an *organically* separate, sovereign realm resonates with many net participants. His description highlights the absence of bodies in cyberspace (an absence that others have questioned; see, for instance, Wakeford 1996). This absence posits for cyberspace's "citizens" a bodiless identity that, he claims, negates the effects of privilege and prejudice. For many like Barlow, much of the hype and hope of cyberspace reside in its sovereignty and separation from "real life" and in its ability to correct the inequalities existing outside its boundaries.

However, this hope is called into question by recent research on gender online. A large and growing list of articles suggests that norms of gendered behavior continue to shape online interactions (Cherny 1994; Herring 1992, 1994, 1996a, b; Kramarae and Taylor 1993; Sutton 1994; We 1994). Herring (1994) suggests that women and men use different communication styles online and react differently to flaming. Gladys We similarly found that men tend to post more messages to Usenet newsgroups than women and that "when women speak up, they may be actively harassed" (1994: para. 54). Cherny studied a mud on which, as on BlueSky, many participants have met offline and have participated online together for several years. In mud interactions, she observed, "men use more physically violent imagery during conversation, and women are more physically affectionate towards other characters than men are" (1994: 102).

Cherny's work stands out from other research on muds in its attention to connections between participants' offline gender identity and their online gendered behavior. Her account contrasts with other research that suggests that online "gender switching" can change people's expectations and understandings of gender. Several recent works have proposed that such gender switching can lead to a greater understanding of gender as constructed and of the self as mutable (Bruckman 1992, 1993; Deuel 1995; Dickel 1995; Poster 1995; Turkle 1995; Burris and Hoplight 1996). As quasi-physical "hangouts" that allow for speechlike interactions among groups of people, muds in particular seem to inspire these kinds of hopes. For instance, Turkle states that muds allow people "the chance to discover . . . that for both sexes, gender is constructed" (1995: 223). Similarly, Bruckman suggests that "MUDding throws issues of the impact of gender on human relations into high relief. . . . It allows people to experience rather than merely observe what it feels like to be the opposite gender or have no gender at all" (1993: 4). Bruckman concludes that "the network is in the process of changing not just how we work, but how we think of ourselves—and ultimately, who we are" (5). Dickel also suggests that, rather than "reifying conventional, hegemonic gender bias" (1995: 105), which he acknowledges as a possibility existing on other online forums, muds allow a "play of gender within the imagination[, which] opens up . . . a destabilization of gender positions which might spread beyond the internet into the larger culture" (106). Poster, in even stronger terms, suggests that the ability of mudders to adopt a "fictional role that may be different from their actual gender . . . drastically call[s] into question the gender system of the dominant culture as a fixed binary" (1995: 31).

These accounts rely predominantly on participants' own assertions regarding the liberatory potential of their online interactions. Researchers have not generally contextualized these assertions by considering the social norms and expectations within the online groups or by using examples of online gender enactments. Such research reports thus fail to take into account potential discrepancies between what people say about the online experience and what they actually do online. They also tend to blur distinctions among identity performances, participant understandings of those performances, and the descriptions and assertions participants offer to outsiders.

Before hailing virtual life as ushering in a new sense of self-identity, we need to examine the meanings of online interactions. Without prematurely closing down whatever moment of disruptive possibility exists in the ambiguities of online identities, it is important to examine the ways in which relationships of power influence online interactions and are reinscribed within them. Through this ethnography of BlueSky, I attempt to provide examples of participants' performances of gender, race, and class identities along with their understanding of these performances. I further contextualize these performances and understandings through examination of the social contexts, both online and offline, within which they occur.

Given the popularity of themes of great transformation, many works published to date on the topic of online interactions not surprisingly take overly narrow utopian or dystopian views of such interactions. As Wellman suggests, such "criticisms and enthusiasms leave little room for the moderate, mixed situations that may be the reality" (1997: 446). My hope here is to provide a window into just such a mixed situation, where relationships both suffer and benefit from the conditions of online interactions and where participants both disrupt and reproduce power relations and hierarchies existing in offline social contexts.

In the chapters that follow, I include in my examination of BlueSky's social contexts the effects they have on people's online interactions, with an emphasis on gender. Participants bring particular backgrounds and understandings to their interpretations of each other's presentation of self online. I also look at what people gain from their online participation and what offline experience and knowledge they bring to their online interactions.

Chapters 2 and 3 provide background information about muds, their history and culture. Chapter 2 describes my research project. (Readers interested in more detail about my relationship as a researcher to BlueSky participants may wish also to read appendix B, in which I consider various practical and ethical issues involved in doing research online and discuss the relationship of my project to ethnography generally.) I also provide demographic information about BlueSky's participants and discuss the connections between their work with computers and their choice of BlueSky as a social and leisure forum. To help readers understand the chapters that follow, I also explain in chapter 2 some of the basic technical features of muds. Chapter 3 provides information about BlueSky's subculture and its relationship to other online subcultures. I detail BlueSky participants' use of various mud technological capabilities in the development and maintenance of their culture and interpersonal connections.

Chapter 4 provides the theoretical focus for the book. In it, I discuss gender, focusing on the particular masculinities performed on BlueSky and their relationship to hegemonic masculinity. The dominant masculine identity on BlueSky is connected to computer-related work. BlueSky participants enact masculinity in and through discussions related to work. I also discuss BlueSky participants' understanding of what it means to be a "nerd" and the advantages and disadvantages that BlueSky's male-dominated space provides for female participants.

Chapters 5 and 6 deal with identity and relationships mediated by computers, with particular attention to the effects of gender. In chapter 5, I discuss the effects of the mediated and networked character of Internet communications on online interaction. When combined with the cultural context of the Internet, such effects create a special vulnerability of online social groups. I also describe how exclusively textual communications can facilitate deception and lead to identity ambiguity and confusion. In chapter 6, I describe relationships among people on BlueSky and discuss some surprising advantages and disadvantages of socializing online. I examine some of the reasons people still find face-to-face contact important. Friendships also provide an important arena for the performance of gendered identities, and I demonstrate some of the ways people enact understandings of gender through group conversations. I argue that gender underlies and informs all relationships with others and that friendships recognize, reinforce, and/or reconstruct gendered identities.

Chapter 7 discusses class and race online. The class backgrounds of BlueSky participants enable their participation in a variety of ways and allow them to use BlueSky to support and continue their middle-class status. I also examine participants' perceptions of their own racial identities and the racial character of BlueSky. Online spaces remain predominantly white in both demographics and culture.

Finally, chapter 8 presents a summary analysis of identity and power on BlueSky.

2 Logging On
An Introduction to BlueSky

THE MYSTERY SPOT

On the day after New Year's Day in 1995, several BlueSky participants gather in henri's Bay Area apartment. evariste and Peg are in town from Minnesota, visiting evariste's family for the holidays. Ulysses and Mender have come from Philadelphia and Madison, respectively, for about a week to hang out with other BlueSky people. Several others from the West Coast, ranging from San Diego to Seattle, have also driven or flown in to join the party. I missed a couple of group dinners and the New Years' Eve party and have just barely managed to join the group in time for today's excursion to the Mystery Spot in Santa Cruz (an entertainment center that purports to exhibit unexplained gravitational phenomena). It's the first gathering of BlueSky participants I've attended, and I'm nervous driving up to the large apartment complex and knocking on henri's door.

Jet opens the door and graciously invites me in. A Chinese American, he's very tall and thin, with medium brown skin, straight, shoulder-length black hair, and an unusually deep voice. henri, an equally tall but stockier white man with short, sandy brown hair, comes out from the bedroom. I've met henri before, so he introduces me to everyone else. He refers to each person by both "real life" first name and mud name, thus allowing me to connect faces and offline names to mud names, with which I'm more familiar. Throughout the day, most people refer to each other by their offline first names, although occasionally a mud name slips out.[1] BlueSky participants not present are generally referred to by mud names only.

We're still waiting for a couple more people to join the group, so I sit down with the others in the living room. Four people are sitting on the floor playing a card game called Nuclear War, with frequent references to the rules, since the game is new to some of them. The others are seated on the floor or the few pieces of furniture, reading comic books and magazines or browsing henri's collection of science-fiction books. For a while nobody says much to me or anyone else. I watch the game, feeling aware of how different I am from the others in the room. I am the oldest here, and most of the rest look even younger than their years. They are also aware that I am observing them not just as someone meeting online acquaintances for the first time but as a researcher. Jet breaks the tension around this fact by acknowledging the lack of verbal interaction among them, saying, "Yes, this is what we do."

Finally, we pile into several cars and head off to pick up Susanah, who is currently staying at her parents' house. The plan is to stop at pez's house for lunch, and then drive to the Mystery Spot in Santa Cruz. The house pez shares with her mother and sister is in a semirural area outside San Jose. Everybody makes sandwiches and sits in the living room exchanging gossip about various muds and mudders, reminiscing about other group meetings, and discussing among other topics the value of comic book collections. In regard to the last, everybody defers to Ulysses, who apparently has the greatest knowledge on the subject. At their request, he modestly advises others on the worth of various older comic book issues and critically discusses the careers of particular comic book authors and artists.

We take photos of the group. Several weeks later, Jet will scan some of these in and post them to his website. I download these and store them on a disk along with other photos of BlueSky people I've previously acquired from various online locations. I have a printout of the group photo of me and the others from the Mystery Spot gathering displayed in my office at school. This display is partly motivated by a sort of group pride. But in addition, that photo is one of the few physical artifacts I have from the "field," one of the few things I can point to and say, "There's the subject of my research." For me, the desire for something tangible to display relates to ideas about what constitutes a "real" research site. A similar desire for tangible presence may underlie online acquaintances' efforts to meet in person.

Meanwhile, at the January gathering, we barely make it to the Mystery Spot, located off a winding road in the Santa Cruz mountains, in time for the last tour of the day. Guides take groups of visitors along a paved path through the woods, stopping at various points to provide "scientific" demonstrations, mostly based on the exploitation of optical illusions.

Our guide, a somewhat smug white man in his fifties with a hucksterish patter, annoys several in our group. Later, we get months of amusement from the guide's having called Locutus, with his young, androgynous face and long, wavy, honey-colored hair, "ma'am" and then compounded the error by calling pez, with her short hair and very quiet demeanor, "sir." Since that trip, people periodically refer to Locutus and pez as the "gender-ambiguous twins." These references both play with gender's potential fluidity and emphasize, by making a joke of the guide's "error," the normative expectations and taken-for-granted understanding that Locutus is "really" male, and pez is "really" female.

On the way back to henri's, I ride in the "party barge," a large van belonging to evariste's father. evariste plays a tape by Ministry, which everybody seems to know and enjoy except me. In my field notes, I've recorded, "I didn't care for it much. Growly distorted vocals. Very dark and vicious." The loud music and people's fatigue curtail conversation. This lack of interaction continues back at henri's, where we watch *Ren and Stimpy* cartoon videos for a while. Finally, exhausted, I drive back home. I think to myself that I'm really part of the group now. There's photographic proof.

A SOCIOLOGIST IN CYBERSPACE

Joining an offline gathering constitutes almost a rite of passage for online participants. Other BlueSky participants have expressed an understanding similar to my own feelings of "really" being part of the group after meeting people face-to-face. Such experiences form part of the continuum of online and offline connections among participants on online forums, demonstrating the interconnectedness of online and offline life. People who choose to enter online social spaces do not leave their offline world behind when they do so, but rather begin a process of weaving online communications and activities into their existing offline lives.

Far from being an experienced online participant, when I first decided to study interaction online I didn't even have an e-mail account. I was mostly unfamiliar with the Internet. I thus began my study of muds cautiously, by reading about muds on Usenet. Usenet, a bulletin board system distributed on the Internet, provides thousands of "newsgroups" on different topics of interest. Having heard of muds through people I met at the Computers, Freedom, and Privacy conference in the Bay Area in 1993, I started hunting for more information on the mud subculture by reading posts on the mud-related newsgroups.

By "lurking" on newsgroups (that is, reading posted messages without posting any myself), I gained familiarity with the mudding subculture before interacting with its members. This proved useful, particularly on

BlueSky, since it gave me an idea of the norms and practices on different muds. Reading the mud newsgroups also enabled me to acquire technical knowledge that helped me negotiate the variety of muds available online and the different computer commands necessary to access them. This knowledge proved to be particularly important in my early encounters with BlueSky, given the high level of computer skills and long years of mudding of most of its participants. (It did not, however, prevent confusion on my part during my first few weeks on muds.)

In May 1994, after about a year of familiarizing myself with the Internet and the mud subculture, I began visiting various social muds. I did not employ any single or consistent sampling strategy to select the muds I visited. Some muds I visited because they were "famous," having appeared in magazine articles about muds. Some I knew about because they had provoked controversy in discussions on the mud newsgroups. I visited one mud because it was suggested to me by other mud participants. Finally, I visited some muds because they had interesting names or themes.

This last motive was what drew me to BlueSky. Although I later learned that the theme of the mud was not particularly important to BlueSky's participants, initially I was intrigued to discover what kind of world BlueSky's creators had envisioned in their description of BlueSky's spaces as entirely above ground, among treetops and clouds. In contrast with this pastoral theme, my first encounter with BlueSky inhabitants struck me as disturbingly rough and rude. I seemed not to have full control of my character and thought that others were making it do things against my will. I was also put off by frequent crude references to blow jobs and other sexual activity. A recent rereading of that earliest log revealed to me that in fact the participants present were mainly ignoring me, but my misunderstanding of much of what occurred led me to believe at the time that I was being specifically attacked. After a few minutes of attempting to assert my nonaggressive intent and plead my case for visiting their mud, I finally logged off and sat back to think about the first unpleasant encounter in my initial week of mud exploration.

I was not completely surprised by the level of hostility that I perceived or by the explicit sexual language. In 1994, the image of the Internet as an untamed frontier was already common in media accounts. Nor are representations of cyberspace as less than civilized limited to mass media. One of the earliest and best known organizations attempting to protect civil liberties online is called the Electronic Frontier Foundation.[2] Numerous other references to the Internet as a wild frontier have appeared both online and off, sometimes as warnings to those who expect more "civilized" social graces. Frequently they nostalgically and uncritically present the construction of the United States' historic Wild West as a model of pioneering spirit, now to be found in this new "frontier." As Miller points out, "The Western narrative connects pleasurably with the American romance of individualistic masculinity; small wonder that the predominantly male founders of the Net's culture found it so appealing" (1995: 52). Fuller and Jenkins also suggest that "part of the drive behind the rhetoric of virtual reality as a New World or new frontier is the desire to recreate the Renaissance encounter with America without guilt" (1995: 59). These types of representations thus specifically support the participation of young white ("pioneering") males and suggest that women, children, people of color, and others may be uncomfortable.

Since my early forays into the mud subculture, I have come to believe that the degree of unpleasantness online has been greatly exaggerated in media accounts, but, at the time, I considered that BlueSky might provide an example of an aggressive, male-oriented space and that, as such, it might even be typical of much online interaction. So I mustered my ethnographic courage and resolved to attempt what I anticipated would be a difficult entrance into the field. As brief as my initial conversation on BlueSky was, it did provide me with the information that anonymous guests were not appreciated. I thus felt that choosing a character name and registering a character (essentially acquiring an online "account" on BlueSky) would make a difference in my interactions there. To bolster my confidence, I chose a name, Copperhead, whose aggressive and poisonous connotations might allow me both to fit in and to feel somewhat protected.[3]

For approximately three years I was a regular on BlueSky, participating in online socializing as well as conducting informal online interviews. During the first year or so, I also spent many hours each week on several other social muds. Initially I thought I might attempt a comparative study of more than one mud. Even after abandoning that plan, I found it useful to be able to continue comparing my experiences on BlueSky with the feel of other social muds. One or two BlueSky people also periodically participate on most of the other muds I visited. These include ElseMOO (described in Cherny 1999), EarlyMUD (discussed in more detail in the next chapter), GammaMOO (a very large social mud), AniMUCK (a social mud with an anthropomorphic animal theme), and HappyHour (a social mud reputed to include lots of online sexual activity, which I, in my few casual visits, failed to discover). I also briefly visited several other muds. As my research progressed, I began limiting my mudding time mainly to BlueSky.

Getting to know people and understanding the culture of any particular mud requires significant time.

BlueSky's group seemed particularly worth investigating because of the length of time many of the participants had been mudding (up to six years at that time), the relative stability of the group, and the connections between their participation on BlueSky and their work activities. Because BlueSky participants have integrated muds into their lives over a prolonged period and have maintained their online relationships through a variety of life changes, the group can reveal much about the advantages and disadvantages of online social life.

BlueSky relationships include the participants' offline contacts as well as their online interactions. I attended several informal offline gatherings of BlueSky participants, such as that described at the beginning of this chapter, as well as a few gatherings of participants on EarlyMUD and GammaMOO. During these gatherings, in the San Francisco Bay Area and elsewhere, I had the opportunity to chat face-to-face with online acquaintances.

In addition to these casual offline meetings, I conducted thirty face-to-face, open-ended interviews with BlueSky participants. By the time I met people offline, I generally knew something about what they looked like and had a sense of their personalities. In a few cases, my sense of them changed after meeting offline, but the online identities portrayed by BlueSky participants are generally congruent with their offline identities. These offline meetings thus gave me further information about people's identities, online and off, and provided information about the differences that the online context can make in people's interactions and identities.

Most interviews were conducted in people's homes or in nearby public locales. Twenty-two of my interviewees were regulars, most of whom had been mudding for several years (although one was a very recent newcomer). This group included the three "wizards" (people responsible for running and managing the mud). Two interviewees were previous regulars who had left the group because of personal differences; two were previous regulars whose participation had recently all but ceased because of lifestyle changes; and two were infrequent participants. I also conducted two interviews with long-term mudders who had never been members of BlueSky, although both occasionally associate with BlueSky participants on other muds or face-to-face. Twenty interviewees were male, and ten female. Twenty-five were white; four were Asian American; and one was Mexican American.

Many BlueSky participants also participate on an e-mail list called med-menham (my pseudonym), which provided another source of information for my research. Not all BlueSky participants have joined medmenham, and several on the medmenham list do not participate on BlueSky. Included in the latter medmenham group are several previous BlueSky regulars who now keep in touch with other BlueSky participants mainly through e-mail. Medmenham mostly serves as a forum for exchanging jokes, humorous stories, and similar tidbits gleaned from various online sources. However, participants also occasionally use it to notify others of impending cross-country trips in order to arrange meetings or places to stay.

BLUESKY DEMOGRAPHICS

BlueSky participants form a mostly homogeneous group. Participants are predominately white, middle-class, college educated, and in their twenties. Of the 138 regulars, 37 (27 percent) are female. As the level of participation increases, however, the percentage of females decreases. Only 12 of the 52 most active regulars are female, and among the top 29, only 5 are female. The top 15 participants are all male. Thus, while men still outnumber women online in general, BlueSky may be more male dominated than most of the Internet. Several BlueSky participants have suggested that other muds with which they are familiar have more active female partic-ipants.

All BlueSky participants (except for a couple still in high school) have at least some college education. Most began mudding in college, whether as undergraduates (in most cases) or as graduate or professional students. henri, for instance, was a computer science graduate student at a presti-gious private university when TinyMUD Classic began in 1989, and RaveMage learned about muds while a medical student on the East Coast.

The level of education of BlueSky mudders reflects that of Internet participants generally. Approximately half of Internet users are thirty-five or under and have at least some college experience (only 13 to 18 percent report no college, and 18 to 26 percent have some postgraduate education). The even greater prevalence of college education among BlueSky partici-pants probably reflects the fact that muds were invented by college stu-dents and continue to include significant numbers of students (Rheingold 1993; Turkle 1995). In the early days of mudding, at the end of the 1980s, most student mudders were from computer science, math, or engineering departments. BlueSky participants, not surprisingly, come from a similarly narrow range of university backgrounds.

Felicia, an undergraduate engineering student at a large midwestern university, has a character on BlueSky but rarely visits the site. She knows several BlueSky mudders through their participation on other muds. A mudder since early 1991, Felicia is well-known among the mudding subculture. She has run several muds, moderates one of the mud-related Usenet newsgroups, and is active in mud server development. In a face-to-face interview, she described the group on BlueSky:

> The thing about BlueSky is, because it's the dinomud, it started up at a time when it was mostly guys, because only guys had access to the stuff—computer science and electrical engineering. So, many of the BlueSky people come out of technical disciplines. You've got . . . on BlueSky you get . . . it's white or Asian, usually male. . . . BlueSky is very heavily technical, in fact. That is not true of the mudding population in general any longer. It's [also] older—people who started when they were eighteen or nineteen that are now twenty-four, twenty-seven.

Felicia's description matches the information I obtained through my research on BlueSky. Felicia refers to BlueSky as the dinomud because so many participants have been mudding for many years. Mudders refer to people who have mudded for more than three or four years as dinos (from "dinosaur").

My figures on BlueSky's regulars are derived in part from a listing I acquired on May 6, 1996, from a programmed object (see the discussion of objects in the next chapter) that keeps track of people's time on BlueSky. The listing was ranked by number of active hours. (Hours were accumulated from March 11, 1995, when the object had been reset.) Total hours for characters ranged from 0 to 2,098, but I eliminated all characters whose activity fell below 30 hours. The 146 characters eliminated included very occasional users (usually either newbies who don't stay or dinos periodically reconnecting to contact old friends); and prior regulars who, as of this writing, have disappeared or ceased activity on the mud. Characters who never logged on after March 11, 1995, do not appear on the list generated by the object. Alisa, who handles character registration for BlueSky, indicated that in September 1995 BlueSky's total number of characters (including robots) was 584. This means there are approximately three hundred additional inactive characters. In addition to relatively inactive characters, I eliminated characters who use specialized software to keep themselves artificially active (which defeats the usefulness of their numbers), BlueSky's robots (described in chapter 5), and the guest characters.

The login object attempts to take account of time when a character is logged on but not active (and therefore not participating) and delete it from the total hours accumulated. However, the resulting hours are only a rough approximation of actual activity. Moreover, the definition of activity is somewhat arbitrary: one participant pointed out to me that she frequently reads without speaking, and therefore would be counted inactive by the login object, but considers herself active. The login object also cannot account for the amount of text each character generates. Any command executed within a six-minute span of time counts the character as active for that six-minute span. If, for instance, women on average generate much less text than men do but issue the same number of commands to the mud program, they would be counted by the login object as equally active. The percentages I provide are therefore best read as indicative of overall numbers of women participants and of the tendency of women to participate less than men.

Most muds still draw many of their participants from college and university undergraduates. BlueSky, in contrast, has limited the entrance of newcomers. As its population ages, its average age becomes older than that of many other muds. However, at thirty-nine, I was one of a very few regulars on BlueSky over thirty-five. Most BlueSky participants' ages range from twenty-four to thirty-two. Several other of the longer-running muds, including EarlyMUD and GammaMOO, also have pockets of similarly aged populations. In my experience, it is extremely rare on any mud to meet anyone over forty. (Most exceptions I have encountered are college professors, many of whom either participate on one of the various professional-oriented muds or are themselves studying muds.)

Eight BlueSky regulars are Asian American/Pacific Islander, one is African American, one is Mexican American, and the remainder are white. Most of the Asian American/Pacific Islander participants are among the most active regulars. The African American participant is a relatively infrequent participant, and the Mexican American, once a very active participant, now rarely participates. Almost all BlueSky regulars are from the United States, with about half a dozen from Canada, a few from Australia, and one from the Netherlands. Except for the one participant from the Netherlands (who primarily speaks Dutch but is very proficient in English), all have English as their primary language.

These statistics present a picture of a relatively homogeneous group. However, like the affluent, white Sun City residents whom Fitzgerald (1986) studied, BlueSky participants overestimate the diversity of their members. As evidence for assertions of BlueSky's diversity, many mention the wide range of political positions represented within the group. Participants especially mention two whom they consider to represent the extremes of the political spectrum on BlueSky: Faust, a radical libertarian; and Bilerific-Sid, BlueSky's only avowed socialist. The consistency with which these two names arose exposes, however, the relative similarity of BlueSky participants to each other, even with regard to politics. A handful of liberals (most of whom live in northern California) and a few staunch conservatives are well outnumbered by the majority, who cover a narrow spectrum of conservative-leaning libertarianism.

HAVEN IN A HEARTLESS (WORK) WORLD: MUDDERS AT WORK

Media discussions of people's usage of online services frequently mention the potential for people to "goof off" at work. This was the most common reaction when I divulged to colleagues and friends that BlueSky participants most frequently mud at work. Mudders themselves also sometimes characterize their mudding as a waste of time or feel guilty about participating at work. However, the experiences of BlueSky participants demonstrate that leisure and work cannot be clearly separated. Mudding can be a leisure activity but also often constitutes a work resource for participants.

BlueSky is busiest during the "normal" work day, especially at lunchtime and through the afternoon. Because participants span the North American continent (with a handful connecting from other countries), these busy periods extend from 11:00 A.M. to 2:00 P.M., Pacific standard time, with another period of heavy usage from about 4:00 to 6:00 P.M. As these patterns suggest, most BlueSky participants log on from work, interspersing online socializing with their work tasks.

Very few participants log on before 9:30 A.M. Pacific standard time, but an intermittent "night crowd" sometimes creates a busy period around 7:00 to 10:00 P.M. in that time zone. Some of these people log on from home. Others are still at work, either putting in overtime or working a later shift. Some of the programmers, for instance, have flexible work hours and may not arrive at their offices until noon or later. Frequently a few people are still connected when the mud goes down for an hour each night at 3:00 A.M. Pacific time. Some live on the East Coast, where it is then 6:00 A.M. These late-night participants usually are logged on from home. But the great majority do their mudding from work.

To have standing as regulars in BlueSky, then, group members must have jobs that allow online activity. (By "allow" I mean that workers are *able* to participate, not that their employers necessarily consent to such participation, although some do.) Approximately 80 percent of BlueSky participants work as computer programmers and system administrators or hold similar computer-related jobs. These fields, like BlueSky itself, are male-dominated: the pattern of participation on BlueSky suggests important interconnections among work, leisure, computers, and masculinities.

The social rhythms of other muds and online social spaces may include more evening and weekend hours, but on BlueSky, participation all but depends on either having a middle-class technical/professional job or being a student. (In other online groups, having an occupational status that allows for personal control of time, such as being a homemaker or retired, would also suffice.) As in offline social groups, if a participant fails to show up and regularly interact, he or she risks being forgotten or becoming marginal to the group. In a physical social setting, participants can often show up and merely "hang out." Those who speak little may still have a strong presence in the group. But in a social forum with no physical presence, maintaining a sense of presence and connectedness requires frequent, ongoing participation. Without periodic textual contributions, you are all but invisible online. On BlueSky, participants even consider it rude to remain for long periods of time connected and in the active hangout room without participating.

Communicating on muds also involves typing, which is slower than speaking. (Most BlueSky participants do, however, type very quickly.) Participating in the conversation precludes preparing long speeches. Politeness also prohibits spamming others, that is, transmitting large quantities of text at once. Thus, mud conversations generally occur in short bursts of text. All of these factors mean that, on the whole, mud conversations take longer than similar conversations offline (and there is no way to communicate some types of information easily).

This social dynamic requires a job that provides not only the ability to connect to the Internet or other large networks but also considerable autonomy. Heavily supervised employees who have adequate computer and network access would nevertheless be constrained in their online participation. Data entry clerks whose keystrokes or record-production levels per hour are monitored, for instance, could not converse online.

Caring for young children also renders significant online participation difficult. Two women on BlueSky whose children are already school-aged have been relatively infrequent participants since my participation began. Kate, who had a child last year, has actually increased her time online somewhat, but her pattern of participation has changed. Previously she was out of the house during the day and tended to log on infrequently at night. Now she is often home with the baby and logs on more often during the day, although she remains relatively quiet. Her participation pattern may help her feel less isolated as a new mother, but it depends on her husband's continued employment. Two male participants' wives also gave birth last year. Captin's recent fatherhood has not appreciably decreased his online time, which continues to occur mainly while he is at work. However, elflord's new parenting responsibilities have significantly decreased his online time.

Online participation therefore requires that people's responsibilities allow them to dedicate the time necessary to this form of interaction. The jobs that allow for the types of access necessary for mud participation from work are relatively well paid and dominated by white men.

CODERS AND SYSADMINS

Most (but not all) of the BlueSky participants who work as programmers have degrees in computer science or related fields. Programming usually requires at least some formal training: programmers have to understand both what people want the computer to do and how the computer itself operates. Writing computer code—words and syntax that a computer can understand and translate into desired actions— requires intense concentration.

However, writing programs is usually only a small part of a programmer's job. Other tasks relate to standard business organization. Much of the workday, for instance, may be taken up with meetings at which decisions may be made concerning what features will be programmed, who will program which portion of a job, and other similar organizational and management issues. Like most corporate workers, BlueSky participants profess to hate meetings. Aside from other reasons to dislike meetings, they take participants away from their computers, which precludes active participation on BlueSky.

Other time is taken up with the translation of computer programs from programming "languages," in which the programmer writes the code, into instructions that the computer processor can interpret. Programming languages contain words and syntax similar to those of human (usually English) languages. However, these are not directly readable by computers. Once each program or portion of a program has been written in a programming language (such as C++, a very common language used by many of the BlueSky participants), it must be "compiled." Compiling translates the program into the strings of ones and zeros (on and off), into which all computer commands must ultimately be translated for execution by the machine. Compiling takes time, so sometimes programmers break the compilation of programs into small portions. While waiting for a program to compile, the programmer may have little else to do and is free to participate in a mud. In response to a request for information about work activities, henri sent me the following e-mail, in which he discusses how the rhythms of his workday enable him to intersperse mudding and programming:

> When I'm really paying attention and interacting on the mud, I generally am not really doing anything right at the same time. I'm usually waiting for a recompile to finish (after I've made a change to the code), or waiting for a test run to complete, or talking on the phone, etc. It really is like a computer multi-tasking—there's only one CPU [central processing unit] but it appears to be doing several things at the same time.
>
> The way mudding works makes it easy to appear to be 100 percent active when really you're switching back and forth, too. You can say something when I'm editing C++ code, and I can look back and reply to it after I start the compile, and to you it looks like I was right there the whole time. Unknown thinking, typing, and netlag times make it impossible to tell. If you want to think about it that way, the program I'm working on can't tell I wasn't there the whole time, either—it just "sees" as soon as it recompiled that I'm there running it again.

Both mudding and programming require interacting with a computer. henri takes advantage of the expected conversational gaps on muds produced by the necessity of typing, the processing time of the mud server, and the vagaries of network connections to intersperse his short bursts of conversation with short bursts of programming activity. Accustomed to adjusting his rhythms to those of computers, he even compares this activity to a computer's own method for processing multiple tasks.

While programs often compile easily, they do not necessarily "run"— that is, perform the intended functions—as desired. Usually, the programmer instead receives an error report, listing programming equivalents of bad grammar: half-finished commands, "dangling function calls," misunderstood directions, and so forth. Sometimes the exact location of the error must be painstakingly teased out of thousands of lines of code, not all of which may have been written by the programmer attempting to decipher it. This process of hunting down and correcting errors in software code is known as "debugging." Debugging can be very tedious but does not always require the same level of intense focus as creating code. (Ulysses, for instance, explains that "coding is creative, debugging is analytical.") Hence, programmers can sometimes engage in other tasks while debugging, especially socializing online, which allows them to remain at the computer and doesn't take much concentration. Socializing also provides a welcome relief from what is often not only tedious but also frustrating work.

The next facet of programming work involves testing the program either by attempting to use it or by writing additional small sections of code that will interact with portions of the program to test particular features or functions. Like debugging, this type of activity can involve short periods of concentration followed by short periods of waiting for results from the computer. Here again, as henri describes above, many participants can work and socialize simultaneously.

While this overview generally describes the working day of several BlueSky participants, far more of them work as system administrators than as programmers. System administrators (often referred to as *sysadmins*) keep the computers of an organization (whether an academic department, a corporate division, or a small business) running. Although they may have to write short programs that relate to network connections or that tell the computer which larger program to access when, most of their work involves not writing programs but doing routine maintenance to keep the computers running and fielding user problems. The latter can involve both correcting computer problems and training users. Most system administrators are also responsible for at least light hardware work: moving and installing computers, adding new equipment, and replacing obsolete or defective equipment. Depending on the size and organization of their workplace, system administrators may also be responsible for ordering computer supplies, planning system needs, and making decisions concerning equipment and programs to use in the future.

Some types of system administration work pull the sysadmin away from his or her own computer. However, sometimes user problems can be handled over the phone or by e-mail. Particularly when questions from users involve problems that are familiar and easy to solve, the sysadmin can assist the user and socialize online simultaneously. System administration activity can occur in unpredictable bursts. When everything is running smoothly and no user needs assistance, the sysadmin may have time to relax and spend time online.

Since my aim is to provide insight into BlueSky participants' strategies for blending online socializing with their work, I have described these work patterns from the perspective of the worker, not that of the employer. Employers may have other ideas as to what the programmer or sysadmin should do with time found between debugging or troubleshooting tasks. Some BlueSky participants indicate that their employers know about their online time and have no complaint about it, as long as necessary work gets done. Others know or suspect that their employers would disapprove of their mudding, and they therefore keep it hidden from bosses and co-workers.

My sense from talking to BlueSky participants is that, rather than re-place the time that would otherwise be spent doing work, online socializing tends to replace the time that would be spent socializing within the work-place. During my ride with Jet to the Mystery Spot, he asked about my research and talked about how BlueSky fits into his life. He indicated that his company had just switched him from a night-shift job to a better po-sition during the day, but, he explained, "I still don't know people very well. Even though I work days now, I don't eat lunch with other people at work; I basically eat lunch on the mud. I feel a little guilty about it." Jet compares his own workday with that of his coworkers:

> The nature of my work is such that I often have great periods of intense work and then begin a long-running job, and there's nothing to do for an hour or two. At work people usually go visit other people during that time. They play [computer games]. But I tend to be stuck at my terminal. I really haven't gotten to know most of my coworkers. If I didn't mud, I would probably be out shooting the breeze with my coworkers.

Jet expresses this recognition of his distance from coworkers with some remorse. However, others are just as happy not socializing with their co-workers. Obtuse also socializes on BlueSky rather than with coworkers. He, in fact, prefers BlueSky to ElseMOO, another mud he participates on, because several of his coworkers hang out on ElseMOO.

> What BlueSky has been for me has been an escape. And I'll be honest and say that that's what it was—an escape from the interactions that I had to worry about. Because it's not unlikely that Raymond [who participates on ElseMOO] is going to be my boss in about six months. Raymond and my boss have been friends for years. There's a very close-knit group here at work, which includes Raymond and Maria [another ElseMOO participant] and so forth, and that's just too close.

Obtuse uses the "escape" of mudding to manage his work relationships. He uses mud relationships specifically to avoid work relationships, a strategy that only partly succeeds for him because many of his coworkers also mud. For most participants, BlueSky provides a forum separate from the work environment in which they can talk about their coworkers without fear that their words will get back to those people. BlueSky participants can thus let off steam about work while still on the job. Relieving inter-personal tensions in the workplace may be beneficial. However, people who do not socialize with coworkers may not be perceived as integrated into the company, and they may miss important contacts and information gained through informal interactions.

Having a social group accessible during work but separate from work thus has both advantages and disadvantages for mudders as well as their employers. Online socializing at work may disconnect BlueSky partici-pants from valuable social relationships within the workplace. However, the availability of BlueSky may also motivate participants to work longer hours. For instance, henri comments:

> I try to pretty much work a full day, but after that I will slow down the pace and mud or look at the web. Often I will stay and work for a couple of hours longer than I would have if I just had to sit there and watch things run, because I can talk on the mud while it's going on. Especially when I come in on the weekend—there's no way I would come to an empty building to just work on the computer for hours if I didn't have something else to do as well.

The computer industry notoriously demands long hours from pro-grammers. While programming offers much more creative interest than many jobs, it has its share of tedium. Mudding often demands little or only intermittent attention (I have a mud window on my computer screen next to my word processing window as I'm writing this, for instance) but provides feelings of contact and company, which alleviate boredom or lone-liness while on the job.

THE MUD EXPERIENCE

Muds can be very disorienting to the new visitor. During their busy times, text scrolls by on the screen at an alarming rate. In the party atmosphere that usually prevails when many people are in the same mud "room" at the same time, several different conversations may be going on simulta-neously. Whereas at a physical party, conversational groups separate into different parts of the room, on a mud all conversations occur in the same "space" and, unless "whispered" (communicated privately to one other person), are readable by all in the room. Thus, different strands of conversation intertwine in bizarre juxtapositions and can be extremely difficult to make sense of.

Muds therefore require facility with written language, and this requirement has several implications for participation. First, although muds are available on the Internet and therefore accessible to people from many different countries, each mud is likely to attract people who speak and write the same language. Muds also work well as a social space only for people who are able to express themselves with some facility through written text. As the Internet population diversifies, mud populations may do so as well, but most people on muds will likely still have at least some college experience. This implies, among other things, a particular socioeconomic class identity for most mudders.

The commingling of different conversations on one's computer screen requires not just language skills but also a particular orientation to language and conversation. It requires a capacity for "modular" thinking. Each burst of text that appears on the screen must be considered as a unit and assigned to its place in the exchange without the cues available in face-to-face conversations, such as eye contact, gesture, and tone. Many people learn to make these distinctions through their mud participation. However, the skill involved in treating language this way is analogous to the logic skills and view of language required in computer programming. This is not to say that skill in programming is required to converse on muds, nor will everyone able to converse on muds make a good computer programmer, but the two sets of skills do overlap.[4]

Entering a Mud

A person with a computer account allowing Internet access goes through the following steps to log onto a mud.[5] In the simplest instance, after logging on to their account (usually on a local machine), the user issues a *telnet* command to connect to the remote computer on which the mud program is running. The command looks something like this:

```
telnet machine.university.edu 8888
```

The first word, "telnet," activates the telnet program on the local computer; the second phrase, "machine.university.edu," is the Internet address of the remote computer on which the mud runs (which can also be expressed as a series of numbers); and the number 8888 specifies a particular "port" on the remote machine. (The different ports on a computer allow people to connect to different programs running on the same computer.

Mud participants must specify the mud program's port, because the remote computer will not allow them access to other programs without an account on that computer.)

Participants next see an entrance screen for the mud, which usually includes a welcome message and instructions for logging on, such as the following:[6]

```
**************************
* Welcome to BambiMOO! *
**************************
```

If this is your first time, enter: create <name> <password>

Otherwise use "connect <name> <password>" to reconnect to an existing
   player.

Type "connect guest guest" if you just want to visit.

"news" informs you about recent program changes and items of interest.

"help" gives help on the commands.

Connecting as a guest usually produces a screen of helpful tips for "newbies." (The term "newbie," in general Internet usage, means someone new to the net. On BlueSky it can mean someone new either to BlueSky or to mudding in general.)

Most experienced participants do not use the *telnet* command to connect directly to a mud, because connecting through "raw telnet" results in a messy and difficult-to-read interface to the mud. Instead they use a specialized "mud client" program, which runs on their local machine. This gives a better interface to the mud server program as well as additional command capabilities:

> Clients are programs, usually written in C [a computer programming language], that connect up to servers. . . . Many clients written for MUDs have special added bonus features through which they filter the output; most, for instance, separate your input line from the output lines and wrap words after 80 columns. Some also have a macro-writing capability which allows the user to execute several commands with just a few keypresses. Some allow you to highlight output coming from certain players or suppress it altogether. (Smith 1998)

The clients used by most BlueSky participants provide features such as the ability to connect to more than one mud at once, highlight text from people they particularly want to pay attention to, and suppress text from people they don't want to hear from.

Mud Features

Most muds are composed of several "rooms," each of which has a description. Descriptions usually set an overall theme for the mud. On some muds, particularly role-playing muds, participants integrate the theme and room descriptions into their interactions. By contrast, on BlueSky, participants don't pay much attention to room descriptions, but the descriptions do contribute somewhat to the overall mood. For instance, all of the several hangouts on BlueSky are, like the Falcon, some type of bar. henri, a participant who has built several of the BlueSky group's favorite hangouts, suggested that this feature relates to the gaming roots of muds. Dungeons & Dragons–type games almost always include a pub where adventurers can replenish supplies and gather information.

In part because conversations on muds can be confusing, the main hangout on most muds is usually not the first room the user sees when logging on. Some muds have a default entrance room, which is programmed in such a way that characters are invisible to each other and conversation is not possible unless whispered. New characters and guests thus have a quiet space in which to become familiar with basic commands (which can be learned by consulting the "help" feature). A hint about how to get out of this first room is usually contained in the description of the room.

The Utility Closet

The utility closet is a dark, snug space, with barely enough room for one person in it. It's stuffy and cramped and feels like a good place to get out of. You notice what feel like tools, rags, boots, and cleaning supplies. One useful thing you've discovered is a metal doorknob set at waist level into what might be a door.

The exit hint "you've discovered . . . a metal doorknob" cues people to type a command such as *turn doorknob* or *open door*. (The command *out* frequently works as well.) This moves the participant's character from the entrance room to the next room on the mud. Each room on a mud has one or more "exits," which allow participants to move through the different spaces of the mud. Many exits can be accessed through simple directional commands such as *north, south, up,* and *down,* all abbreviated to their first letters (*n, s, u,* and *d*). Mud rooms may be organized in a logical geographic or sequential manner. Also, most muds include some form of *teleport* command, which allows the participant to "jump" from the current room to any other room on the mud.

Usually all participants can build rooms. Often the first thing participants will build is a "home base" for their character, sometimes modeled
after a familiar real-life space or an appealing fantasy location. Many mudders view these rooms as private spaces on the mud. Whoever builds a
room owns that room and may restrict access by other participants.

Participants may also build more public rooms in which they hope others will hang out or visit. On most muds, some rooms become favorite
hangouts, either because they are easy to get to or because their particular
descriptions or features appeal to other participants. Sometimes the main
hangout is the room the participant moves to from the entrance room.
However, on muds where this is not the case, finding social action can
require paging someone for information on where to go or being proficient
with mud commands. (*Paging* allows one-to-one communication with
other participants in either the same or a separate mud room.)

Newbies are likely to spend some time wandering around before they
find things to do or figure out where people congregate. My own first
experiences with muds included several days of fumbling around before I
could consistently locate groups of people to talk to. It was months before
I had any real facility with mud commands. (I was probably less motivated
to learn commands than some, since my main aim was to talk to other
participants. Other mud participants may have more interest in creating
mud objects or spaces.)[7]

Characters

People interact on muds through characters, which are programmed "objects" that act as a surrogate for the participant. The participant types
commands that cause the character to move through different mud rooms,
perform actions (within the program), or "speak" to other characters. This
description may make the character sound like a puppet operated by the
participant, which is a relatively accurate understanding. However, over
time, many participants come to understand their characters not as separate entities that they manipulate and cause to communicate nor as dramatic parts they perform, but as a type of interface through which they
remotely communicate with other people. Although the word "character"
implies a separate persona, for many experienced mudders, characters are
merely mouthpieces through which they speak.

Each character has a name and description as well as a gender "attribute," all of which are chosen by the participant. Other participants can
view a character description (or any room or object description) using the

look command. The gender attribute allows the program to assign the appropriate pronouns to the character when text referring to that character is generated by the mud program. This constitutes one of the ways in which gender's treatment on muds is different from that of other aspects of identity, such as race and class (and also reflects the connections between gender and language). On most social muds, participants are not similarly required to choose a race, sexual orientation, and so forth, for their character.[8]

On BlueSky, a desired character name must be submitted along with an e-mail address to the wizards for character registration through e-mail. Wizards are participants with responsibility for the maintenance of the mud program itself.[9] BlueSky's three wizards include Corwin and Alisa, who have run muds together since the earliest TinyMUDs, and elflord, who was recently given wizard status. Although Corwin does not own the computer on which the mud is run, he has permission from his academic workplace to run the mud there. He has primary responsibility for the practical tasks involved in maintaining the program. Alisa handles character registration. elflord's responsibilities include moderating disputes between participants. Social conflicts can threaten the efficient and smooth running of the program. (It is possible for disgruntled or malicious participants to "crash" the program, causing it to cease to operate.)[10] Alisa muds far less than she used to because of increasing job responsibilities, and Corwin tired of dealing with social issues, so elflord was invited to be BlueSky's third wizard, specifically assigned to "social" duties.

Character registration serves several purposes. It attaches the character to an e-mail address, although a skilled participant can pass off a fraudulent address without detection. Registration also allows the wizards to reserve names for people known to have used them previously. This encourages identity consistency and decreases confusion. Registration can help keep the database free from one-time-only characters. Given the delay (sometimes several days) in receiving a character and password, one-time visitors will more likely use the guest character. Perhaps most important, registration also presents a barrier to full participation, indicating to potential participants that a certain level of identity consistency and accountability are expected on BlueSky. Many BlueSky people have kept the same names through years of participation in a variety of different muds run by Corwin and Alisa. Others change names frequently, but members of the group often still refer to them by their original, best-known, or longest-used name. (For instance, during the course of my research, Corwin used three different names. I have changed all of these to "Corwin" to avoid confusion.)

The potential identity confusion caused by these name changes is alleviated by other identifying information. A set of commands that Corwin added to the mud allows people to attach to their character such information as e-mail address, birth date, and so forth. One feature included in this set of commands is an "alias," which most people use for their "true" mud name (if they have recently changed it to something else) or for a commonly used abbreviation of that name. My alias, for instance, is CH.

The gender choices available on BlueSky are male, female, neuter, and plural. They are set for one's own character using a command that reads "@sex me = _____," with the blank being filled in by text indicating gender. The program reads only the first letter of this text: "Genders that start with *M* or *m* are considered male, those starting with *F, f, W,* or *w* are considered female, those starting with *P* or *p* are considered plural, and anything else is considered neuter."[11] Most BlueSky participants all but ignore this feature, using the gender setting for joke purposes such as "not lately," "no thank you," and "Grrrreek letter" (the last from a character whose name was represented by a Greek letter). Gender designations are unnecessary as personal information, since most participants know each other and have met face-to-face. (Those who haven't met in person have usually met someone who has met the others.)

BlueSky participants treat descriptions similarly. Most muds include the default character description "You see nothing special." Characters sporting this description on BlueSky give themselves away as newbies and are likely to be told, "Get a description!" However, most regulars do not strive for realism, nor do they seriously attempt to enact a fantasy character consistently. Descriptions are rarely looked at or referred to. People usually call attention to descriptions on BlueSky only to make jokes or to show off programming proficiency. One participant, for instance, set his description to "You see nothing special. Really. Go away. Stop looking at me." Another created a program that mirrored the description of the last person who looked at his description, displaying that description for the next person to see.

BlueSky participants' attitudes toward standard mud features reflect in part their years of experience on muds. In keeping with their reputation as dinos, they are sometimes blasé about technical aspects of online communication. In addition, BlueSky participants distinguish themselves from other mud participants through their shared view of the mud as a communication medium rather than as an alternative (or virtual) reality.

BAD HABITS: MANAGING MUDDING AT WORK

Although mudders and nonmudders alike sometimes characterize mudding and similar online activities as goofing off, the situation is more complex. While employees may indeed find online time a convenient way to have fun instead of working, even very social (and arguably frivolous) forums such as BlueSky can provide important work resources. Furthermore, while many employers feel that every second they pay for should be spent in productive efforts, this expectation is rarely met, and work and leisure intertwine in people's day-to-day experiences (Calagione and Nugent 1992; see also Nippert-Eng 1996 for a discussion of people's blending of home and work; and Hochschild 1997 for discussions of quality versus quantity work time).

In addition to mastering the necessary technical skills and becoming familiar with the peculiar rhythms of mud conversation, mudders must find ways to integrate their online socializing into their daily lives. BlueSky mudders who mud from work must decide whether to do so openly and to what degree they wish to integrate the different environments, and people within them, experienced electronically on the mud and physically at work.

BlueSky participants' degree of openness with coworkers about mudding activities varies. People like Obtuse, whose job requires participation on a workplace mud, can generally acknowledge their other mudding activities to coworkers, at least to some degree. Obtuse, who works as a system administrator, indicated that his bosses were aware of the job-related benefits that were likely to derive from his socializing on muds with other people in similar work positions.

People working alongside others with similar computer backgrounds and skills also frequently mud openly. Jet received his degree in engineering several years ago and now runs computerized editing equipment for an entertainment production company. Many of his coworkers have similar skills and technical backgrounds.

> People at work have actually asked me what that window is, because it's a very distinctive window, and people sort of walk by and figure out that that's not a usual C-shell window. And they say, "What is that?" "That's a mud." And I just explain it: "So I talk to people by typing to them." And they go, "Oh, that's interesting," and they walk away. No one's ever really given me any grief about it.

Some BlueSky participants acknowledge online participation to co-workers but hide the degree of such activity or imply that their participation involves noninteractive media such as e-mail lists or other bulletin board–type services. Noninteractive online activities tend to be viewed as "information-seeking" behavior and sometimes carry less stigma than interactive activities such as games or chat rooms. Donatello says this was the attitude toward mudding at a previous job he held. "I had a job where I was sitting in front of a computer and I mudded very, very, very infrequently. But that was how I learned about the World Wide Web. It was considered fairly inappropriate to mud while you were working. It was *not* considered inappropriate to use Mosaic [a tool for browsing the World Wide Web], because it was an information source rather than a time sink." The attitude of Donatello's employers reflects American culture's bias toward "instrumental" or "goal-oriented" behaviors. This in itself reflects the predominance of values associated with middle-class morality. BlueSky participants often reflect this bias in their discussions of mudding activities.

For instance, pez has alternated between enrollment as a student and employment in various computer support positions. She mainly muds during leisure hours but has recently cut down the level of her participation. She says, "I consider it a bad habit. . . . Just not being online makes me feel like I'm more productive." She views "merely" socializing as less valuable than "getting things done." This perspective also suggests that divisions between work and leisure are shifting, ambiguous, and permeable. Although reading Usenet newsgroups can just as easily be unrelated to work, the value of this activity tends to be judged on the basis of content. By contrast, online gaming and socializing are deemed unproductive and in some cases improper uses of company (or school) resources, regardless of whether the games sharpen work-related skills or whether a chat group provides information important to work performance.

Depending on their job situations, BlueSky participants may or may not hide their mudding activities from coworkers. During my first summer of fieldwork, I also worked full-time as a legal secretary. Like other BlueSky participants, I frequently spent my lunch hours logged on to BlueSky. When people in the office noticed that I was logged on, I sometimes indicated that I was checking my e-mail. Even on my lunch hour, I was reluctant to let people know that I engaged in chat activities online. Although checking school-related e-mail (as opposed to intraoffice e-mail) was no more related to work than chatting online, engaging in that activity provoked little comment at work and was probably viewed similarly to making personal phone calls on work time.

People with windowing systems on their computers can quickly "icon-ify" (shrink) their mud window or cover it with another window. Having no windowing system at the law firm forced me to come up with alternative strategies for hiding my mudding activity. My dilemma was complicated by the frequent sexual and scatological references in BlueSky conversations. Even supposing I could hide the source of those references, having them on the screen at work could prove embarrassing and possibly even violate sexual harassment laws.

In the following conversation, which became sexually explicit, I attempted to shield my screen by soliciting assistance from other BlueSky participants, and I learned their past and current work strategies in the process. In addition to providing examples of different participants' strategies for managing work and mudding, this conversation also demonstrates the BlueSky norm of providing technical assistance to other participants.

Copperhead turns her screen _away_ from the corridor.

Faust laughs

Copperhead prepares to type WHO if necessary.[12]

henri LAUGHS at Ch

Copperhead fervently wishes she had windows here.

Perry snickers at ch

henri says "I used to hit the 'setup' key on my vt220 at my previous workplace, Ch; it effectively clears the screen"

Copperhead says "I don't think I have anything like that."

Perry hides his tf[13] window behind something that actually looks like work, aligned so he can see the first character of each line in the tf window, so he can see if anyone said anything

Faust leaves it up, iconifies if someone needs to talk to him or look at the screen. The cubicles here at work are actually quite private, all things considered

Copperhead says "is there a tf command that will clear the screen?

henri says "you can hit ctrl-Z and then type 'clear'"

Perry says " L, CH"

Bilerific-Sid says "Not only don't I hide my MUd screen, I read massive chunks of it aloud to my bald acolytes who surround me and toss dates at my feet."

Corwin uses a virtual root window manager

Corwin doesn't use it to hide anything in particular, however

As the above excerpt indicates, BlueSky participants employ different strategies for combining their mudding and work activities, depending both on their own feelings about the appropriateness of mudding at work and on their particular work environments. Some, such as Bilerific-Sid (who was not at work during the above conversation) and Corwin (who was), take pains to indicate they do not hide mudding activities. Others, like Perry and henri, while not necessarily feeling guilty about mudding, doubt their bosses will share their lack of concern. No one is particularly surprised by my desire to hide my mudding.

Some BlueSky participants do feel that mudding detracts from their work or ties up limited online connections at work. A few ceased daytime mudding completely on taking new jobs. Donatello, a biology graduate student, talks about mudding as a waste of school resources.

> I might mud again in the future, but I don't think I'll be doing it while I'm in school. I don't think it's appropriate use of the resources. If I were an undergrad and I was just spending some of my free time on the computer, sure, but when I'm here for school, I feel that I should be working when I'm on the computer, because someone else might want to use the computer for work, and it would be terrible if I was on the computer [just to mud].

Others have no online access from work or insufficient privacy. When Faust was a student, he was one of the most active participants. However, after graduating he obtained a full-time job from which he has no network access. When I interviewed him, his time spent on BlueSky had dropped to almost zero.

FAUST: Up until I got this job, I was mudding a fair amount. Some days a lot. Now I hardly ever do it.

LORI: Why is that?

FAUST: Uhm. It's easiest to do it at work, and I think that's the most useful. Working, you've got a window open [you can ask people questions]. . . . [Now] I don't have net access from my work, so that really took care of that. When I get home it's not really worth it to get on. There's other things I would rather be doing. In addition to that, I have to pay for my net access now, so it's not cheap. It's certainly not free.

Faust's lack of network access on the job forced him to reconsider the value of his online time. Rather than displace other leisure activities, he decreased his mudding participation.

3   Mudding History and Subcultures

MUDS AND THE "SURLY GANG"

Muds began as multiplayer text-based adventure games, usually based on Tolkienesque scenarios in which players, represented by fantasy characters, could search for treasure, solve puzzles, and kill monsters (and sometimes other players' characters).[1] Single-player versions of such games have existed since the early 1970s, when they were available mainly to computer hobbyists and people associated with academic computer departments. As computer networking emerged, various people began writing networked, multiplayer versions of such games.

The first such game, called MUD for Multi-User Dungeon, was written in 1979 by Roy Trubshaw and Richard Bartle, both students at Essex University (Bartle 1990). After a year of availability only to students at the university, the game allowed access to others by means of modems. Very few people in the United States found out about the game at that time. More learned of the program in the mid-1980s when "a flurry of articles in computer hobby magazines" appeared (Bartle 1990: 9). Some of these people then began writing their own versions of multiplayer networked games.

Alan Cox, who played the original MUD, wrote AberMUD in 1987 and, as became typical for mud programs, distributed it freely to anyone interested. Corwin, who currently runs BlueSky, was a computer science student at the University of Montana in 1988 with several years' experience on local computer bulletin board systems. He picked up a copy of AberMUD and began running a game played mostly by local students.

Meanwhile, Jim Aspnes at Carnegie-Mellon University wrote a mud program that he called TinyMUD. TinyMUD had two significant differences from previous muds. First, Aspnes restored to all players the capability of building their own objects. Bartle had removed this capability from the original MUD, feeling that "the hodge-podge of items created by players detracted from rather than enhanced the game" (Reid 1994). Second, Aspnes removed the scoring command, which in previous multiuser games gave points for monsters or players killed and for treasure gathered. Aspnes described the reasons for his decision:

> Most adventure-style games and earlier MUDs had some sort of scoring system which translated into rank and often special privileges; I didn't want such a system not because of any strong egalitarian ideals (although I think that there are good egalitarian arguments against it) but because I wanted the game to be open-ended, and any scoring system would have the problems that eventually each player would hit the maximum rank or level of advancement and have to either abandon the game as finished or come up with new reasons to play it. This approach attracted people who liked everybody being equal and drove away people who didn't like a game where you didn't score points and beat out other players. (Rheingold 1993: 162–63)

Aspnes's changes also opened up muds to uses other than playing games. The ability for all players to build objects has allowed people to use muds for academic and professional purposes, incorporating teaching tools and texts as objects within the programs. As Aspnes points out, the focus on activities other than hack-and-slash gaming and the lack of scoring encourage a broader range of participants, including people with no interest in Dungeons & Dragons–type games.

Since the early 1990s, people have written many different mud servers. While the type of mud server does not determine its use or purpose, AberMUDs and similar muds (with scoring systems and limitations on user extensibility, that is, the ability of all users to build objects) have tended to continue in the tradition of hack-and-slash gaming spaces. TinyMUDs and their descendants are mainly used for social, role-playing, professional, and educational purposes.

Most mudders who began mudding on Aspnes's original TinyMUD now refer to it as Classic, to differentiate it from later muds built using the same TinyMUD server program. Classic was available over the Internet and accumulated people by word of mouth and "word of net" (i.e., through e-mail lists and Usenet newsgroup posts). Many BlueSky participants first mudded on Classic. The players who populated Classic with thousands of characters and objects did not share Bartle's disdain for user extensibility. For those who discovered mudding in its early days (mainly college students), much of the appeal came from the excitement of being able to create virtual worlds through text as well as from the novelty of communicating in "real time" with large numbers of geographically remote people.

Because Aspnes made the TinyMUD program freely available, people began using it to create other muds; some developed other mud programs. Among the many other muds that opened in early 1990 was TinyFarm, the first "Surly Gang" mud. This began a series of muds run by Corwin and his wife, Alisa. The interest in exploring different facets of mud technology as well as the inherent instability of many of the earlier mud programs led Corwin to run a mud for (usually) several months to a year and then abandon it, beginning a new one using a different mud program. But these muds tended to attract many of the same players. This roughly bounded group became known over the years as the Surly Gang by others in the mud subculture. BlueSky, the longest-lived of the Surly Gang muds, had been up for three years at the end of my research. By that time, some of BlueSky's participants had been mudding together for eight years. Membership in the group has fluctuated over the years, changing with various personal and political arguments. The group acquires new members as more discover mudding and loses people for various reasons.

Some of those who have left BlueSky continue to mud elsewhere; some who leave mudding simply tire of it. Others find that as their circumstances change, they can no longer easily integrate mudding into their lives. BlueSky participants also tell stories of people, particularly in the early days, who "mudded too much" and dropped out of school, losing their Internet access. Thus, over time the BlueSky group has been shaped by factors such as the availability of computer network access; a continuing interest in muds (or at least in the group of people the participants have met through muds); the ability to integrate muds into other aspects of their lives; and an affinity for or tolerance of the particular interactional style of BlueSky.

Some BlueSky participants speak nostalgically of the early days of mudding, when everyone built new rooms and objects and explored each other's creations. Many of my dino interviewees told stories of building elaborate textual worlds on muds that, for various reasons, "went down" (that is, ceased to be available online), often with little or no warning. Many early muds were created and run by students on university machines, which they may not have had permission to use in this way. The demands of student life, coupled with occasional discoveries and shutdowns of illicit muds as well as the notorious instability of many early mud server programs, resulted in frequent disappearances of favorite mud hangouts. Many mudders decided that the medium was too unreliable and ephemeral to justify investing large amounts of creative energy. On some other muds where dinos hang out, people do still build, and a few such muds have run continuously for as long as seven years. But almost no one builds anymore on BlueSky, and nearly everyone hangs out in the same room (although the choice of room shifts from day to day). For this group, socializing emerged as more appealing than the creation of virtual worlds.

ROLE PLAYING VERSUS IDENTITY CONTINUITY

Researchers writing about muds have tended to overgeneralize in their characterization of the social interaction that occurs on muds, relying on superficial characterizations or ignoring significant variation to support a particular view of online interaction. For instance, even while acknowledging the use of muds for different purposes, including education, professional meetings, game playing, and so forth, several researchers characterize all muds as forums for "role playing" (Porter 1997; Poster 1995; Turkle 1995). Many mudders would object to this characterization as trivializing their experience. In addition, like the quote from Barlow's manifesto in chapter 1, it relegates mud interaction to a sphere of meaning separate from everyday norms and assumptions regarding sociability and identity continuity.

While many muds encourage role playing, others do not, and the types of role playing also vary. Some role-playing muds derive their scenarios from popular science fiction or fantasy works. Participants on these muds engage in elaborate character and scene development and liken their participation to interactive theater. On other muds, participants play roles in accordance with a loosely defined theme, such as anthropomorphic animal characters. In this type of setting, a participant may invent a character (a talking, tool-using cat, for instance) and play aspects of that character, but then converse with friends about offline life, rather than enact elaborate online dramas. Participants may understand the meanings of their online actions as "keyed" differently from everyday life (Goffman 1974) and thus differentiate their role playing from their "true" selves.

Several BlueSky people also participate on role-playing muds where everyone is "in character" except on specifically designated communications channels. Such muds are usually based on fictional universes inspired by popular media representations such as *Star Trek* and Anne McCaffrey's *Pern* books.[2] Most role-playing muds have fairly strict rules concerning the creation of characters, plot development, interactions among characters, and designation of specific limited spaces where out-of-character communication may occur. Such rules facilitate the difficult process of enacting what Peg, a BlueSky mudder who also participates on role-playing muds, described to me as "improvisational drama." Such explicit rules may also reflect the perceived dangers of online masquerade. On role-playing muds, rules keep such masquerade within well-known and clearly specified boundaries.

On BlueSky, people do not play roles, and they expect that others will represent themselves much as they appear offline. Participants share information about their offline lives, and some sneer at role-playing muds where people act as if the mud were a reality separate from other aspects of life. Those who do play roles elsewhere rarely discuss these activities on BlueSky, since other participants disdain role playing or condemn conversations about it as boring. BlueSky participants view the mud as a means of communication that enables them to "hang out" with a group of friends and acquaintances. Although they compare BlueSky to a bar or pub, they do so to explain a style of interaction that preexists the analogy rather than to set up a theme to which their online behavior should conform.

This stance toward online interaction, emphasizing identity continuity and interpersonal responsibility, contrasts with representations by participants and researchers that emphasize the flexibility of identity in online interaction. For instance, Turkle quotes a participant as saying, "You can be whoever you want to be. You can completely redefine yourself if you want" (1995: 84). Turkle goes on to characterize most muds as anonymous, indicating that "you are known only by the name you give your characters" (85). On BlueSky, by contrast, people generally have only one character and are identified not just by their character name but also by their own personality characteristics, their shared history with others in the group, and usually by considerable knowledge of their offline lives.

Some mudders may indeed use muds as anonymous forums and may find the capability to change their identity freeing. The example of BlueSky suggests, however, that the ability to remain anonymous varies from mud to mud and, by extension, among other online forums as well. Further, few people can remain known for long only by the name they give their character. Online participants seek additional information with which to identify others, and on most muds participants make use of program features such as character descriptions to project an identity of some sort, even if that identity bears little resemblance to the identity they present offline.

The example of BlueSky suggests that while anonymity may work for people who use their online activities as an escape or as fantasy play, integrating online participation into one's offline life requires more continuity between online and offline identities. BlueSky participants share considerable information regarding their offline lives, often soliciting advice or assistance with work or personal problems. Such personal exposure requires a level of trust that would be difficult to achieve in an environment full of shifting, ambiguous personae.

Because of the length of their association, the Surly Gang members provide a rich example of an online subculture. BlueSky participants have developed various means of conveying identity, and they incorporate many of these means into their cultural norms. They have also developed strategies for compelling others to conform to these norms. Examining their norms and strategies illuminates aspects of offline identities and understandings that underlie online performances. Even on muds where fluid and shifting identities are encouraged, participants cannot easily invent new types of identities that have no relationship to the other participants' offline experiences.

FURRIES VERSUS THE SURLY GANG:
BLUESKY AND OTHER MUD SUBCULTURES

A split even more profound than that between BlueSky participants and role players exists between the Surly Gang and mudders who participate on muds with anthropomorphic animal themes, known as *furries*. The furry subculture exists offline as well as online. Numerous comic books and other media are based on furry characters, and fans of such media sometimes attend conventions, much as other media fans do (Bernardi 1998; Jenkins 1992; Penley 1991). Some furry fans began mudding on TinyMUD Classic; on some of the earlier Surly Gang muds, furries participated alongside the people who later became loosely designated as the Surly Gang. That moniker arose when a rift began forming between furries and antifurries. Objections to furries among BlueSky participants include disapproval of the "overly cutesiness" of cuddly animal characters and the explicitly sexual descriptions and behaviors of some furries. Flames directed at furries on muds and in the mud-related newsgroups frequently suggest that most furries are male and that their portrayal of fuzzy, sexy, anthropomorphic female characters is considered disgusting or immature.

While a very few BlueSky participants also participate on furry muds, others have mounted vigorous campaigns against such muds, logging on and harassing other furries by creating vile characters and behaving obnoxiously or by posting antifurry diatribes to the mud-related newsgroups. This has intensified enmity between furries and BlueSky, cementing a particular reputation for the BlueSky participants as intolerant, "crusty old dinos."

BlueSky thus differentiates itself from other muds on the basis of the activity or purpose of the mud as well as the themes of various muds and the relationship of participants to those themes. Some BlueSky participants also participate on muds with other activities, such as role playing or hack-and-slash gaming. Others profess to visit despised muds purely for the enjoyment of sneering at or harassing the participants on those muds. A few continue to participate quietly on various different muds, including some muds that are theoretically antagonistic to each other.

BlueSky participants recognize a few other muds as acceptable and share some participant overlap with those muds, which therefore periodically appear in my descriptions. For instance, as mentioned in chapter 2, a handful of BlueSky participants frequent EarlyMUD, one of the longest continuously running muds online. EarlyMUD has a social atmosphere similar to that of BlueSky, although more women participate, and (perhaps as a result) the overall feel is less contentious. EarlyMUD participants also put a greater emphasis on puzzle-solving activities.

BlueSky also overlaps in membership with ElseMOO. ElseMOO, another social mud, is a forum for discussing and exploring mud programming and other related programming. (See Cherny 1999.) Because several very active BlueSky participants also participate on ElseMOO, there has been significant overlap between the two subcultures. A variety of cultural references on BlueSky originated on ElseMOO and vice versa.

PROGRAMMED OBJECTS AND MUD CULTURE

Because most people on BlueSky have known each other for years, the group has developed a rich culture of relationships, standards of behavior, in-jokes, and norms. They use particular features of the mud program to express these traditions. BlueSky norms reflect the social history and technological development of muds: participants compensate for the limitations of text-only communication through repetition, manipulation of mud technology, and traditions of information exchange.

Mud servers are in part databases of the various rooms, characters, and other objects that form the environment. As Jennifer Smith (1998) explains: "A server is a program which accepts connections, receives data, mulls it over, and sends out some output. In the MUD world, the server keeps track of the database, the current players, the rules, and sometimes the time (or the *heartbeat*). Servers are usually very large C programs which maintain a small-to-enormous database of the objects, rooms, players and miscellany of the MUD."

Characters are one type of object within the mud program; rooms are another. Objects that participants create within the mud can be used to imitate objects that might be found in analogous spaces in real life, to enhance the experience of the mud as a virtual space and to communicate information to each other. Once an object has been created, it generally responds to text that participants type by outputting text of its own. In this way, objects add to the experience of the mud as a "virtual space" through their quasi-autonomous reactions to stimuli.

Many of the objects on BlueSky function as information exchanges. For instance, a job-listing object allows people to type in jobs that might be of interest to others or to read the list for job information. A login object records weekly active time of all characters, allowing people to find out how often someone else has been on recently. Some commands are also built into the mud program itself, allowing participants to display additional information about themselves if they wish, including e-mail addresses, "snail-mail" addresses, birth dates, and so forth.

Other objects function more as toys, which participants play with when conversation flags, when they are bored, or just for fun. For instance, one of the bars on BlueSky contains a "diving platform" (written by elflord). The command *up*, when typed in the bar, causes the character to climb "bravely up the ladder to the platform." Once at the top, a special help command informs the participant of actions possible from the platform:

Help for diving platform commands:

dive—execute controlled dive

jump—leap wildly from platform

yell <msg>—yell message down to bar

push <person>—attempt to throw person from platform

You can also set visible "myjump" and "mydive" attributes on yourself. To test
them, "give jumper = 100" and "give diver = 100" respectively.

In the example below, several BlueSky participants show off by executing silly preprogrammed "dives" (using the "mydive" attribute). Episodes of play like this are common on BlueSky, but in this case the tomfoolery was probably sparked by a discussion of my research project and was essentially a demonstration of an element of BlueSky culture for my benefit. To illustrate the ways in which objects and other elements of the mud program work, I have highlighted in bold type the text that was specifically typed by participants using the *say* or *pose* commands. I have italicized text that was previously typed in by a participant, then displayed to the other participants through use of a short command. (In this case, people have set "mydives," which they then trigger by typing the command *dive*.) All other text was generated by objects or the mud program in response to short typed commands by the participant (such as *u* for *up*). During episodes of playful behavior such as the following, participants may generate very little text "on the spot," relying instead on preprogrammed objects or their own preprogrammed responses.

Jet DEMONSTRATE YOUR MYDIVE ROLL CALL
Jet climbs bravely up the ladder to the platform.
Jet has left.
Jet executes a perfect swan dive into the tub of water.
Jet has arrived.
Locutus has no mydive
Locutus weeps
Gravity climbs bravely up the ladder to the platform.
Gravity has left.
Gravity shouts, "I HAVE NO MYDIVE!" and does a bellyflop into the tub. Water
    SPRAYS throughout the bar.
Gravity has arrived.
Roger Pollack gets soaked
Roger Pollack says "hey, watch it with the no mydive there"
Jet HOWLS
henri climbs bravely up the ladder to the platform.
henri has left.
henri shouts "AIEEE A SPIDER" and HURLS himself from the platform, SMACKING
    into a table. He sits up groggily and mutters, "or was that a piece of lint"
henri has arrived.
Roger Pollack giggles at henri
henri grins
Roger Pollack laughs
Locutus climbs bravely up the ladder to the platform.
Locutus has left.
Locutus shouts "RESISTANCE IS FUTILE! YOU WILL BE ASSIMILATED! and falls
    off the platform.
Locutus has arrived.

After watching the fun, I attempt to join in as well. henri joins me and unsuccessfully attempts to push me off, after which I use the *dive* command. The text below starting with "Copperhead attempts" was generated as a default dive by the diving platform in response to my typing the command *dive*. (I was unable to figure out quickly how to set a "mydive" attribute.)

> You boldly climb the spindly ladder, up, up, up . . .
>
> Atop the platform
>
> This small platform teeters high above the Falcon. You may attempt to "dive" into the bucket of water far below, or simply "jump" and hope for the best. It's a long way to the bottom—better not look down!
>
> henri climbs bravely up the ladder to the platform.
>
> henri has arrived.
>
> **Ichi yells up from below, "Jump Jump Jump"**
>
> henri tries to push Copperhead over the edge, but Copperhead manages to shove henri over instead!
>
> henri has left.
>
> **henri yells up from below, "AUUUGH"**
>
> Copperhead attempts the Double Boontit with a Half Twist, from the handstand position. The crowd grows quiet, then exclaims "AWWW" as Copperhead WHAPS into the rim of the tub.

Play with objects on the mud can generate large amounts of text in a short period of time, as this example shows. This quickly moving text also has a relatively low level of intrinsically useful content, so it is referred to, on BlueSky and elsewhere on the net, as *spam*. (The term derives from the canned meat of the same name, particularly as referred to in a Monty Python skit in which the listed menu items in a breakfast cafe include increasing amounts of Spam.) Spamming with objects is considered objectionable during busy times, when it disrupts ongoing conversations.[3]

Objects used in play can serve as repositories of culture and history, particularly of stories told by participants or jokes about them. For instance, in one of the BlueSky bars, a "bartender" object (written by henri) reacts to "spoken" names of drinks or food. Several of these names derive from media references, such as "Spam," "tranya" *(Star Trek)*, and "pan-galactic gargle-blaster" *(Hitchhiker's Guide to the Galaxy)*. Others refer to specific participants. For instance, "shub" refers to the character Shub's interest in guns and his tendency to use the *kill* command frequently:

> Copperhead says "shub"
>
> The bartender suddenly produces a .45 and shoots Copperhead. *BLAM*

Whenever a participant says "shub," the bartender interprets this as a drink order and "kills" the character who requested the drink. The *kill* command can be used by objects such as the bartender or by one character against others. On some gaming muds, kills occur in the course of battles with other characters, usually governed by intricate rules of the game. In some cases, these sorts of kills actually delete the character from the database. However, on most social muds (some of which have eliminated the *kill* command entirely), *kill* merely sends a character back to its "home base" (usually either the entrance room to the mud or a location built by the participant). Several of the bartender's drinks kill the person ordering the drink.

Other menu items have much more benign effects and serve mainly to transmit various in-jokes. For instance, one drink order, "Mountain Dew," refers to Corwin's reputed fondness for the soft drink of that name:

> Copperhead says "mountain dew"
> The bartender shakes its metallic head, "Corwin drank it all."

The restroom in the bar (also created by henri) pokes fun at the virtual reality aspects of muds by playing off the character gender designation. henri and Bob, noticing that I have failed to set my character's gender, encourage me to try it out.

> henri says "ch has no gender"
> Copperhead says "New Gender-Free Copperhead"
> Bob says "Try the restroom, Ch."
> henri says "ch you must go into the restroom and type 'pee'"
> Restroom
> You're in a green-tiled room with fluorescent lights in the ceiling. There seems
>   to be some sort of complex plumbing apparatus over in the corner.

When I type the command *pee* in this room, the room takes note of the gender setting of my character and displays a message accordingly.

With character setting of female:

> You lower the seat, but before you can do anything else, a couple of robotic
>   arms grab you by the shoulders, lift you into the air, and squeeze you
>   completely dry. A light comes on over the plumbing apparatus which reads,
>   "THANK YOU FOR YOUR PATRONAGE"

With character setting of male:

> You unzip, but before you can get any farther, a hose descends from the
>   ceiling, making an ominous sucking sound. To your horror, it attaches itself

to your crotch and drains your bladder dry. A metallic voice announces:
"THANK YOU FOR USING AUTO-POT"

With character setting of neuter (or plural):
The plumbing apparatus seems to go crazy, and a red light starts flashing and
you hear a mechanical voice say "GENDER UNKNOWN GENDER UNKNOWN."
You just pee on the whole thing.

In addition to its in-joke wink about character attributes, this object's responses also play with ideas about gender. Much of the humor in the final response to a neuter gender derives from ideas about the connection between gender and genitals and the difficulty people have in imagining their way out of the gender binary.

Familiarity with objects and the stories to which they allude marks one as an insider to the culture (Fine 1987b). The ability to program objects that people enjoy also gives a measure of status within the group. henri enjoys a high level of respect on BlueSky in part because of the humorous and interesting objects he creates. Similarly, Beryl has written both useful objects, such as the login object that records people's online time, and several fun objects, most of which allow people to add customized messages, a particularly popular form of toy.

The use and creation of mud objects, similar to that of artifacts in offline cultures, become part of the production of culture, and the objects themselves embody and perpetuate that culture. As seen above, people's practices with mud objects become part of the culture. These objects also transmit and repeat aspects of the group's culture, such as people's likes (e.g., Mountain Dew) and hobbies (e.g., gun collecting). Although mud objects are merely programmed textual descriptions, their similarity to physical objects lies in their ability to embody cultural meanings that can be perpetuated or changed through manipulation of the object. Objects also serve as avenues of information exchange between participants.

Two of BlueSky's objects also provide important ways of managing online interactions. The first, a "lom lever," exists in some form in each of the BlueSky bars. This object allows certain participants (who must be approved by the owner of the object) to expel others from the room using the command *lom*, which is sometimes done to express annoyance and is particularly used to harass newbies, who cannot similarly retaliate.

Lom differs from the *kill* command in a couple of important ways. First, all participants (except guest characters) have access to the *kill* command, but the *lom* command works with an object associated with a particular room on the mud. Since rooms are owned by their creators, meaning that changes cannot be made to them by other participants, a participant can acquire lomming capability only through the room owner.

Also, the *lom* command does not cost the character anything, whereas using the *kill* command costs participants a certain number of "credits," some of which must be paid to the killed character. Credits are a form of mud money. Each character receives a certain number upon creation and gradually receives more from the mud program as the participant spends more time on the mud. Credits are "spent" through the use of cpu-intensive commands, that is, mud commands that place a heavy burden on the computer on which the mud is operating. Charging the character credit for these commands discourages profligate use and helps protect the mud program from crashing. All building commands are so taxed, meaning that anyone who wants to build his or her own room or objects needs to acquire a certain number of credits and is presumably discouraged from "wasting" it killing characters. Because *lom* does not cost credits, its capability is desirable to whatever extent that a participant also values building.

On BlueSky, not many people build, and many people amass far more credits than they use. But people still use *lom* more often than they kill. Both commands can be used to indicate displeasure with someone or to tease or harass them. BlueSky participants view *kill* as somewhat more extreme than *lom*, rather analogous to using a harsher swear word.

The following example demonstrates the use of a couple of different objects, including *lom* and the jack-in-the-box. First, Mender activates the jack-in-the-box (built by Beryl), which serves as a repository for joke objects that various other participants program and add to it. (Six-Foot Tall Hello Kitty was inspired by a display of the popular Japanese cartoon character Hello Kitty in a San Francisco Sanrio store.) After I imitate the Six-Foot Tall Hello Kitty, RaveMage suggests I'm participating too fully and loms me.[4] Since I am not yet on the lom list, I am unable to lom him back, and I receive the command failure message, "a humongous buzzer goes off." Mender chivalrously steps in to lom RaveMage for me. Roger Pollack also attempts to do so and finds he is not on the lom list. Meanwhile, Bob loms George just for being a newbie.

> Mender cranks the jack-in-the-box.
> Six-Foot Tall Hello Kitty comes ROCKETING out of the jack in the box!
> Six-Foot Tall Hello Kitty shouts "I WILL EAT YOU LIKE A SAUSAGE!"
> Six-Foot Tall Hello Kitty is shooped back into the box!

Copperhead says "yay! Six-Foot Tall Hello Kitty!"

Copperhead makes big eyes and runs around the room, "I WILL EAT YOU LIKE
A SAUSAGE!"

George says "THAT'S NOT A SAUSAGE"

Rostopovich says "hey, George, I haven't seen you before, are you just a
infrequent visitor?"

George is a NEWBIE SWINE.

RaveMage says "whoa, CH, you're getting too much into the spirit of things
. . . TIME TO COOL DOWN"

RaveMage pulls a large lever, and a trapdoor opens right underneath Copperhead!

Copperhead SHOOTS out into the sky!

The Eyrie [my new location after being lommed]

There is nothing around you save clouds. [description of the Eyrie]

@tel #288 [my command to return to the Falcon]

The Falcon

This spacious chamber is furnished with myriad tables and chairs of every
conceivable material, height, and design, as though a used furniture store
had exploded. Booths tucked against the walls offer a modicum of privacy.
Panels in the curving walls provide diffuse lighting for the patrons who sit
about drinking and talking. At the far end of the chamber, a vertical
extension provides room for a very tall high-diving platform.

Mender says "NEWBIE SWINE MUST BE DESTROYED"

lom RaveMage [here I use the command to attempt to lom RaveMage]

Copperhead pulls a large lever, and a humongous buzzer goes off!

Copperhead hmphs

Mender says "ALLOW ME"

RaveMage says "hee hee :)"

Bob pulls a large lever, and a trapdoor opens right underneath George!

George has left.

Mender pulls a large lever, and a trapdoor opens right underneath RaveMage!

RaveMage has left.

Copperhead bows and says thanks

Roger Pollack says "no, please, i insist"

Roger Pollack pulls a large lever, and a humongous buzzer goes off!

Roger Pollack pulls a large lever, and a humongous buzzer goes off!

Roger Pollack says "well fine"

henri originated both the object and the term "lom." He told me that
in previous versions of this object, everyone theoretically could use the
object, but the command was changed periodically to different nonsense

words, enabling only those with an up-to-date password to use the object. Participants using an old password were subjected to an embarrassing command failure message. Eventually, a list of approved people was developed instead, which was more effective at keeping the expel capability out of the hands of people who abused it. At the time of the creation of this list, "lom" was the current nonsense password and stuck as the object name. "Lom" is also used as a verb to describe the act of expelling someone from the room and has become an important part of BlueSky culture.[5] Some participants lom guests and newbies almost on principle, or as a hazing ritual, or for the amusement of regulars. To some extent, lomming a new participant serves as instruction in the local culture as well.

A second important object, the "magic recording device," or "mrd," stores up to a hundred lines of public text (i.e., excluding whispers and pages) for rereading. The mrd serves several useful social functions. It provides conversational context for people who have just entered the room. It also guards against "spoofing," since it precedes each line of text with the name of the originating character.

Spoofing is a way of transmitting text to others on the mud without that text being attributed to your character. Most commands that generate text, such as *say* and *pose,* precede each line of text with the character name. Spoofing uses a command to generate text that does not include one's character's name. On BlueSky this command is usually used for joke effect, particularly since all participants are aware that others present will immediately make use of the mrd to check the identity of the spoofer. Some muds have made spoofing more difficult by restricting the use of such commands. Others have altered the commands to include the name *after* the line of text, enabling such commands to be used for joke or other effect without giving up character accountability.

Like many of the objects on BlueSky, the mrd demonstrates the importance of identity and continuity for BlueSky participants. In its protection against spoofing (which occurs very rarely on BlueSky), it guards against misrepresentation of identity. Its function as a context provider also supports a social environment in which people are expected not to disrupt conversations already in progress. The ability of others to read the last hundred lines also tends to discourage negative speech about participants not present, lest that participant suddenly appear and read the comments just uttered. (On the other hand, anyone who wants to "clear" the mrd of such speech can easily create enough spam with other objects to do so.)

DOING POLLS, ROLL CALLS, AND QUOTE FESTS

In addition to creating objects, BlueSky participants also use features of the mud program, and of online text-based communication in general, to share information regarding each other's identity. Three of these are doing polls, roll calls, and quote fests. Doing polls appear almost every day as a semiformal part of BlueSky's social practice. Roll calls and quote fests emerge more spontaneously from ongoing interactions. All three form a part of BlueSky's history and culture, enacted much like elements of an oral tradition, which is continually re-created through repetition.

Doing polls resemble play with participant-created objects in that they rely on a mud programming feature that functions much like an object on the mud. The command *WHO* on BlueSky (and, in some form, on most muds) enables a participant to view a listing of everyone connected to the mud at that time. This listing on BlueSky consists of four columns: the first contains names of characters, the next shows how long the character has been connected, the third shows how many minutes it has been since that character last typed something into the mud program, and the fourth is a column labeled "Doing," where participants can provide information about their current activities (either online or off). Following is an example.

WHO

Player Name	On For	Idle	Doing
Eeyore	00:39	38m	
Crotch	00:41	1m	
Rostopovich	01:29	35m	
devnull	01:40	10m	
BJ	02:25	3m	
Amanda	02:58	5m	
doc	03:57	13m	
Ichi	05:28	13m	
Conductor	09:59	11m	
Xena	10:02	18s	
Xavier	10:02	3s	Robotic stuff

11 Players logged in.

As this WHO listing illustrates, BlueSky participants rarely use the "Doing" feature as intended. (Xavier, a robot, has a preprogrammed default "doing." For more about robots, see chapter 5.)

The above WHO listing was obtained on a weekend, when the mud tends to be slow. On weekdays, henri generally changes the "Doing" column to something that invites joking responses from other participants. (henri is the only participant other than the three wizards who can change the "Doing" heading.) These responses are referred to as *doing polls* and provide opportunities for display of wit as well as for the repetition of running gags tied to aspects of people's character or personality. If participants do not "set a doing" immediately on logging on, others (especially henri) will frequently remind them to do so. (The chalkboard I described at the beginning of chapter 1 is my description of an offline analog to this practice.)

In the following, Xavier's "doing" is in the form of a wizard command that can be used to force a character to teleport to the room the wizard is in, thus making a joke about the differences between mud character life and real life. Media references, such as the reference to Barney in Lestat's doing, are also common in doing polls.

WHO

Player Name	On For	Idle	How to Get CowOrkers[6] to Come to Meetings
Guest1	00:02	0s	
elflord	00:09	6m	mind control
Mike Adams	00:20	3m	advertise it as retro night
BJ	00:20	2m	
Phillipe	00:24	8m	
Captin	00:33	29m	have meeting in their office
devnull	01:20	20m	schedule over top of even worse meetings
Bang	01:33	3m	
doc	01:45	12m	
Jet	01:57	8m	By force majeure
Lestat	02:03	2s	have Barney sing over their desk phones
henri	02:13	4m	donuts
Tempest	02:18	6m	fondle the barrel of your .45
Corwin	02:20	16m	
Obtuse	02:28	45m	Announce a simultaneous network outage
fnord	02:29	9m	pay raises for good attendance
Mender	03:05	39m	free nookie
Ichi	03:32	2m	
cycle	05:22	2m	
Rostopovich	05:42	18m	remote controlled motor-chairs

Conductor	08:08	13m	
Xena	08:10	53s	promise to do dance of seven veils
Xavier	08:11	13s	@force CowOrker = @tel here
24 Players logged in.			

Sometimes doing polls are based on media events, such as the capture of the Unabomber suspect or coverage of the O. J. Simpson trial. Polls may also be based on random topics that come up in conversation or on events in participants' lives, such as a poll about marriage when one person announced his engagement and another poll about "features in rat heaven" after a participant's pet rat died.

Roll calls are similar to doing polls in that a topic is announced and various participants respond. Roll calls were invented by henri at a time when it was technically difficult to tell which logged-on characters were actually active, and all created characters were visible (that is, listed in the room contents description) in the rooms they were last active in. In popular hangouts, this could become confusing, since the room might contain many characters whose participants were not actually present and participating. A roll call offered a way to see who was actually present and participating in the conversation.

After some changes in the ways mud programs treat characters not currently logged on and the development of a more sophisticated *WHO* command, roll calls became a way to poll participants in a room for information or opinions. Some, like doing polls, include joking responses. However, many function as an exchange of personal information. Roll calls usually emerge from the ongoing conversation, as in the following example. Conversation also continues while the roll call is being answered, particularly when the answer takes some thought. In the following excerpt, I've edited out nonresponsive comments after the roll call to make the example clearer.

> Copperhead says "PAL when were you in high school anyway?"
>
> PAL says "I graduated in '69."
>
> Barbie says "you GRADUATED in 69??"
>
> henri says "Pal is old, BB"
>
> PAL nods.
>
> Corwin NOTABLE EVENTS IN YOUR LIFE IN 1969 ROLL CALL
>
> Corwin born
>
> Sparkle not even a glimmer in my mom's eye
>
> Barbie says "9th birthday"
>
> Farron was born in late '69, by comparison.

henri first grade

Locutus glint in father's eye

Perry parents were attending college together

PAL came within one jump of beating Olympian Reynaldo Brown at the state
track meet.

fnord had surgery when he was a few months old

Copperhead entered jr. high (I think)

As in real-life roll calls (in school or the military, for example), roll call replies tend to be given agrammatically and in incomplete sentences. Among the topics I've seen for roll calls are personal statistics (including roll calls on age, income, hair length, number of hours worked so far this month, etc.); miscellaneous opinions on current events, movies, or the like; jokes (such as "expert witness on _____ at O. J. trial roll call" inviting a fill-in-the-blank response); and roll calls that require performing an action on the mud first, such as "page Nightcrawler roll call." In the last case, a participant first does the action (paging Nightcrawler) and then performs a "null emote" (the *emote*, or *pose*, command with no text afterward, resulting in a line with just the participant's name and no other text) to respond to the roll call. In the following example, a similar roll call requires people to perform a physical action offline: "RL" refers to "real life." (Previously, a discussion of a "Dr. Smith" called up associations with the old *Lost in Space* television show, resulting in people imitating the robot from that show.)

Half Life waves her arms around shouting "DANGER DANGER"

henri waves his arms around shouting "DANGER DANGER"

Half Life waves her arms around RL and bursts out laughing

henri WAVE ARMS AROUND RL ROLL CALL

henri

Half Life

Ulysses no

Locutus

Half Life says "doit doit"

Corwin no, too tired

Copperhead can't bring herself to do that one.

This roll call took on a "dare you" quality, because many participants were at work at the time, and completing the roll call would have required them to perform a potentially embarrassing action offline. Although other participants had no way of verifying the actual performance of this action, people took it as a point of honor to respond honestly about their compliance with the roll call, as evidenced by several participants' verbal refusal on the mud. This again demonstrates the insistence of BlueSky participants on continuity between online and offline activity and identity.

Less formulaic than doing polls and roll calls, quote fests don't usually start by a call for participation. Instead, they emerge spontaneously from conversation. Some reference in conversation will remind a participant of a previous quote, which he or she will then call up and display for other participants. Sometimes this sparks a long series of quotes from past conversations called up in such a way that the new context renders them humorous. In the following example, all lines where a character name is followed by the | symbol and another character name are quotes, and other lines are original text being "spoken" in between quotes.

> henri | Alisa says "BJ, tell me when it's back up again."
> henri | DelSol says "well, mine's slightly thicker than other people's"
> Faust | Stem4 opens up a desk drawer to reveal: a 15-inch long "Slim Jim".
> henri | DelSol gotcher little professor right here
> devnull | BJ got about an inch and a half down here
> Faust | Susanah says "oh and the thousand little grippers so it doesn't slip"
> Jet says "why are quotes about sex from women funnier? Or is it just me"
> Faust | henri pops up on the screen
> Jet | You say "i hate coming to work early"
> Jet | symmetry whispers "I hate working to come early."
> henri says "quoting whispers is Right Out"
> henri BONKS Jet
> Jet says "OIF"
> devnull says "not if it's a fake whisper, henri"
> henri says "true"

As indicated by henri's reproach of Jet, quote fests follow particular social rules. Anything said "out loud" is fair game, but whispers and pages are not.

Jet's response of "OIF" to henri's BONKing him is a formulaic performance with years of history on muds. This convention has extended to other computer subcultures. The *Hacker's Dictionary* describes this convention: "bonk/oif interj. In the MUD community, it has become traditional to express pique or censure by *bonking* the offending person. There is a convention that one should acknowledge a bonk by saying 'oif!' and a myth to the effect that failing to do so upsets the cosmic bonk/oif balance, causing much trouble in the universe. Some MUDs have implemented special commands for bonking and oifing" (Raymond 1991: 74).

In addition to having rules against quoting private communications, BlueSky participants also frown on the quoting of partial lines (usually done to enhance the humor).

> Ulysses holds the peanut butter with his thighs as he shifts books and beer
> bottles on the computer table to make room for the bagels
> Ulysses <—deft
> Perry <—daft
> Copperhead | Ulysses holds the peanut butter with his thighs
> Perry snorts
> Ulysses says "partial quoting is no fair"
> Copperhead hangs her head.
> Copperhead couldn't resist
> Jet says "Disks the world over would fill should we start partial quoting"

As Jet's admonition indicates, participants engage in quote fests by saving quotes in files on their local machines for later use. Most participants use some type of windowing system that allows them to open a quote file in one window while the mud is running in another window and paste or retype text from their quote file into the current mud conversation.

Quote fests are sometimes sparked by particular words. Everyone might call up all the quotes they have with the word "penis," for instance. Quote fests can also be directed at a particular person, when everybody calls up the quotes they have of that person. These sometimes take the form of duels, in which two people hurl each other's quotes back and forth.

> Corwin | henri squirts water out of his blowhole at Corwin
> henri | Corwin is over 200 pounds, and not to be taken to bad opera
> Corwin | henri has never fizzed over the top
> henri | Corwin says "Good guess, except totally wrong"
> Corwin | henri says "I feel so. . . . plastic"
> henri | Corwin chants: shut the fuck up
> Corwin | henri says "tie a finger around your string"
> Copperhead howls outloud at Corwin/henri quote war
> henri | Corwin says "not quotes of me, you nitwit"
> Corwin | henri ? henri
> henri | Corwin says "henri will quote that"
> Corwin concedes, having run out of henriquotes

henri has a ton more

fnord I Corwin can just stop talking now, and let henri quote him periodically
    instead

Corwin has 13 henriquotes

henri has 59 Corwin quotes

henri I Bilerific-Sid says "A few more quotes, and I'll never have to log on
    again."

These examples illustrate that quotes most likely to be saved are sexually suggestive when taken out of context or in some way embarrass the
quoted participant. This limits the content and tone of quote fests, causing
some participants to complain that they are silly, tedious, or spammy.
However, regardless of their content, they exhibit interconnections among
participants. A character who is quoted has a demonstrable history on the
mud. Being quoted is also deemed a recognition of wit, which can lead to
discussions of quote file sizes and comparisons of different participants'
wittiness.

devnull NUMBER OF BJ QUOTES YOU HAVE ROLL CALL

devnull 22

Perry 0

henri says "23"

Faust 5

henri NUMBER OF BARBIE/COALGHOST/HACKMISS/etc.QUOTES ROLL CALL

Copperhead no quote file yet

henri 80

Jet ose, barbie is coalghost

Perry didn't know that

devnull 3

Jet rethinks coalghost quotes in this context

Faust 8? dunno

This example also demonstrates the confusion generated by participants
changing their mud names. The participant "Barbie" used several different
names over the years. Because they began their participation on BlueSky
later than some others, Jet and Perry knew Barbie's other mud names
through quote fests but had not connected those names to Barbie's current
mud name.

Doing polls, roll calls, and quote fests all display wit or personal information in ways that explicitly compare the contributions of individual
participants. Sometimes this can be competitive, but more often on

BlueSky it is a friendly exchange and a search for commonalities and differences among participants. Like other groups of friends, BlueSky participants compare ages, histories, wittiness, and so forth, creating, reenacting, and strengthening bonds of friendship and knowledge about each other. These cultural practices can also help compensate for the limitations of communication in a text-only environment. Through these traditions, BlueSky participants manage to exchange information that might be more readily available in a face-to-face setting, such as age and other personal statistics.

RUNNING A MUD

BlueSky participants consider their mud more entertaining and interesting than most muds, and they often mentioned to me in interviews that they valued the wit and intelligence of other participants. They also pride themselves on the egalitarian quality of the social group. My interviewees acknowledged some differences in status, attributing them primarily to the different abilities to contribute to the group culture either through wittiness or through building and programming skills. However, most felt that these status differences were minimal.

Yet all muds have a separate class of participants—wizards—who have more control over the mud's operation than other characters. Even on BlueSky, where participants' extensive mud experience and their familiarity with each other demystify the wizard role, the role of wizard still confers some status difference.

Although anybody connected to the Internet can access hundreds of muds, including BlueSky, muds do not constitute truly public space. Each mud program requires a host computer on which to run and uses some of the resources of that computer. Someone must provide the computer, which must have enough spare memory and processing capacity to run the mud, and someone must also take responsibility for keeping the mud program running. The people who undertake these tasks have a different status from that of the average participant.

The person with control of the host computer essentially controls the existence of the mud. Similarly, the person or persons who control the mud program have the power to decide whether the mud continues to operate. Wizards, and possibly others to whom wizards give access, can view any part of the mud database, including communications such as whispers, which would otherwise be inaccessible to any except the two parties involved. This can have a significant impact on the social environment. For instance, BlueSky participants discuss rumors that the wizard of HappyHour routinely eavesdrops on unwitting participants, and they wonder why anyone would participate on that mud under those circumstances.

How a wizard administers a mud affects the social norms of the group. Wizards' relationships to the other participants and their decisions controlling access and participation, also give them a degree of social power. Their actions affect the social norms of the group in much the same way as club rules affect the types of interactions that can occur in private social clubs.

Ulysses joined the BlueSky group several years ago. Although technically not a dino, he was already acquainted with several long-term BlueSky participants through common newsgroup participation. More important to his continued popularity have been his facility with language and a quirky, acerbic wit. He describes the operation of BlueSky as more or less a benevolent dictatorship.

> The way things are administered is basically very autocratic. You've got two or three wizards, and what they say goes. It's not a democracy. It's basically a private club. That's the way it's administered. People would come in and expect that it would be a democracy. There's lots of sort of democratic experiments on the net. Like LambdaMOO and its millions of petitions and votes and everything else.[7] This is really the opposite.

Under such circumstances, the philosophy of the wizards clearly can significantly affect norms of behavior. But although wizards with control over access to the mud itself can ultimately control membership in the group, many have learned that social groups pruned too heavily die out quickly. Stories abound on the mud newsgroups of wizards whose style of governance, perceived as too heavy-handed, resulted in a steadily decreasing membership. Such cautionary tales, combined with the Internet's historical bias toward libertarianism as well as Corwin's and Alisa's own views on free speech, have led these two to a very laissez-faire style of mud governance. Corwin stated his philosophy as follows:

> I have some very serious ideas about what's appropriate and what's not. And I'm not relativist about them at all. On the other hand, I feel that if I regulated what kind of communication was going on on my mud, someone else might do it on another mud. Let me give you an example. If I said that I found something, some topic—I'm not even going to pick out one—to be personally obnoxious (and there are some, there are some that we discuss on BlueSky in the event of which

I'll either idle or leave) . . . if I said that was not appropriate for BlueSky, what if religion were no longer appropriate on another mud to talk about?

As a person whose fundamentalist Christian views are unpopular among the other members of BlueSky, Corwin understands the benefits of allowing for different opinions among the group and not attempting to select group membership according to particular political affinities or others.

The "ruling" style of the BlueSky wizards also results from the long association of the group members. Alisa indicated that on previous Surly Gang muds, wizards had to intervene more often in conflicts, but that by now the remaining group understands which types of behavior are tolerated. She described BlueSky's current culture and attitudes:

> It's gotten through their thick heads how to behave—what they can do and what they can't get away with. There are no holds barred and no one hesitates to make fun of anyone else. Killing is a pastime, just to make people shut up or whatever. You just don't see that on other muds very often. Other muds are more attuned to newer users. If a very new-to-muds user walks on our mud, they've got to have a thick skin. And a lot of them may be put off by it, and a lot of them will leave and that's it. I've never had any complaints. I've gotten people who are completely confused by it, or they can't find the Falcon and are baffled and wonder why this is so different from other muds. . . . If they're curious they'll stick around, and if they're curious they'll usually hang in the back. If they're not, then they'll go somewhere else.

As these descriptions from Corwin and Alisa indicate, they rarely intervene in social affairs on BlueSky (although elflord, given wizard status specifically to handle the social side of mud administration, intervenes more often). Even more rarely do they use the formal sanctions against characters available to them. However, general knowledge of the existence of these sanctions, based on BlueSky participants' years of mudding experience, nevertheless affects people's behavior.

Several formal sanctions are available to wizards against other characters on muds. The ultimate sanction is character destruction. Every character consists ultimately of bits in the database. Wizards with complete access to the mud database can destroy any object at will, including characters. Participants sometimes refer to this as *toading*. (Originally "toading" referred to a command that merely turned a character into a toad that could only croak, robbing the participant of the ability to communicate through the character. On some muds, this type of toading is still practiced and is differentiated from sanctions involving actual destruction of the character.)

I know of no one on BlueSky who has had his or her character toaded. However, on several occasions, elflord has resorted to the next most severe level of discipline, known as *newpasswording*, which consists of the wizard changing a character's password so that the participant can no longer log on and use his or her character. Usually this serves as a strong warning that if the participant's behavior does not change, the character will be toaded. It also imposes a temporary exile on the participant (although he or she can use the guest character in the interim).

elflord is a quiet, scholarly young man who works as a system administrator and lives in a medium-sized western town with his wife, Carla. He expressed a degree of pride in being "the first non-Corwin or -Alisa wizard on a Corwin and Alisa mud" and takes his wizardly responsibilities very seriously. During my interview with him, we discussed a recent incident that led to his newpasswording the character shorthop. He also explained his views on the effect of his wizarding on the social environment on BlueSky.

> I think people pay more attention to my pronouncements now because
> I am a wizard, and I've shown that I will boot you [or] I will
> newpassword you if you cross the line. Just having [my] presence
> there probably contributes somewhat to stability. The only people who
> really push it have been Florin and shorthop. And I view them as
> the lunatic fringe. Florin just gets his jollies out of poking people, and
> I can understand that to a certain extent. He tends to push it a little
> too far in my opinion. shorthop's just nuts. The less said about him the
> better. . . . Florin got his password back eventually. shorthop [was]
> gone for a while and got his password back eventually as well, but I
> don't think he's going to get it back this time, because I don't think he
> can stop his stream of invective at me long enough to apologize, let
> alone ask for something back.

As elflord indicates, participants can plead their case and request the restoration of their password. In the incident elflord alludes to involving Florin's newpasswording, Florin refused for weeks to apologize or ask for his character back, using the guest character in the meantime. (Guest characters cannot build rooms or create objects. Nor can they "teleport," making it more cumbersome for them to move from room to room. These and other limitations on the guest character make it an undesirable character to use for very long.)

shorthop has a long history of annoying other BlueSky participants.

For some, his worst offense was writing a description of BlueSky for an Internet guide. That description included details about the lives and personalities of several BlueSky participants. Despite having been asked not to do so, shorthop included these participants' character names. Some felt this violated their privacy and exposed them to potential harassment from outsiders. I was warned on several occasions not to repeat shorthop's mistake.

But while shorthop's breach of social norms may have contributed to reduced tolerance of his behavior generally, it did not lead directly to his newpasswording. Given the raucous, raunchy, no-holds-barred discourse tolerated on BlueSky, the only behaviors deemed worthy of incurring newpasswording have been those that threaten the actual running of the mud. Both shorthop and Florin were newpassworded for this reason. shorthop incurred official wizardly sanction when he went on a rampage of indiscriminate building, using an automatic feature to duplicate rooms that, if left unchecked, would likely have crashed the mud. Florin actually did crash the mud through extremely fast-paced automatic spamming. Florin finally apologized and requested use of his character back. shorthop has not returned.

Florin's and shorthop's behaviors demonstrate the ambiguity on muds between speech and action.[8] Since all communication on muds occurs through text, it all resembles speech of a sort, and BlueSky participants generally regard it as such. BlueSky regulars repudiate the suppression of speech, no matter how vile or vulgar. However, Florin used "speech" to create a tangible effect, crashing the mud program. This suppressed the speech of other BlueSky participants through the temporary destruction of the social space itself. Thus, forms of speech that cross the line to effects on the program also exceed the limits on behavior. Conversation on BlueSky, however annoying or emotionally disturbing, does not usually cross this line, although extreme personal attacks usually arouse the ire of other participants.

The problem of database maintenance suggests one of the ways in which online relationships are vulnerable to offline interference. The existence of a coherent social group such as the group BlueSky depends on the continuous and consistent existence of a forum in which the group can interact. Somebody, somewhere, must agree to the use of his or her computer for this purpose, and that computer must run more or less reliably.[9]

Although behaviors that do not threaten the BlueSky database itself rarely invoke official sanction, on rare occasions wizards do "boot" characters. This command constitutes a third level of sanctioning, less severe than either toading or newpasswording. It kicks a character off the mud but does nothing to the character or password; thus the participant can log back on immediately. Booting functions as a warning to the participant that stronger sanctions may apply should the current behavior continue.

BlueSky participants de-emphasize the importance of these commands and the exclusive power of wizards to wield them. However, BlueSky participants do accord wizards some extra measure of respect, in deed if not in spirit. Taunting a wizard, tantamount to spitting in the face of a police officer, rarely happens on BlueSky. This stems in part from the fact that until recently Corwin and Alisa were the only wizards on their muds, and the BlueSky group treats Corwin and Alisa with additional respect as the founding "parents" of the mud group. Alisa, who currently rarely logs on, receives enthusiastic greetings when she appears. Corwin, a much more frequent participant, is considered to be rather prickly online. Participants argue with him regularly over political issues but very rarely criticize him personally. When any participants feel the need to express displeasure with Corwin's behavior (or religious views), they generally do so using a command called *mutter*, which allows them to transmit text to everyone in a mud room *except* a chosen character.

A recent incident demonstrated the norm against harassing wizards in the breach. During a minor altercation in which Corwin killed several characters for generating annoying amounts of spam, Rostopovich, one of the characters killed, returned to the room angry at the perceived injustice. Several others reacted with surprise, partly because others saw Corwin's kills as justified and partly because Rostopovich rarely directly criticizes anyone. Part of the surprise also stemmed from the rarity of this direct challenge to a wizard. henri's reference below to an alien in Rosty's chest (derived from the famous scene in the movie *Alien*, where a parasitic alien emerges from a human crewmember's chest) demonstrates the degree of strangeness he attributes to the scene.[10]

Rostopovich has arrived.
Rostopovich says "Twist in the wind, Corwin"
Rostopovich says "or go somewhere else"
RaveMage says "heh"
henri says "as the little alien living in rosty's chest pokes its head out"
Copperhead buh
Corwin says "GO SOMEWHERE ELSE?"
Corwin killed Rostopovich!
Rostopovich has left.

Itchy says "spooky"

Rostopovich has arrived.

Corwin says "no I did NOT hear you tell me go somewhere else on my mud"

Corwin's proprietary reaction to Rostopovich's suggestion that he go somewhere else demonstrates his opinion (and also group knowledge) that, in the last instance, BlueSky belongs not to the group but to Corwin.

In the next portion of log from this incident, Itchy chants the command for toading a character, demonstrating his view of the road Rostopovich is on. Later Itchy also suggests booting Rostopovich. henri indicates Itchy himself may be out of line by lomming him. After Mender borrows a commentary that media reports often use (concerning people who perpetrate random violence but were previously known as "quiet sorts"), Rostopovich accounts for his behavior (although he does not directly apologize to Corwin).

Itchy chants "@toad, @toad"[11]

Rostopovich says "yes you did hear me tell you to go somewhere else on your mud"

Itchy jeers, "BOOT HIM!!"

henri runs over and SHOVES Itchy onto the green circle, then DIVES for the lever! Ka-CHOING![12]

Itchy has left.

Rostopovich says "and it felt good."

Itchy has arrived.

Mender presses the HAIL button on the intercom and says "I remember Rosty, he was always quiet and kept to himself." into it.

Itchy loves being Corwin's toady.[13]

Rostopovich says "I'm just bored crosseyed, and being gratuitously rude to Corwin keeps me from keeling over insensate."

That Rosty's behavior elicited such surprise demonstrates both the departure it represented from his normal behavior and the perceived gravity of his breach of conduct. Both Rosty and Corwin also signal their understanding that the mud *belongs* to Corwin:

Corwin says "no I did NOT hear you tell me go somewhere else on *my mud*"

Rostopovich says "yes you did hear me tell you to go somewhere else on *your mud*"

Similarly, Itchy's suggestion that Rostopovich is about to be toaded or booted demonstrates the expectation that wizards will use the power they have available. Corwin does not do so, however, given his general noninterventionist wizarding strategy. Perhaps the rarity of this confrontational behavior from Rostopovich also leads Corwin to be lenient.

BlueSky participants mostly de-emphasize the degree of respect that wizards gain simply by being wizards. However, as the above incident demonstrates, that status nevertheless exists. Both the understanding that BlueSky "belongs" to Corwin and the expectation that he will therefore be accorded greater respect than other characters fit with comparisons of BlueSky to a private club or bar. Private clubs and bars are owned by somebody and therefore do not constitute truly public spaces. All online spaces are similarly owned in that all must be run on and accessed through computers owned by various entities. Although the Internet was begun as a government project, the government no longer runs it and does not (nor did it ever) provide within it a guarantee of a sort of "town square" public space.[14] This situation has some effect, however small in particular instances, on the interrelationships among people in online spaces.

The examples in this chapter only begin to depict the character and complexity of BlueSky's culture and humor. Much of that culture stems from social solutions to the technical limitations of mud communication. Whereas in face-to-face conversation, annoyance with another participant might be conveyed through tone or expression, on muds, the lack of these cues can be compensated for somewhat through the use of *kill* and *lom* commands. More positive expressions such as approval and solidarity tend to be communicated on BlueSky through group in-references rather than through automated commands.

As in other small groups that interact on a regular basis, BlueSky culture reflects elements of other subcultures to which its members belong (Fine 1987b), from science fiction fandom, to the larger mudding subculture, to the subculture of computer engineers. Cultural practices within muds such as BlueSky also sometimes migrate to these larger groups, as in the example of BONK and OIF. BlueSky participant acceptance of sexual humor, the authority of wizards, and other aspects of their online interpersonal relations draw on, reflect, and re-create cultural understandings formed offline.

Although most of what occurs on BlueSky resembles interactions that occur in other small groups, the limitations and potentialities of online textual communication do exert some influence on the style of BlueSky culture. For instance, that style includes a slightly greater emphasis on repetition, which helps compensate for the lack of daily face-to-face contact. Repetition and ritualized text help substitute for repeated visual contact with familiar faces.

4 Hanging Out in the Virtual Locker Room
BlueSky as a Masculine Space

I've found that in most cases gender becomes one of the least important things about a person. [I choose] male or female as the mood strikes [me]; on many muds I'm almost exclusively female. I think that when you get down to it, if people really think about it, gender matters for little ultimately. Like take you for example—your @sex is set to "female"—but does that mean anything other than the 6 bytes it takes up to store the text? Not really. I treat you the same whether it says female, male, neuter, or whatever—assuming that we're not roleplaying something or the like.

Carets

I'd like to think . . . I don't really know, because I'm not a guy . . . but I would like to think that when you're online as a woman that the fact that you're a woman is backseat to the personality.

Peg

A female newbie will be given more breaks & more attention, even (especially?) by women.

Beryl

Women get treated differently from men. It's not that they get more slack or anything, but they get chased out differently. Part of it is that most women tend not to talk immediately, just by normal socialization. Guys are much more likely to mouth off early. But women often get turned off by less nasty hazing than men.

Spontaneity

Online participants, like the researchers who study them, present a range of views about the significance of gender online. Carets believes gender doesn't matter at all, while Peg more ambivalently hopes it doesn't. Beryl, on the other hand, has noticed different patterns of treatment based on characters' declared online gender identity. Spontaneity further notes that people bring different behavior patterns to their online interactions on the basis of their previous gendered (offline) socialization.

Unless they attempt to use nonstandard or invented pronouns, text-based forums require some acknowledgment of gender. People must choose pronouns to refer to themselves and others, and mud servers use character gender designations to pick appropriate pronouns when generating text about characters.[1] Gender's connection to sexuality also brings it to the fore in online interactions. Many mudders engage in personal, social, and sexual exploration on muds (Deuel 1995; McRae 1997; Turkle 1995). Mudders thus acknowledge and discuss gender more readily than they do either race or class. Mudders almost never ask about others' real life race or class identities (although they do sometimes ask about age). But the interconnection between specific gender identities and sexual identity, the expectation that both gender and sexual identities form a core part of the self, and the prevalence of homophobia in U.S. culture lead participants online to ask each other's "real life" gender designations routinely.

Such questions almost never occur on BlueSky, where people know each other's offline identity and also distance themselves from the "pickup" atmosphere of some mud public areas. Many of BlueSky's female participants appreciate that people are not likely to hit on them on BlueSky. (Participants do sometimes flirt.) Yet some people on BlueSky also recognize its gendered nature. As RaveMage commented online when I suggested BlueSky could be characterized as a "male" space, "i'd say totally male, ya; I mean, look at all the sexist banter." Patterns of speech, persistent topics, and a particular style of references to women and sex create a gendered environment on BlueSky that favors males.

MASCULINITIES AND COMPUTER TECHNOLOGY

The masculinity of BlueSky's environment relates in particular to computer use. As Connell (1995) has pointed out, masculinity does not constitute a single uniform standard of behavior but rather comprises a range of gender identities clustered around expectations concerning masculinity, which he terms "hegemonic masculinity." Connell defines hegemonic masculinity as "the configuration of gender practice which embodies the currently accepted answer to the problem of the legitimacy of patriarchy, which guarantees (or is taken to guarantee) the dominant position of men and the subordination of women" (77). While few men actually embody the hegemonic masculine ideal, they nevertheless benefit from the "patriarchal dividend" of dominance over women. However, they must also negotiate their own relationship to that ideal.

This negotiation, along with the performance of specific masculinities, occurs through interaction with others. As Messerschmidt points out, "Masculinity is never a static or a finished product. Rather, men construct masculinities in specific social situations" (1993: 31). Segal describes masculinity as not only emerging through relations with others but as relational by definition: "As it is represented in our culture, 'masculinity' is a quality of being which is always incomplete, and which is equally based on a social as on a psychic reality. It exists in the various forms of power men ideally possess: the power to assert control over women, over other men, over their own bodies, over machines and technology" (1990: 123).

Perhaps the most salient of these forms of masculine power for the men on BlueSky is power over technology. Not all BlueSky participants currently work with computers, but most have done so at some time. In addition to their socializing on BlueSky, many participants employ computers for other leisure uses, including playing computer games at home and participating in networked games on the Internet. BlueSky participants thus enact a form of masculinity congruent with computer culture, itself a largely masculine domain (Spertus 1991; Turkle 1984, 1988; Ullman 1995; Wright 1996). Wright discusses the particular style of masculinity in both engineering and computer culture as "requiring aggressive displays of technical self-confidence and hands-on ability for success, defining professional competence in hegemonically masculine terms and devaluing the gender characteristics of women" (1996: 86).

MASCULINITIES AND WORK TALK ONLINE

Many conversations on BlueSky revolve around computers, including discussions of new software, planned purchases, and technical advice. Participants stress the value of the work-related computer information they have obtained on BlueSky. When people log on with a particular question or problem from work, they give other participants the opportunity to demonstrate technical knowledge and reinforce a group identity connected to computer technology. Following are several log segments from a long conversation in which one participant asks for help with rewriting a segment of software code. During this conversation, participants negotiate group norms and their relationships with each other. They also demonstrate their computer knowledge and membership in the computer subculture in ways that specifically relate to masculinities. In the following excerpt, henri asks for help in figuring out how to execute a command in a particular computer language, which opens up discussion of various computer languages.

> henri says "what's the /bin/sh equivalent of goto"
> henri d'ohh there doesn't seem to BE a goto in /bin/sh
> Perry says "of COURSE there isn't a goto in sh. why do you need one?"
> henri says "I CAN'T BELIEVE THERE'S NO GOTO IN 'SH'"
> Perry says "sh is the lily-white pure programming language"
> elford says "Perl is the One True Language"
> Corwin says "is not"
> elford says "Well, it's a damn fine language anyway :)"
> Faust says "Perl is the One True language for Many Uses"

As the conversation continues, participants implicitly compare their preference for particular languages to adherence to different religious doctrines. The discussion allows them to demonstrate the extent of their programming knowledge as well as to indulge in a joking argument about the virtues of the various languages. In the next segment, Perry initiates a roll call polling of the Perl "faithful." Perry and Faust list their names as agreeing with the roll call statement, while Corwin indicates disagreement. The other participants tease Corwin about his dislike of Perl, suggesting it relates to his religious beliefs as a born-again Christian.

> Perry THINKS PERL IS A DAMN FINE LANGUAGE ROLL CALL
> Perry
> Faust
> Corwin pfeh
> Faust says "Corwin doesn't like Perl because of the comment in the docs
>   about 'You're going to hell anyway, might as well program in Perl.'"
> henri LAUGHS
> Perry heh
> Corwin eyes Faust

After this digression, henri attempts to draw the conversation back to his programming problems, introducing a new snag he has hit. This time participants respond more directly to his question.

> henri says "goddamit how do I put a embedded newline in a string in sh"
> Corwin says "\n"
> Corwin says "maybe"
> henri tried that and got a literal n

elflord says "What's the context? Just an 'echo' or something?"
henri says "setting a variable to a string that includes newlines; to be used in
    an echo later"
elflord says "Ah. Try just slapping a literal newline in there."
Faust thought you used that ENDLINE thingy
henri says "that didn't work either"

While BlueSky participants often get quick and accurate responses to work-related questions, in this case, no one has the right answer for henri. He gets annoyed and frustrated that people respond to his questions without really knowing the answer.

henri can guess as well as anybody
Corwin laughs
Corwin says "use \012"
henri BONKS Corwin
Corwin says "ow, what"
henri says "stop guessing"
Corwin says "it's a GOOD guess, try it"
henri tried it before he bonked you

Although several things can confer status on BlueSky, including a quick wit, participants respect extensive programming knowledge. henri, with a Ph.D. in computer engineering and a job in which he works on complex and specialized programs, has high status on BlueSky.[2] henri's reputation as a superlative programmer makes this conversation somewhat different from more routine occurrences in which less experienced programmers ask for help. Without his intending it to, henri's question becomes a challenge to the other participants. In the next section, elflord, apparently after consulting online documentation, responds to henri's original question.

elflord says "okay, in sh, \ only escapes \, ', ", $, and newline; no nifty c-like \n
    or \r or anything"
henri says "it doesn't seem to work when I'm setting the value of a macro to
    be echoed later"
henri gave up on the sh problem
Perry says "right, it has to be inside an echo"
Faust says "write it in perl :-)"
elflord's literal newline gets turned into a space in a variable value
henri says "it's a 2000 line sh script I'm trying to improve"
henri ain't rewriting it

henri says "my mistake 2892 lines"

elflord says "Well, bummer, henri."

elflord says "If you remove \n from $IFS you might be able to include it literally
in a variable value"

henri stares at elflord

elflord stares back

henri says "(i) you're still guessing (ii) I gave up on that problem"

elflord says "Okay, fine, forget it, just trying to help"

henri says "JUST SAY I DON'T KNOW"

henri's last remark plays off Nancy Reagan's anti-drug-use slogan "Just
say no." In BlueSky's cultural context, this also implies that elflord suffers
from MAS, or male answer syndrome, as defined in this earlier conversation:[3]

Jet says "What is MAS?"

henri says "Male Answer Syndrome"

Jet ose

Obtuse ew

Rostopovich says "that's when you answer everything with a question?"

Jet says "You attempt to answer any questions asked of you no matter your
actual knowledge of the subject at hand"

Barbie says "a thoroughly knowledgeable SOUNDING answer to everything"

henri's reference to MAS in the discussion about programming calls attention to the ways in which discussions of computer work reinforce particular middle-class masculine identities.

Like most statements on BlueSky that call attention to norms of masculinity, accusations of male answer syndrome tend to be offered and taken
in good humor. As an example, henri described for me an object called the
Male Answer Syndrome Clinic, which he'd built on a previous mud. The
clinic functioned as a type of puzzle common to the text-based adventure
games that were the precursors of muds. A participant who entered the
clinic had to solve a variety of puzzles. The final puzzle, which had to be
completed in order to exit the clinic, required typing the words "I don't
know," at which point the participant was declared cured of MAS. elflord's
familiarity with MAS and with henri's earlier puzzle allows him to interpret henri's accusation of MAS without henri actually using the acronym
in this case.

BlueSky participants' discussions of MAS suggest a critique of hegemonic masculinity. However, BlueSky's culture in general includes a high

degree of sexist banter and comments about women. Significantly then, the critique of MAS is leveled at a type of behavior that has nothing to do with women or sexuality. Rather, it has to do with male conversational style and accusations of posturing. In this way, it relates more to relationships among men than to relationships between men and women. It also leaves intact a standard of aggressively answering all questions, as long as the answers are correct. Accusations of MAS denigrate inaccuracy more than they denigrate a particular style of interaction. Many people on BlueSky in fact self-accuse as a way of letting the hearer know that the information they are imparting is not verified.

In the following, final segment of the programming conversation, henri's MAS accusation angers elflord, who "shouts" at henri. Corwin also suggests that henri's response to others' attempts to help is unreasonable. (The phrase "man page" in the following refers to online manuals of commands that are available on computers using Unix operating systems.)

> elflord says "I DON'T KNOW BUT I'M TRYING TO HELP BY VIRTUE OF READING THE DAMNED MAN PAGE"
> elflord says "BUT NOT ANYMORE"
> henri points at the man page sitting on his xterm window
> Corwin says "henri asks just so he can abuse helpful attempts"
> henri asks in case someone who has some specialized knowledge is present, not so N people can duplicate what he's already tried
> elflord says "Well how the heck are we supposed to know what you've already tried?"
> henri says "just believe that I would try the obvious strategies like reading the man page, trying n"

Here, the participants negotiate potentially discrediting facets of their relationships and computer knowledge. Computer culture depictions of end users suggest that they are not capable of looking up basic questions in available documentation. For instance, the *Hacker's Dictionary* offers as one definition of user, "A programmer . . . who asks silly questions" (Raymond 1991: 364). This dictionary also offers a definition and etymology for the more derogatory term "luser" (pronounced "loser"), also used to refer to end users of programs (see 229–30). Computer engineering culture, and especially hacker culture, values self-instruction and the ability to figure things out. The belief that "lusers" lack this ability is expressed in the well-known acronym RTFM, for "read the fucking manual." The *Hacker's Dictionary* offers the following definition for RTFM: "1. Used by gurus to brush off questions they consider trivial or annoying. . . . Used when reporting a problem to indicate that you aren't just asking out of randomness. 'No, I can't figure out how to interface UNIX to my toaster, and yes, I have RTFM'" (307). In the BlueSky conversation, henri expresses frustration at people's guesses and also asserts his own competence in answering basic questions, distancing himself from derogatory depictions of "users."

While the preceding conversation illustrates henri's attempts to gain information necessary for his work activities, it serves several other purposes as well. The discussion of the relative merits of different programs confirms the status of various participants as sharing programming skills and knowledge. It also augments and perpetuates BlueSky's connection to computer culture. Further, the argument over the proper response to a call for help constitutes negotiation of BlueSky's social norms.

Through such discussions, not only do BlueSky participants gain work information; they also enact and reinforce a particular type of masculine culture. They receive affirmation of their computer knowledge and work abilities and of the value of such skills. In addition, by obtaining answers to their questions from online sources rather than from coworkers, BlueSky participants can appear more self-sufficient and knowledgeable and bolster their status at work.

"DEAD BUG WALKIN'":
PROGRAMMING AS SPECTATOR SPORT

Work-related talk on BlueSky does not always involve information exchange. Some people also use BlueSky to engage in running commentary about their work, which further illuminates BlueSky's role in supporting a particular work-related, masculine, middle-class identity. For instance, some computer tasks are so tedious and routine that a person can perform them while participating in a mud conversation. The most common of these is "bug fixing"—hunting down errors in computer code. In the following, Locutus comments on his progress in attempting to fix a particularly problematic bug. He begins his commentary with a mock-sexual suggestion common to masculine discourse in various forums. (This conversation occurred on a relatively quiet night. I've inserted spaces into the log excerpt to indicate pauses in the conversation.)

> Locutus says "man this bug can blow me"
> Locutus hate hate hate
> Copperhead snerts
>
> Locutus prays to the gods of mail merge

Locutus thinks it's grandma's cookies time
Locutus says "bringing out the big guns"

In suggesting that a computer software error can "blow" him, Locutus almost certainly has no explicit image of sexual activity in mind. His expression derives from widespread slang usage particularly common among males. Although the sexual imagery therefore serves as an expression of general displeasure, it nevertheless suggests that the "bug" holds a subservient (feminine) position to Locutus's masculine prowess as a programmer. Such routine usages demonstrate the degree to which the concept of competence, both at work and in life, is intertwined with expectations and assumptions about masculinity.

Locutus says "mother FUCKER i just figured out this bug"
Locutus debug debug "hey that looks bogus" look at code "how did this ever
    work?"
Locutus says "answer: it didn't"
Copperhead says "go Locutus go"
Thistle watches Locutus demonstrate the Heisenbug Uncertainty Principle.
Locutus says "nah; you could repro it, but it was just tricky"
Locutus bets no user has ever run into it, even

Locutus debugs
Locutus is a CODER AFIRE
Locutus says "AAHAHAHAH bugs who know me know FEAR"
Thistle says "DEAD BUG WALKIN'!"

Thistle, a newbie who ultimately logged only ten hours on BlueSky, attempts to assert his or her own programmer status by bringing up the rather arcane discussion of the Heisenbug Uncertainty Principle. Raymond defines a heisenbug as "a bug that disappears or alters its behavior when one attempts to probe or isolate it" and identifies the reference as wordplay on "Heisenberg's Uncertainty Principle in quantum physics" (1991: 198). In the line following Thistle's comment, Locutus indicates that Thistle is wrong, because this does not describe the bug Locutus is working on. Locutus's relatively gentle correction acknowledges the potential relevance of the phenomenon Thistle identifies by pointing out the specific difference between Locutus's own problem and a "heisenbug," that is, reproducibility. This kind of discussion again demonstrates knowledge of programming and computer culture minutiae and establishes the work identities of the participants involved. By contrast, my lack of similar programming knowledge relegates my participation in this conversation to a cheerleader role ("go, Locutus, go").

Debugging can be an extremely tedious and frustrating part of programming. By commenting on progress in this way, programmers on BlueSky can express their frustration regarding difficult problems and receive encouragement and congratulations when they manage to fix them. In a way this turns programming into a spectator sport; something with a higher degree of masculine status—that is, greater congruence with hegemonic masculinity—than sitting in front of a computer.

"HOW DID I GET SO NERDY?"

While their computer skills help BlueSky participants gain and maintain employment, and their connections with computers have cultural cachet as well, U.S. culture is ambivalent toward computer expertise and those who hold it. This ambivalence extends particularly to the perceived gender identity of people skilled in computer use and centers on the figure of the "nerd." For instance, Turkle discusses the perception that MIT students (when compared with, for instance, Harvard students) are nerds because of their connection to technology and that MIT computer science students are "the ostracized of the ostracized" and "archetypal nerds" (1984: 197–98).

In addition to its (relatively recent) connection to computer use, "nerd" connotes a lack of masculinity. For instance, researchers have documented its pejorative use in regard to nonhegemonic white males (Connell 1995; Addelston and Stirratt 1996). Euro-American men sometimes also denote Asian American males (often stereotyped as feminine in U.S. culture) as nerds (Cheng 1996). "Nerd" thus is not necessarily limited to designating a technologically savvy male, but in recent years the term has been increasingly connected to computer use.

However, as Wajcman discusses in reference to descriptions of computer hackers as disheveled loners and losers, the connection to technological knowledge conveys masculine status, even while it complicates that status.

> The question that this poses is whether for these men technical expertise is about the realization of power or their lack of it. That in different ways both things are true points to the complex relationship between knowledge, power and technology. An obsession with technology may well be an attempt by men who are social failures to

compensate for their lack of power. On the other hand, mastery over this technology does bestow some power on these men; in relation to other men and women who lack this expertise, in terms of the material rewards this skill brings, and even in terms of their popular portrayal as "heroes" at the frontiers of technological progress. (1991: 144)

The growing pervasiveness of computers in work and leisure activities has changed many people's relationship to this technology and thus has also changed the meaning of the term "nerd." Since the 1980s, the previously liminal masculine identity of the nerd has been rehabilitated and partly incorporated into hegemonic masculinity. The connotations of this term thus vary depending on the social context. As an in-group term, it can convey affection or acceptance. Even when used pejoratively to support structures of hegemonic masculinity, it can confer grudging respect for technical expertise.

Men on BlueSky are well aware that the extent of their computer use places them within the definition of the nerd stereotype. Many also have some of the other personal or social characteristics that brand them as nerds. As represented in the "Nerdity Test," available online, such characteristics include fascination with technology, interest in science fiction and related media such as comic books, and perceived or actual social ineptitude and sartorial disorganization.[4]

In the following statements, culled from several different conversations on BlueSky, participants illustrate their recognition of the nerd as both a desirable and a marginal masculine identity in their discussions about nerd identity.

> Ulysses looks in henri's glasses and sees his reflection, and exclaims "Oh NO! I'm a NERD!"
>
> Mender says "when you publish please feel free to refer to me as 'nerdy but nice'"
>
> Jet says, "HOW DID I GET SO NERDY"
>
> Randy <— fits one of the standard nerd slots

BlueSky participants humorously identify themselves as nerds and connect with each other through play with that identity. But they also indicate their understanding that this status disqualifies them from a more hegemonic masculine identity. Ulysses' mock dismay at his nerdy looks and Mender's phrase "nerdy but nice" indicate that they see the nerd identity as not completely desirable.

The nerd stereotype includes elements of both congruence with and rejection of hegemonic masculinity. Its connection to a reconfiguration of middle-class male masculinity partly redeems its masculine status. The nerd identity thus constitutes one type of masculinity that Connell identifies as complicit "with the hegemonic project" (1995: 79–80).

Not surprisingly, given the nerd's contradictory masculinity, BlueSky participants both support and call into question societal norms regarding masculinity. Their conversations about women, men, and sex are often wry and self-deprecatory.

> henri says "[Mender], if we meet a couple of supermodels in NYC, the rule is:
>   you take the brunette, I take the blonde"
> Mender says "what if they are both blonde?"
> henri says "you take the shorter one"
> Mender says "hsm"[5]
> henri says "you are shorter than me after all"
> Mender says "OK"
> fnord says "what if you meet a short blonde and a tall brunette?"
> Mender says "trouble"
> henri says "hair color overrides height"
> henri says "domehead and I used to use the blonde/brunette system when
>   scoping babes (from afar) at basketball games"

In such joking conversations, the irony derives from the men's knowledge that they do not meet the standards of hegemonic masculinity and also indicates some degree of rejection of those standards. However, this self-referential irony encompasses only the relationship between these men and other (presumably more hegemonic) men. It does not include women, who become adjunctive definers of status. Mender and henri poke fun at expectations that masculinity includes the easy possession of women but do not question the desirability of "supermodels." Although they distance themselves from normative standards for masculinity, BlueSky participants do not necessarily embrace a more egalitarian standard between the sexes.

For example, the term "babe" is ubiquitous on BlueSky. Usually it denotes a woman outside the mud group. The woman's connection with a mud participant is usually romantic or potentially romantic, although that connection may exist only in fantasy. In the following brief excerpt (taken from a much longer conversation), Mender and henri (who live in different areas of the country) discuss possible plans for the evening; people offer joking responses to Mender's request for entertainment ideas; and Tempest waits for a response to a phone call.

> Mender says "What should I do tonight henri"
> henri says "Mender, rent The Quiet Earth"
> Roger Pollack says "find a babe and rent the fisher king"
> Roger Pollack says "okay, okay, forget the first part"
> Mender stares at Roger
> Mender says "I HATE YOU"
> Tempest waits for his party to respond
> Roger Pollack says "is this the babe, tempest"
> Tempest says "babe?"
> Tempest says "not, just some woman"
> Tempest says "i mean, she's a babe, but not any specific babe :)"
> Roger Pollack says "weren't you eyeing some babe? or was that madmonk"
> Tempest "that was madmonk :)"
> Roger Pollack ose
> Mender says "what should I do tonight"
> Mender says "the bar with all the babes isn't serving alcohol tonight"
> Mender says "no point going if there's not even a chance of me getting tipsy
>   enough to talk to them"
> Perry says "so get drunk beforehand"
> Mender ! @ pairy [= Mender looks very surprised at Perry]
> Mender says "YOU'RE A GENIUS"

Mender's request for suggestions concerning what to do that night sets a joshing tone, and both his statements and others' suggestions include ironic insinuations regarding their inadequate social lives. (I've reproduced only some of these insinuations in the excerpt above.) Mender in particular implies with his continual requests for suggestions about what to do that he needs to be talked into undertaking social activity. He also indicates that he needs alcohol to talk to women. This conversation demonstrates BlueSky's use as a place in which guys can share anxieties about socializing with women and strategies for decreasing those anxieties. In this context, Mender particularly uses "babe" to denote anonymous women of potential sexual interest.

Roger Pollack and Tempest demonstrate uses of the term "babe" connoting attractiveness and also a specific relationship. (I've excerpted a portion of their conversation again here for ease of reference.)

> Roger Pollack says "is this the babe, tempest"
> Tempest says "babe?"

Tempest says "not, just some woman"

Tempest says "i mean, she's a babe, but not any specific babe :)"

Roger Pollack says "weren't you eyeing some babe? or was that madmonk"

Tempest's correction of Roger Pollack's use of the term "babe" demonstrates the relational quality of the term and also exposes the element of sexual attractiveness in its definition. Tempest refers to the woman he phones as a "babe," in the sense of "attractive woman," but stresses that she is not a babe in the sense of being a potential sexual object, such as the one madmonk was eyeing.

These uses of the slangy, offhand term "babe" fit the casual, clubby atmosphere while also keeping concerns about sexuality and relationships at a distance. BlueSky participants refer to "the receptionist babe," "the Yale babe," "the swim babe," and so forth. This allows them to designate sexually attractive women by monikers describing their connection to the participant or to some outstanding but still relatively generic feature. But even with these particularizing classifications, all of these women remain just "babes." This allows the guys to discuss potential (or unlikely) exploits and to bemoan their inability to connect with babes without it reflecting too negatively on their masculinity. Further, they can deflect the loss of masculinity connoted by the inability to get dates through their comradery in bemoaning the situation. "Babes" become an abstract, an unattainable; talked about and theoretically longed for, they are always a distant object.

"DIDJA SPIKE 'ER?": HETEROSEXUAL MASCULINITY ONLINE

As Segal points out, " 'gender' and 'sexuality' are at present conceptually interdependent" and "provide two of the most basic narratives through which our identities are forged and developed" (1994: 268–69). Understandings of one's own and others' gender identity include assumptions about sexuality. While not all BlueSky participants are heterosexual, heterosexuality is an important component of the particular style of masculinity enacted on BlueSky. However, in this forum, in which relationships are based so heavily on "talk," talk about sex and about men and women not surprisingly becomes more important to acceptable masculine performance than avowed conformity to particular sexual desires, practices, or relationships.

For instance, two very active and well-respected BlueSky male regulars define themselves as bisexual. One of these has never had a sexual relationship with a man. The other had a relationship with another male mudder (who only rarely appears on BlueSky), which most other BlueSky participants knew about and accepted. Both of these BlueSky regulars currently live with women in long-term relationships. Thus, arguably they are not viewed by other BlueSky men as having strayed very far from heterosexuality. However, they also actively participate in jokes and conversations depicting women as sexual objects as well as in other forms of BlueSky banter connected to performance of masculinity.

In keeping with acceptable performance of hegemonic masculinity, both men and women on BlueSky distance themselves from femininity and, to some extent, from women in general. Conversations that refer to women outside the mud, particularly women in whom a male participant might have a romantic interest, bluntly depict such women as sexual objects. However, participants' allusions to sexual activity are so far removed from the circumstances described that these references again incorporate a high degree of irony. Participants further enhance this irony through the use of formulaic joking patterns, as in the following variations on the question "Didja spike her?"

> Mender says "did I mention the secretary babe smiled at me today"
> Roger Pollack WOO WOO
> Jet says "cool Mender"
> Jet says "did you spike 'er"
> Mender says "No, sir, I did not spike 'er."
>
> McKenzie wonders if he should continue this email correspondence or just wait
> till he can meet her tomorrow
> McKenzie siigh
> Locutus says "meet whom"
> Locutus shouts into a microphone, "SPIKE HER"
> Locutus had a short conversation with a 50–55 year old wrinkly well dressed
> woman in the wine section of the grocery
> Mender says "didja spike 'er, Locutus?"
> Rimmer says "DIDJA SPIKE HER LOCUTUS"
> Locutus says "hell no"

In each of these conversations, mere mention of a woman provokes the formulaic question "Didja spike her?" Such joking formulas constitute techniques of group identity construction. Through jokes regarding women's status as sexual objects, the men on BlueSky demonstrate support for hegemonic masculinity. As Lyman explains, "The emotional structure of the male bond is built upon a joking relationship that 'negotiates' the tension men feel about their relationships with each other, and with women" (1998: 173). The ironic sexism of much BlueSky discourse maintains "the order of gender domination" (172), almost irrespective of other aspects of BlueSky men's activities and behaviors with and toward the women in their lives.

For instance, in a later discussion, Locutus and Rimmer indicated that they used the term "spike" to refer to any heterosexual activity (whether initiated or controlled by the man or by the woman). But the phrase "Did she spike him?" would provoke considerable confusion for most people. Further, its suggestion of nonhegemonic heterosexual practices gives it a very different meaning from "Did he spike her?" The metaphor "spike" contains an obvious male bias. It also contains a discomforting conjuncture between sex and violence, which corresponds to standard expectations about hegemonic masculinity.

Further, the joking quality of the "Didja spike her?" conversations points to an uneasiness with hegemonic masculinity as well. During a period when several participants had read a piece I'd written analyzing references to gender on BlueSky (which did not include a discussion of the term "spike"), Rimmer asked me about "spike her" references:

> Rimmer says "So if I now said to Locutus 'So did you SPIKE her?' would that be offensive?"
>
> Copperhead does find the "did you SPIKE her" stuff a bit offensive, actually
>
> Rimmer says "Wow; the SPIKE stuff wouldn't be funny if there was any chance in hell that anyone ever would"
>
> henri nods at rimmer
>
> Locutus says "the 'didja spike her' joke brings up the whole 'women as conquest' idea"
>
> Rimmer says "Boy I don't think it's a woman as conquest thing at all"
>
> henri says "what you find offensive (and I agree) is people thinking any time a guy interacts with a woman they should ask if their pants fell off and they locked hips"
>
> Rimmer says "I think it's more of a 'Mudders never have sex' thing"
>
> McKenzie agrees with Rimmer, "asking 'didja SPIKE her' is more parody than anything else"
>
> Rimmer doesn't think he's ever asked "DIDJA SPIKE HER" and expected someone to actually say YES
>
> Rimmer says "It would be tacky as all hell in that case"
>
> McKenzie says "actually everyone would say 'I HATE you'"

Rimmer points out the joking nature of the question "Didja spike her?" His assertion that "the SPIKE stuff wouldn't be funny if there was any chance in hell that anyone ever would" specifically highlights the mildly mocking intent of the joke. In this and similar conversations, participants illustrate their perception of the connections between nerd identity and heterosexual incompetence. The irony of "spike 'er" humor relies on and reproduces the image of the sexually frustrated, and therefore perpetually adolescent, nerd.

However, as Locutus and henri recognize, the joke also relies on the continuing portrayal of women as sexual objects. Women's unattainability as sexual objects to *some* men provides the sting in the self-deprecatory joke, leaving in place a normative expectation that masculinity involves the sexual possession of women and that this is a desirable norm to attain. Rimmer and McKenzie indicate this in their statements that "Didja spike her?" is a rhetorical question, because it is expected that mudders never have sex with women and wouldn't talk about it if they did, because the other "less fortunate" participants would, as McKenzie indicates, say, "I HATE you." The joke is intended to be on the participants themselves, regarding their nonhegemonic masculinity, but women are the ultimate butts of the joke. As Butler points out, heterosexuality (and, as one of its terms, I would add hegemonic masculinity as well) "can *augment* its hegemony *through* its denaturalization, as when we see denaturalizing parodies that reidealize heterosexual norms *without* calling them into question" (1993: 231, emphasis in original).

The sexual practices of BlueSky participants also may diverge from the aggressive hegemonic model implied by the word "spike." The potential discrepancy between sexual practice and group identity practice demonstrates some of the dilemmas involved in negotiating masculinities. Like adolescent boys who feel compelled to invent sexual exploits about which they can brag, men in groups create sexual and gender narratives that may not resemble their lived experience but nevertheless form important elements of their masculine identities and their connections with other men. Such connections to other men can come at the expense of connections to and empathy with women.

"BLUBBERY PALE NERDETTES": NERDS, GENDER, AND SEXUALITY

BlueSky discussions also demonstrate the dilemma that nerd identity introduces into connections between gender identity and sexuality. Nerdism in both men and women is held to decrease sexual attractiveness, but in men this is compensated by the relatively masculine values attached to intelligence and computer skills. In women, lack of sexual attractiveness is a far greater deficiency. The following excerpt of a conversation among several male BlueSky participants about attendance at science fiction fan conventions ("cons") demonstrates this:

> Mike Adams says "that's half the reason I go to cons. Sit and have these
>   discussions with people"
> Bob . o O (No it isn't)
> Mike Adams says "well, okay it's to ogle babes in barbarian outfits"
> BJ says "*BABES*?"
> BJ says "you need new glasses"
> BJ says "pasty skinned blubbery pale nerdettes"
> Locutus laaaaaughs
> Locutus says "ARRRRR 'tis the WHITE WHAAALE"
> BJ wouldn't pork any women he's ever seen at gaming/other cons, not even
>   with Bob's cock.
> Perry says "that's because pork is not kosher, drog"
> Locutus says "women-met-at-cons: the Other White Meat"
> Perry LAUGHS
> BJ HOWLS at locutus

While apparently quite misogynistic, the impetus for this conversation relates at least as much to the BlueSky love of wordplay (another "nerdy" pastime) as to negative attitudes toward women. The word choices and the source of the humor in the above banter also reveal some key assumptions about, and perceptions of, nerd identity. Besides the implication in BJ's description that female nerds, like their male counterparts, do not spend much time outdoors or engage in exercise, his and Locutus's statements represent nerds as white. While the term "nerd" may be applied to non-white males who meet other nerd identity criteria (see, for instance, Cheng 1996), the stereotypical nerd is white. Similarly, nerds are presumed male, as evidenced by the term "nerdette." This term, like the term "lady doctor," defines the normative case of nerd as *not* female.

This connection between nerdism and masculinity may be what makes a nerd identity so damaging when applied to women's potential and perceived sexual desirability. The participants express the assumption that "nerdettes" who would attend science fiction conventions by definition lack sexual desirability, and they quickly join in the joke set by BJ's critique of Mike Adams's potentially transgressive desire. Mike Adams, on the other hand, dropped out of the conversation until the topic of cons had passed.

Although some versions of these types of "guy talk" likely occur in most male groups, this group enacts a particular style of masculinity relating to their use of computers and the accompanying social stereotypes. Their rejection of some aspects of hegemonic masculinity led them to reject my attempt to construe their interaction in male-specific sports-related terms, as in the following.

> Copperhead makes some quick notes about "lockerroom atmosphere" and
> "male bonding".
> henri says "what did we say that was locker room like"
> Mender exposes himself to Copperhead
> Mike Adams I henri thinks about the cool guys girlfriend "MAN she is a babe"
> henri says "that's not locker room, that's angst"
> henri says "locker room is 'well my date with so and so last night was hot, she
> was all over me' etc."
> Mender snaps henri with a towel
> henri YEEOOWWW
> Copperhead was referring more to the general repetitiveness of topic than to
> the flavor of any particular comment.
> henri says "the only things people talk about on muds are (i) technical issues,
> (ii) sex, (iii) idiots"
> Mike Adams says "lessee, common repetitive topics here: computers, dating,
> lack of dating, computers, sex, sexual deviance, computers, jobs making
> money, lack of jobs making money, computers . . ."
> henri says "see I'm right"

The other participants (in this case, all male except for myself) object to my characterization of the space as a locker room. They also demonstrate their understanding that I may be accusing them of sexism (as in Mender's joking comment that he is exposing himself to Copperhead) and their knowledge of the cultural code I have evoked through their pantomime of locker-room behavior (Mender's snapping of henri with a towel, and henri's yelled response). While more or less agreeing with my identification of repetitive topics, they disagree with my characterization of the space as therefore potentially excluding women. They represent their discourse as just normal topics of conversation, to which anybody can contribute. But henri's and Mike Adams's descriptions of these "normal" topics nevertheless reflect the identities of the majority of participants on BlueSky as young, white, male, and middle-class.

HETEROSEXUAL "DROPOUTS"

Several BlueSky males are bisexual or gay, including some of the participants in the conversations above. Of the 138 regulars, I know the self-reported sexual identities of 75.[6] Of those 75, 7 (both men and women) are either bisexual or gay, and a couple of infrequent participants are as well. Although participants' sexual orientations occasionally become a topic of conversation, for the most part they are ignored. Homophobic jokes generally are not tolerated, although participants known in general for crassness sometimes get away with homophobic remarks. Significantly, in a forum where outspoken opinions are a normal feature of discourse, several of the more politically (and/or religious) conservative participants, understanding that their views on homosexuality are in the minority, express such views quietly and only when asked, if at all. Through their tolerance of different sexual orientations, men on BlueSky thus diverge again from hegemonic, heterosexual masculinity, which "is also defined according to what it is not—that is, not feminine and not homosexual." (Herek 1987: 73.)

Further, some of the ways in which BlueSky participants enact and express heterosexual identities suggest that in examining connections between sexualities and masculinities, we need to problematize notions of heterosexuality as a single, uniform sexual identity. A standard, Kinsey-style spectrum of straight to gay identities based on sexual behaviors or feelings does not adequately describe sexual identity on BlueSky, because it leaves out important information concerning affectional connections and orientation toward sexuality in general. As Segal states, "It is men's fear of, or distaste for, sex with women, as well known as it is well concealed, that the heterosexual imperative works so hard to hide" (1994: 257). Discussions of sexuality on BlueSky sometimes reveal this distaste as well as the unorthodox solutions some men find for the dilemma imposed on them by the tension between distaste and hegemonic masculine identity, including its heterosexual component.

For instance, several of the straight men on BlueSky report that they have "given up" on women or romantic relationships and have been celibate more or less by choice for several years. In occasional discussions on BlueSky focusing on this issue, these men complain of rejection that derives from their nonhegemonic status.

Stomp has problems with dating and women and stuff, but also has serious
  reservations about the accepted male-female dynamic in the USA, to
  the point where he's never felt much point in getting over the first set of
  problems.
BJ says "Sides, women LIKE scumbags; it's been proven"
Ulysses nods at BJ
BJ should have been gay, he can relate to other guys
Stomp says "as far as I've been able to observe, abusing women (subtly) is
  one of the fastest and most efficient ways of getting laid."
BJ will agree with that
Stomp says "Once I realized this, I just sort of went: Well, forget it, then."
BJ says "guys get to be assholish and abusive cause that kinda attitude is richly
  rewarded"
Ulysses says "Nice guys end up being the friends to whom those women say
  'You're such a good listener, let me tell you about the latest horrible
  thing my inconsiderate sweetie did to me'"
Stomp says "Expressing interest in a way that isn't assholish invites getting
  cut down brutally."
Ulysses says "We tried opening our mouths a few times, and got laughed at"
Ulysses says "End of experiment"
Stomp says "You get seen as weak."
Ulysses says "self-assurance and confidence are not options for me. I'd have
  to go back to infancy and start over"
BJ says "this mud is full of 'nice guys.' it's also full of guys who haven't been
  laid in epochs if ever"

The male participants in the above conversation express considerable ambivalence toward predominant standards of masculinity, portraying themselves as "nice guys" left out of the standard (in their understanding)
heterosexual dynamic of violent conquest. Although they designate more
sexually successful men as (by definition) jerks, a degree of envy tinges
this discussion. Rather than merely rejecting a heterosexuality they view
as abusive, they represent themselves as reacting to having been "cut down
brutally," "laughed at," and "seen as weak" as well as used as a sympathetic ear without regard for their own potential desires.

The rather stereotypical depiction of women in the above, as not only
tolerating but desiring abuse, leads to some potential interpretations of the
male angst expressed. Hegemonic masculinity's requirement of heterosexuality contains an inherent contradiction. As Lyman points out, "The separation of intimacy from sexuality transforms women into 'sexual objects,'

which both justifies aggression at women by suspending their relationships to the men and devalues sexuality itself, creating a disgust of women as the sexual 'object' unworthy of intimate attention" (1998: 178). While the hegemonic gender order thus depicts women as inferior and not acceptable identity models, it nevertheless requires that men desire these inferior (even disgusting) creatures. The men in the conversation above represent casualties of this contradiction. Their discomfort blends a rejection of perceived expectations regarding hegemonic masculinity, especially those involving violence toward women, with a more hegemonically congruent discomfort with women themselves.

While not all of the men on BlueSky share this orientation toward sexuality or the discomfort with women that it entails, conversations such as the above elicit no surprise and little censure. A closer look at reactions of BlueSky participants to the situation of one of these men, Ulysses, helps further illuminate the connections among nerd identity, hegemonic masculinity, and sexuality.

Ulysses' sole sexual relationship has legendary status on BlueSky, partly because it involved Elektra, another BlueSky participant who was formerly a regular but currently participates very infrequently. Ulysses and Elektra initially met online and, after meeting offline, lived together for several months. BlueSky participants frequently retell or allude to the story of Ulysses and Elektra's relationship as one in which Ulysses, a shy and retiring intellectual male, became involved with Elektra, a promiscuous and exploitative woman, who subsequently abused Ulysses and ruined him for all future heterosexual contacts.

> Ulysses has only kissed one person, and does not remember it fondly
> Anguish wows.
> Copperhead says "only one person?"
> Ulysses says "One"
> BJ imagines sucking face with eleqtra and GIBBERS in abject horror
> Anguish says "gee . . . are you asexual, Ulysses? Or is that an entirely inappropriate question to ask?"
> Ulysses says "No, I'm straight, just completely unappealing"
> BJ says "anguish. you haven't seen or talked to his last slamp;[7] it's a wonder he talks to women"
> BJ would have been either a monk or gay by now
> Anguish has had some horrible "partners"
> Ulysses is a hermit, basically, especially since Elektra
> Anguish says "oh oh, I think I've heard of Elektra stories."

BJ is even less appealing than ulysses, but still manages to get laid or at the
very least kissed at semi regular basis

Stomp says "Ulysses is dapper and appealing, but cannot admit it to himself,
because he's scarred so much."

In the above, Anguish and Copperhead (both female) express amazement
at Ulysses' lack of sexual experience, while BJ and Stomp (both male)
demonstrate their familiarity and sympathy with his story. In other online
conversations, references to Elektra usually allude either to her lack of
willingness to pay back the large amounts of money she reportedly owes
Ulysses and others or to her many sexual contacts (including several other
BlueSky participants). My aim here is neither to dispute nor to confirm
claims regarding Elektra's actual behavior or those regarding Ulysses'
status as her scarred-for-life ex-lover. The notable aspects of this story and
its frequent retelling are (1) the representation of Elektra as the archetypal
manipulative (and promiscuous) female, and (2) the acceptance of Ulysses'
claim that because of Elektra, he will never have another heterosexual
relationship. These themes have taken on a mythic quality in BlueSky's
culture and, as such, represent important expressions of ideas about sexuality and women, even if they do not represent the feelings or experiences
of the majority of men on BlueSky. The concerns expressed in this story
demonstrate some of the strains and contradictions involved in enacting
heterosexual masculinity.

Ulysses represents himself in the above conversations as unappealing
and lacking in self-assurance and confidence. While this assessment may
or may not represent his actual estimation of himself, it does not match
the opinions others hold of him. Ulysses has relatively high status on
BlueSky, and others consider him witty and intelligent. Furthermore,
Stomp's description of him as dapper and appealing fits my own impres-
sions from spending several days as Ulysses' guest while doing interviews.
Far from the awkward portrait that the above discussions likely convey,
Ulysses' actual comportment is suave, gracious, and considerate. His wry
sense of humor and quirky wit enliven the mudder gatherings he attends.
The discrepancy between, on the one hand, Ulysses' demeanor and the
high esteem in which others hold him and, on the other hand, their account
of his relationship status highlights the danger that BlueSky participants
perceive from heterosexual relationships.

BJ, Stomp, and Ulysses still represent themselves as heterosexual (and
not, for instance, asexual, as Ulysses indicates to Anguish), despite their
lack of sexual involvement. Their support of each other's stories and the

acceptance of these stories by other BlueSky participants reflect the connection between this form of heterosexuality and the nerd identity. As Wright says about hackers (a closely related category), "Hackers take pride in being 'nerds' and being antisocial, not needing women in their lives" (1996: 89). BlueSky participants can hardly be considered antisocial, given the many hours they spend socializing with each other online. However, many of them strengthen their bonds with each other through common commiseration over the poor quality of their offline social lives, especially their romantic and sexual lives. Such commiseration represents an ironic understanding of the expectations connected to the stereotypical nerd identity, but it also stems from actual dissatisfaction with offline social experiences.

These "victims of masculinity" are all in their late twenties and may in time change their views of heterosexual relationships. However, their current divergence from normative heterosexuality relates directly to the performance of masculinities. Categorization of men according to sexual identities based solely on sexual object preference fails to consider significant differences among the relationships of men to other men and women and the meanings that their own sexual preference or behaviors hold for them.

ONE OF THE BOYS:
WOMEN PERFORMING MASCULINITIES ON BLUESKY

The sexist attitudes toward women sometimes expressed on BlueSky and the mud's status as a male-dominated space do not preclude the active participation of several women. The sexual objectification of women usually refers to women "out there." Any woman on BlueSky itself is one of the gang. This means that sexual harassment and the experience of "being hit on" is almost unheard of on BlueSky.

Lisa has been a member of the Surly Gang for many years. Like both her parents, she has a degree in engineering, providing clear proof of her ability to get along in male-dominated settings. She pointed out in her interview that one of the advantages of being accepted as "one of the guys" in a male-dominated setting like BlueSky is the lack of attention to sexuality.

LISA: I think the atmosphere of the Surly Gang muds is kind of different from the other muds [in terms of] just being hit on. That's one of the reasons that that's where I hang out primarily—you're not hassled.

LORI: Have you found that a problem on other muds?

LISA: Occasionally, yeah. Someone will just start paging you stuff. You have no idea. Someone who doesn't know you will presume familiarity at you. And that happens a lot less on Surly Gang muds. Part of it may be that it is kind of a smaller community. There are fewer strangers.

The general obnoxiousness on BlueSky tends to keep out potential new female participants. But the harassment of outsiders also benefits the women who are already there. Most participants are known, and harassment from strangers, sexual or otherwise, is not tolerated.

Slightly more than one-quarter of BlueSky's regulars are women. Most of these women have histories of participation in male-dominated groups, as Beryl, a female regular, indicated to me in our interview:

BERYL: I've always been around men, groups of men, because I've been interested in role-playing games and science fiction and computers.

LORI: Those are all pretty male dominated.

BERYL: Yeah. So I feel totally comfortable. Even though it's weird to notice that sometimes I look around and there's ten guys in the room and—me. But then sometimes there'll be four or five women in the room and just a couple of guys. It swings the other way. Not as far.

Beryl's previous experience with male-dominated groups has given her social skills and understanding that help her to deal with BlueSky's rough social ambience. BlueSky's other active women participants also have experience in male-dominated groups, which helps them fit in well.

Peg notes some differences in men's and women's experiences on BlueSky. But in the following excerpt from my interview with her, she suggests that gender doesn't strongly affect how people are treated on BlueSky.

LORI: You've talked a little bit about women getting different treatment on BlueSky. What have your experiences been?

PEG: Really, I don't pay attention to that. When I just started mudding, people flirted, but that's when I wasn't thinking about how people were treated. Half the time you couldn't tell what sex somebody was anyway. I think on BlueSky it's the classic geek thing. I still get the feeling sometimes that the guys think of themselves as . . . they're all sitting around in this guy geekhold and any woman who comes in it's like the things will be—

LORI: Different?

PEG: Yeah.

Here and in her comment at the beginning of this chapter, Peg connects gender to sexuality. In the earlier quotation, she assumes that she can't know whether being a woman online really matters, since she isn't a guy and therefore can't know what they might think. She assumes then that her status as a woman online means something different to guys from what it means to other women. Here, she replies to my question about differential treatment with reference to flirting. In both comments, Peg reveals a degree of uncertainty and ambiguity in her characterization of the mud social space. Although she claims not to pay attention to differential treatment, she nevertheless characterizes BlueSky as a "guy geek-hold" that changes when women enter it.

Beryl, Peg, and I all share histories either of personal interest in science fiction and computers or of primary friendships with men or boys with those interests. Our previous experiences in male-dominated subcultures prepared us for the tone and character of BlueSky's social atmosphere. While we all have female-designated characters and make no efforts to hide our female status, our familiarity with the dominant topics of conversation and our ability and willingness to conform to the social norms of the male-dominated space enable us to perform (at least in part) masculine identities and enjoy the enhanced social status attendant on being "one of the guys."

However, the few participants who do not work with, and are not interested in, computers can sometimes feel left out of the culture of the group and hence outside the group's norm of masculinity. Because Western culture in general associates computer competence and interest with masculinity, femininity can come to be associated with lack of competence and an inability to fit into the dominant social norms. Shelly, a woman who muds on BlueSky only infrequently, told me that she wasn't interested in all the "tech talk" that occurs on BlueSky and that therefore "they all consider me a bimbo here." BlueSky participants do tend to evaluate Shelly's intelligence negatively and may do so because of her lack of interest in computers. Significantly, in Shelly's mind if in no one else's, that negative evaluation takes a gendered form in the term "bimbo."

Another frequent regular, Sparkle, said:

> In the bar [on BlueSky], I most likely seem more flakey than I am, but that's mostly because they don't talk about things I know anything about. All I can do is crack jokes and laugh when I read something

that's funny to me. . . . For the longest time, I was too scared to talk to anyone on here. I just hung out in the bar and laughed, which is why people think I am a ditz.

Both Shelly and Sparkle refer to themselves using terms that both denigrate their intelligence and connect that denigration specifically to femininity. They thus connect their lack of technical knowledge to negative female stereotypes. On BlueSky, as long as a woman participant shares the group's interest in computers, she can fit into the taken-for-granted conversational pattern by becoming one of the guys. Women such as Shelly and Sparkle, however, remain gender outsiders.

These social norms tend therefore to reify connections between technical competence and masculinity. Because the male-dominated nature of the social space combines with an emphasis on technical talk, people who join the technical talk more successfully perform the type of masculine identity dominant in the subculture. As Cockburn explains, "Technology enters into our sexual identity: femininity is incompatible with technological competence; to feel technically competent is to feel manly" (1985: 12). To the extent that conforming participants, whether male or female, are defined as "one of the guys," participants perceived as not technically competent are also perceived as *not* one of the guys. They become, in both cultural and gendered terms, Other.

Several people, both male and female, nevertheless participate successfully in the group without any particular computer interest or expertise. For these participants, joining into the general style of conversation becomes more important than the ability to participate in any particular topic of conversation. Both men and women agree that conversations on BlueSky frequently become insulting and obnoxious. Most women do not consider obnoxiousness normal in friendship groups or a usual requirement for group membership. Many men, however, are used to this as a feature of male group sociability. Women on BlueSky, including myself, must negotiate a stance within this unfamiliar social terrain.

After several months of mostly quietly observing the conversations (or "lurking," as this activity is generally referred to on the net), I decided to attempt to become a more active participant on BlueSky. In the following excerpt of a conversation on BlueSky, I deviate from my previous, relatively quiet comportment and attempt to respond in kind to the obnoxious banter. allia is the only other woman present.

Florin has arrived.
Shub says "Baron Florin of Shamptabarung!"

Copperhead says "hi Florin"

Florin says "shub, copperhead. who the hell is copperhead?"

Shub says "copperhead is your future wife, Florin."

Copperhead WHULPs at the thought of being Florin's wife

Florin says "bah. every woman on this earth bleeds from the crotch at the
    thought of being my wife."

Florin isn't sure whether it's GOOD or BAD, but that's what they DO.

allia thinks every woman on this earth gets a yeast infection at the thought of
    being florin's wife.

Florin SILENCE, UNSHORN HUSSY

Shub wondered why they all bleed from the crotch . . .

Florin says "because their WOMBS are FERTILE"

Florin must PROCREATE

Copperhead says "uh-oh"

Copperhead hands Florin a Petri dish

Florin says "well, if you're nasty looking, CH, i'll just hand ya sperm in a petri
    dish. i understand."

Florin won't deny any woman the chance to bear his offspring; he only denies
    them the chance to touch his Captain Happy, when they're unacceptable.

Like many forms of bantering among groups of young males, this conversation revolves around sexual references and insults. As a woman entering the group, I have limited options for dealing with this masculine
pattern of interaction. As Fine suggests:

> Women who wish to be part of a male-dominated group typically
> must accept patterns of male bonding and must be able to decode male
> behavior patterns. They must be willing to engage in coarse joking,
> teasing, and accept male-based informal structure of the occupation—
> in other words, become "one of the boys." While some women find
> this behavioral pattern congenial, others do not, and they become
> outcasts or marginal members of the group. (1987a: 131)

Hacker also describes women students in engineering (a culture closely
related to BlueSky's computer culture) as becoming "one of the guys"
(1989: 49).

In this regard, my performance in the above exchange can be read as
an attempt to become one of the boys, that is, to perform a masculine
identity. My efforts partly fail because of people's previous knowledge of
my female identity, as evidenced by their references to my female status
(as potential wife) and body. On the other hand, my performance succeeds
to the extent that the other participants accept my behavior as normal. My

own obnoxiousness, while out of character with my previous demeanor, fits into the conversation without apparently causing any of the other participants to change their definition of the situation or their understanding of my identity.

The above conversation probably had little effect on my status on BlueSky. However achieving "regular" status on BlueSky depended on my ability to participate actively during similarly obnoxious conversations. In my conversation with Beryl about participating in male-dominated groups and feeling comfortable on BlueSky, she for a time switched roles, interviewing me about my own participation on BlueSky. I tried to explain to her my occasional discomfort with the style of interaction on BlueSky.

BERYL: I feel totally comfortable. Do you?

LORI: Yeah, most of the time I do. Sometimes I don't.

BERYL: How come?

LORI: Um. When, I guess sometimes when the guys are talking about babes or are being very graphic in some ways . . . not really mean or gross or anything, just guys goin', "Oh man, the so-and-so babe just walked in. Oh boy, but she's got a boyfriend, and I don't have a chance." It's kind of like AAUGGH!

BERYL: I think it's hilarious.

LORI: I guess. Sometimes it will strike me that way, and sometimes it doesn't. I would say that as time has gone by, I've been more and more comfortable. So there's fewer times now when I'll just go, "I just can't handle this anymore." But there used to be times when I'd log off for a week or two weeks at a time. I just would not go back in. It's like, I can't take this anymore. I just . . . I don't like it.

Beryl makes clear to me that she isn't bothered by the aspects of BlueSky that cause me to stay away for periods of time. Her support of the interactional status quo provides an example of the ways in which women sometimes not only perform masculinities but also support and perpetuate social structures requiring that they do so to fit in.

Although I have brought up issues of sexism on BlueSky (as demonstrated by examples in this chapter), these critiques have had little impact on BlueSky's culture. On the contrary, BlueSky has probably changed me more than I have changed it. In an earlier article (Kendall 1996), I commented that I was almost the only woman on BlueSky who participated in one of the standard (and arguably sexist) joking patterns. In my eagerness to fit in, and in accord with my own personal historical tendencies to distance myself from other women, I have become a full (and sometimes enthusiastic) participant in BlueSky's male-dominated culture.

Other participants recognize that the style of interaction on BlueSky favors participation by men and excludes most women. Spontaneity, a male regular, explained some of the differences he sees between men's and women's participation on BlueSky in the quote at the beginning of this chapter: He also mentioned that he knew several women who had given up on BlueSky as entirely too "vulgar and mean." Similarly, in an informal face-to-face conversation with Jet, a male BlueSky regular, I mentioned that the generally obnoxious tone on BlueSky tends to keep women out. Jet agreed and said that none of the people on BlueSky "know how to deal with women. We just treat them like we treat men, which is fine for equal rights but doesn't seem to work too well socially."

While Jet and Spontaneity differ somewhat in their opinions about whether women get treated differently from men, they both recognize that treating people "the same" doesn't necessarily result in equal treatment. Spontaneity points out that "women get turned off by less nasty hazing than men," and Jet recognizes that a supposedly egalitarian stance still somehow excludes women. They understand that, even when male and female characters are treated identically, as occurs for the most part in my encounter with Shub and Florin, different participants in the interaction will nevertheless have different experiences of it because of their different histories and the gendered nature of that treatment. As Hacker says about engineering, "Women's entry into the traditionally masculine is important, but it is only one aspect of degendering technology and eroticism. It strengthens the masculinization of both and includes but few women" (1989: 49). Similarly, the gendered social context on BlueSky casts women as outsiders unless and until they prove themselves able to perform masculinities according to the social norms of the group. Women who are able to do so find acceptance within the group, but their acceptance reinscribes masculine norms, which continue to define women as assumed outsiders and outsiders, by definition, as not men.

GENDER MASQUERADE ON BLUESKY

Although muds have been male dominated, they can sometimes provide a relatively anonymous forum in which to experiment with gender identity. Mudders' own awareness of these facets of mud experience sometimes leads them to question the gender performances of others. BlueSky participants treat the question "Are you male or female?" as a joke, because it is so frequently asked in large public rooms on muds and other online chat spaces. Mudders also warn newbies that exaggerated femininity probably indicates that the participant behind the female character is male (Deuel 1995). These understandings of mud gender performances mean that participants may read only particular types of gender enactments as "actually" female. An examination of the few "gender switchers" on BlueSky highlights this.

For the rare gender switchers on BlueSky, portraying an online gender identity different from their offline identity need not disrupt their existing understandings of identity norms. As in other forms of gender masquerade, whether on the stage, in carnivals, or on city streets, motivations for such masquerade vary. So too do the potentials for masquerade to disrupt existing gender norms. Following are excerpts from discussions with two BlueSky participants, Fred and Toni, who, for significant lengths of time, enacted gender identities on BlueSky different from their offline gender identities. Their experiences provide evidence that the online enactment of gender identities differing from participants' offline gender identities need not call into question existing beliefs and assumptions about gender. Fred's and Toni's gender strategies thus highlight both the potential for and the limitations of fluidity in online gender enactments.

Fred/Amnesia: "Her Femininity Shows through Easier via Text"

Fred is a long-term male participant on BlueSky who for a year portrayed himself as female, with the character name "Amnesia." Although Fred revealed his offline male identity to other BlueSky participants several years ago, ending his masquerade, he retains the online name "Amnesia" and continues to self-refer using female pronouns.[8] I asked Amnesia about this in a whispered conversation on BlueSky.

Copperhead whispers "so I'm curious—if everyone knows you're not female, why still the female pronouns? Continuity?"

Amnesia whispers "'Amnesia' is a woman, and always has been. Amnesia was (is) my 'ideal woman', and so is more caricaturial than any real woman can be. I think that means her femininity shows through easier via text."

Copperhead whispers "your 'ideal woman' is caricaturially female?"

Amnesia whispers "no, I mean that I have no real experience in being a woman,

> so can only draw a crude image with a broad brush when I'm acting. Also,
> my 'ideal woman' has qualities not available in humanity, so there's another
> thing that doesn't translate into reality well."

Fred considers himself to be acting and does not expect characteristics of his "ideal woman" to translate into reality: he relies on stereotypical notions of femininity to accomplish his masquerade. Fred also specifically separates the "crude image" he portrays online from his offline identity, suppressing any gender-blurring effect his online masquerade might have on his sense of identity.

This type of gender enactment, while clearly performative, does not necessarily lead to an understanding of gender as performative in *all* instances. In addition, Fred's understanding of gender switching emphasizes rather than diminishes differences between males and females, as seen is this exchange:

> Copperhead whispers "okay, but why do you need experience as a woman to
>   play a woman on-line. I mean, look at me. What experience would you
>   need to come across like I do?"
> Amnesia whispers "in the short run, not a lot. For a year, quite a lot."
> Copperhead whispers "I've been here six months. I haven't needed any special
>   experience yet! ;) "
> Amnesia whispers "now try pretending to be a 50 year old man for 6 months."
> Copperhead whispers "ah, but what if I just talked like I've been talking and
>   *told* people I was a 50-yr-old man?"
> Amnesia whispers "if one isn't exceedingly careful, one slips just slightly and
>   the entire game is up."

While the slips to which Fred/Amnesia refers could result from any inconsistency in online self-presentation, he specifically emphasizes gender. Pronouns in particular are easy to forget. Amnesia is considered by other BlueSky participants to be obsessive about using female pronouns, perhaps because everyone does relate to Amnesia as male (since they have met or know about Fred), and the constant use of female pronouns strikes them as somewhat incongruous. In treating Amnesia as male, BlueSky participants give greater weight to offline identity than online identity and continue to treat gender as immutable and rooted in the physical body. Despite having previously believed that Amnesia was actually female, they treat that earlier understanding as a mistake, now corrected by their greater knowledge of Fred's offline identity.

As Amnesia and I continued to discuss gender portrayals online, it became clear that, at least with Fred's orientation toward role playing online and gender portrayal, ideas about gender and appropriate gendered behavior might become even more rigidly defined through such online enactments.

> Amnesia whispers "'Oblivious' was my male persona briefly, but it was less fun"
>
> Copperhead whispers "less fun? how so?"
>
> Amnesia whispers "hard to say. Perhaps less attention is paid male characters."
>
> Copperhead whispers "hmmm. I've heard that from other people as well."
>
> Amnesia whispers "when I was full-out a woman, the differential was unbelievable and measurable."
>
> Copperhead whispers "but you know, I haven't really noticed it. 'Course, I haven't been on here as a male, but comparing myself to other people, it doesn't really seem to me that I get more attention. Heh. Maybe if I was male, I'd get *no* attention."
>
> Amnesia whispers "you don't 'act female' in the traditional sense, as far as I've seen."
>
> Copperhead whispers "ah. I suppose that's true. So maybe it's not females that get more attention, per se. Am I less a woman than Amnesia? ;) "

Fred interprets my presentation of myself online, in which I make no particular effort to emphasize a gendered identity, as not "acting female." With the limitations inherent in text-based online interactions and the absence of cues we usually use to assign gender identity to others, Amnesia's caricature of femininity becomes potentially more real—more female—than my less stereotypical enactment as Copperhead. However, other participants' understandings of both Amnesia's and Copperhead's online gender presentations remain subject to correction and reinterpretation upon acquisition of further information about our offline identities. Several BlueSky participants acknowledged that Fred had "passed" as female for a year. But rather than interpret Fred's ability to fool them as evidence of gender malleability (and rather than credit Fred with skill at deception), they generally attribute their mistakes to their earlier naïveté and unfamiliarity with the medium. As discussed in chapter 5, BlueSky participants make ironic references to their earlier naïveté, using the phrase "I feel so betrayed" to refer to potential gender switching.

Toni/Phillipe: "Me with Different Pronouns"

Toni has been mudding for several years but joined the group on BlueSky fairly recently. She portrays herself on BlueSky using the male character name "Phillipe." Unlike Fred, Toni de-emphasizes differences between male and female character portrayal. But she too distances herself from her male character, attaching little significance to her online gender switching. In a face-to-face interview, she described for me the process of choosing a name for her character.

> When I was sitting there thinking, "What am I going to name this character?" I had heard so much about what a weird place GammaMOO was that I just didn't want to go there as myself. It wasn't like I decided, "Oh, I'll make a male character because it's safer to be male online, or something like that." I didn't really ever feel that. I just liked the notion of not being myself. I wasn't really sure of the environment or anything. . . . And so I just . . . I had a cat named Phillipe, and so I just borrowed his name. So then I got in the habit of naming characters Phillipe or Phil, some variation of that whenever I went somewhere that I wasn't sure I was going to be comfortable.

At the time of this interview, very few BlueSky participants knew that Phillipe was female offline. Since then, Toni has "come out" as female. However, just as Fred continues to go by the name "Amnesia" and to use female pronouns, Toni retains the name "Phillipe" online and continues to self-refer using male pronouns. This leads to occasional confusion among other participants:

> evariste says "mckenzie won't even dance"
> Phillipe won't dance either; why is this bad?
> evariste says "women like dancing dudes"
> Phillipe says "i don't"
> evariste says "are you a woman?"
> Peg says "yes, she is"
> evariste says "phillipe is a woman?"
> evariste says "niiice name choice"
> Phillipe says "evariste, we've had this discussion before; every few months
>   you find out i'm female and boggle like that"
> evariste forgot it
> evariste has a profound aversion to cross-sexing, that's why
> evariste says "i'm sure i block it out"
> henri says "your illusion is JUST THAT GOOD"
> evariste says "or i care JUST THAT LITTLE"

evariste indicates that he expects online names to reflect offline gender identities (perhaps particularly since those names can be chosen rather than merely received from one's parents). His "profound aversion to cross-sexing" voices the sentiment, common on BlueSky, that online personae should match offline identities. Toni's ability to convincingly portray the male character Phillipe threatens the view that gender, to some extent at least, determines personality: being fooled by gender masquerade is potentially discrediting. Hence, when henri suggests that evariste was fooled because of the quality of Phillipe's illusion, evariste counters that he doesn't care enough to pay attention.

Fred emphasized the difficulty of portraying a character with a gender different from one's offline identity. But Toni claims to have little problem maintaining Phillipe's male persona consistently. She indicates that she makes little distinction between her own personality and that of Phillipe. Toni describes others' mistakes in portraying gendered identities and outlines her own enactment strategy:

> You know a lot of people, if they make an alternate gendered character, they'll make it really exaggerated. I think Phil's kind of this wimpy guy, kind of a pretty boy. I think Phillipe is just more me with different pronouns. I suppose it's a lazy kind of a disguise. He has a guy's name and he has male pronouns. I guess the wimpy part is, it's a stupid name. I have this notion that probably lots of people think that Phillipe is gay.

Toni's masquerade both reinforces and calls into question stereotypical assumptions about masculinity and femininity. Like others I spoke with, she suggests that the attempt to be different when switching genders leads many to perform exaggerated and easily unmasked caricatures. She, on the other hand, successfully passes as male, theoretically without making any effort to behave in a "masculine" fashion. (Participants less frequently question male character enactments, because the assumption is that more online participants are male than female, and our cultural tendency is to view "neutral" enactments as male.) Unlike Fred's contention that lack of experience as a female hampers his ability to portray a female character, Toni's low-key masquerade suggests greater similarities between male and female gender enactments.

Toni's portrayal of Phillipe may indeed be based on her own offline enactment of herself as female. However, few other BlueSky participants would agree with her characterization of Phillipe as wimpy. Given the social norms on BlueSky, gender enactments of all participants, regardless of online or offline gender designations, tend to conform to standard cultural expectations of masculine behavior. For instance, in the following discussion, Phillipe and two other participants (who both present themselves as male, online and off) engage in flirtatious horseplay. The other characters present know that Phillipe is female offline, and some have met Toni in person. (The paged comments between Phillipe and Locutus at the end of this example were private communications, not visible to the third participant, Mender.)

> Mender mewmewmewmewmewmew
>
> Phillipe doesn't really think that's how you attract pussy, Mender
>
> Phillipe says "AHAHAHAHA"
>
> Locutus laughs
>
> Mender says "So how DO you do it"
>
> Phillipe says "i think it's abundantly clear at least to some of us in this room that I don't"
>
> Locutus says "you say 'come to madison' over and over until someone gives in"
>
> Mender says "Locutus, come to madison"
>
> Locutus says "no"
>
> Mender says "Locutus, come to madison"
>
> Locutus says "STILL no"
>
> Locutus says "mender, hint, I'm not female"
>
> Mender says "oh yeah"
>
> Phillipe says "what locutus said, only first we need to have a little talk about genders; and clearly i'm the best person to talk about genders"
>
> Phillipe HOWLS at himself
>
> Mender says "we've had that talk"
>
> Phillipe pages Locutus with 'mender knows i'm a girl, btw. he started telling me a lot of personal stuff and i outted myself cuz it seemed unfair'.
>
> Locutus pages Phillipe: aw you're so sweet

In the above, male and female alike flirt with each other and joke about gender identities. Significantly, Toni/Phillipe indicates that she felt bound to reveal her "true" gender identity when Mender began revealing "personal stuff," that is, information about his offline life. She thus reciprocates his revelation of offline information with her own confession of her offline identity.

As with Copperhead, Toni's online and offline presentations of self fit neither feminine nor masculine stereotypes. Yet because she is female offline, Toni characterizes her less "exaggerated" male character as "wimpy" and believes others may perceive him as gay. Toni's evaluation of Phillipe's wimpiness relies on cultural standards of masculine behavior. Her view of Phillipe as not very masculine and possibly gay also depends on expectations that connect heterosexuality with standards of hegemonic masculinity (Connell 1995). In her interactions as Phillipe, her participation fits into the general banter and passes for male unless she makes a point of "outing" herself. Thus, her characterization of Phillipe as wimpy represents an interpretation that reinstates gender as an essential category of identity. Her passing as a male becomes irrelevant to her own gender identity as long as she passes as only an imperfect or wimpy male. For Toni, as for Fred, caricatured or exaggerated gender enactments are potentially more "real" online than less stereotypical portrayals.

In *Gender Trouble*, Butler asks, "What kind of gender performance will enact and reveal the performativity of gender itself in a way that destabilizes the naturalized categories of identity and desire?" (1990: 139). In that work and in the later *Bodies That Matter* (1993), she suggests that drag, as a form of gender parody, does not necessarily call normative, naturalized gender into question, but rather that the disruptive possibility of such actions "depends on a context and reception in which subversive confusions can be fostered" (Butler 1990: 139). Online performances of gender, whether construed as "masquerade" or as serious and "realistic" performance, may or may not be parodic. But in either case, they are probably even less likely than offline parodies to "drastically call into question the gender system of the dominant culture as a fixed binary" (Poster 1995: 31). The electronic medium that makes gender masquerade possible and conceivable for a wider range of people also enables both the masqueraders and their audiences to interpret these performances in ways that distance them from a critique of "real" gender. The understanding that the limitations of the medium *require* performance allows online participants to interpret online gender masquerade selectively as *only* performance.

Gendered meanings permeate and inform all aspects of BlueSky interaction. The cultural connections on BlueSky among work, masculinities, computer use, and sociability ensure a male-dominated atmosphere regardless of the number of women present. For the most part, BlueSky participants, including myself, conform to dominant masculinity standards. They relate to each other in ways that support heterosexual masculinity (although not all identify as heterosexual) and in the process continue to objectify women. This demonstrates that even as members of nondominant groups increase, their effect on existing social norms may be minimal. Without the constant visual reminders provided by physical copresence, the dominant group can ignore or forget the presence of members of other groups. Because of this, members of subordinated groups may more easily join interactions with the dominant group *as long as they conform to its norms.* Thus online forums have the potential to be nominally more inclusive but in terms that still effectively limit participation.

5 Identity Crises

Late summer in southern California has a drowsy quality—a bit hazy but warm enough for outdoor parties, which take on that bittersweet, "fall's coming" feel. The one I'm driving toward provokes more than my usual party anxiety, since I have never met any of the other attendees face-to-face, and many of those expected to attend I have barely encountered online. This is not a BlueSky party but one for EarlyMUD participants. I have a character on EarlyMUD and considered doing a comparative study of EarlyMUD and BlueSky. However, my main purpose today is to meet several BlueSky participants who also hang out on EarlyMUD.

Parking on an older residential street with houses that sit back from steep embankments about ten feet above the street, I gather my party contributions of 7-Up and potato chips and look for the right address. The house has a deck in front, on which a young man with sandy reddish hair is standing. He observes me with the slightly curious but disinterested gaze of an aloof cat as I ascend the stairs. When I reach his level and approach the house, he gives me no acknowledgment whatsoever, continuing to stare out over the street. Disconcerted, I walk shyly past him to the front door.

Although I had no way of knowing it at the time, this was my first encounter with the BlueSky participant MadMonk, whom I knew as brash, active, rude, and challenging online. Although later during the party he came across as much less aloof, he still spoke little and struck me as shy. Of the participants I've met face-to-face, MadMonk remains the person with the greatest discrepancy between his online and offline presentations of self.

My reception inside the house differs little from that outside. Of the several people sitting about in the living room, a few acknowledge me slightly with a nod while others ignore me completely. As I move through the house, people lean forward to look at the name tag I've made for the occasion, but this mainly provokes confusion. It turns out I have made some erroneous assumptions about the offline use of names in this group.

Because my parents, with whom I am staying during this visit to southern California, have a new color inkjet printer with which my dad delights in playing, he and I created a fancy name tag. I assumed people would primarily use their "real," or offline, name in this offline setting, but I decided I needed to include my EarlyMUD name on the tag as well, so that people could connect my offline face to my online persona. In addition, because I was particularly interested in meeting up with BlueSky people, I felt that I needed to include my BlueSky name. Unlike most of the people at the party, who use the same name from mud to mud or, in some cases, participate only on EarlyMUD, I had chosen different names for myself in different social spaces. In particular, because my BlueSky name was specifically chosen to bolster my courage in what I initially perceived as a hostile environment, I didn't wish to carry that name, with its antagonistic connotations, into every social group. On EarlyMUD I chose instead the name "Redwood" (which I connected thematically, albeit tenuously, to Copperhead). My conference-style, tricolor, printed name tag thus has the name "Lori" in large type, with "Redwood" and "Copperhead" in smaller type in different fonts and colors.

I was correct that people would use name tags to identify themselves at the party, connecting their online identities to their offline bodies. However, everyone else has used an available pile of sticky labels and felt pens to make casual tags. My name tag sticks out as embarrassingly over-produced, but this also fits me into the group in an odd way. It fits people's idea about one type of person likely to attend such gatherings, branding me the type of nerd for whom technology is an end rather than a means. My name tag is thus as much an asset as a liability.

What causes confusion, however, is my prominent use of my offline name. As my notes from that day describe:

> *Absolutely everybody used their mud name.* It caused some confusion that my real-life name was most prominent on my tag. Atropa, for instance, didn't figure out who I was until too late to really talk to me. I felt a bit uncomfortable to be one of the only people with her real name showing, but at that point it was too late.

People clearly knew each other's offline names, which sometimes came up when referring to others in third person. But everyone addressed each other using mud names, unless that failed. Again, from my field notes:

> Calla was trying to get Max's attention and, unable to get his attention
> using the name Max, turned to the person next to her on the sofa
> and said, sotto voce, "What's his real name?" Getting the answer (I
> think it was Mike or some equally common male name), she called
> across the room with his real name and got his attention that way.

Although the attempt was to make this gathering an extension of
EarlyMUD sociability through consistent mud name use, this example
demonstrates that people accustomed to responding to their character
names online have not necessarily developed the habit of answering to
them offline.

Names constitute an important "identity peg" (Goffman 1963) on
which we hang our knowledge of a person, summoning up that knowledge
by reference to the name. Offline, we also connect people's appearances to
their names. Online, where these visual cues are unavailable to us, names
assume even greater significance. BlueSky participants sometimes discuss
whether they have ever seen another mudder with a character name iden-
tical to their own. Most have not. Thus BlueSky character names serve as
unique identifiers, even when BlueSky people visit other muds.

Both EarlyMUD and BlueSky contain populations of experienced mudders who have met each other offline many times. Whereas at BlueSky
face-to-face gatherings people generally refer to each other using offline
names, at EarlyMUD parties people use their mud names. EarlyMUD's
preference for mud names may stem from the large size of their regular
biannual gatherings (often including thirty or more people), which can
make unfamiliar offline names difficult to remember. By contrast, the largest BlueSky gathering I have attended included eleven people. Perry, who
frequents both EarlyMUD and BlueSky, suggests that EarlyMUD can get
larger parties together partly because of the less acerbic tone of EarlyMUD
interaction and partly because Peter, EarlyMUD's founder and chief administrator (at whose house this party was held), likes giving parties. Corwin, Peter's counterpart at BlueSky, has far less interest in playing host.

Despite these differences, the two muds share similar attitudes toward
names and identities. Most participants have only one character and, with
a few exceptions, such as MadMonk, conduct themselves online much as
they do offline. Those who frequent both EarlyMUD and BlueSky usually
use the same name on each. This contrasts with frequent reports regarding
the appeal of anonymity in online interactions. Porter, for instance, characterizes online interaction as, by definition, anonymous and disconnected
from offline identity, stating that "the majority of one's correspondents in
cyberspace, after all, have no bodies, no faces, no histories beyond what

they may choose to reveal" (1997: xi). Turkle similarly reports several mudders themselves emphasizing this feature of their online lives. She claims that "you are known only by the name you give your characters" (1995: 85) and quotes a mud participant as saying, "You can be whoever you want to be. You can completely redefine yourself if you want" (84). However, the name consistency of EarlyMUD and BlueSky participants and the close, long-term relationships they have formed suggest that not all online interaction can be characterized as anonymous or even pseudonymous.[1] People on BlueSky, for instance, know a good deal about each other's offline lives and identities. Different online social spaces have different understandings about the degree of anonymity they expect and will tolerate from others.

While online interactions or mudder relations are thus not anonymous by definition, they do introduce the potential for identity ambiguity. Exclusively textual communication precludes certain conversational cues that allow nuanced expression in face-to-face encounters. Online names can be changed much more easily than offline faces. People can segregate their online and offline lives and identities if they wish to do so. BlueSky participants' experiences with these aspects of online communication have affected the history and culture of the group, and they have developed particular expectations for identity presentation and strategies for managing information about their own and others' identities.

The possibilities for identity masquerade, ambiguity, deception, and confusion on muds can make it difficult to know to whom you are talking. Muds that do not require registration impose few limits on people's ability to change identity representations at will. Some muds also allow single participants to use more than one character. Even on muds like BlueSky, which more or less limits participants to a single character, a participant can easily change the name of that character.

People also cannot be sure that the identity characteristics presented online match the participant's offline identity. As Turkle (1995), Bruckman (1992), and others have discussed, many people engage in various types of identity masquerade (most frequently gender masquerade) online. In some cases, the character of a known participant might even be usurped by another. Because participants log on to muds using a password, someone possessing the password of another's character could log on as that character. Usurpation of another's character can also occur temporarily through spoofing. In addition, although likely a rare occurrence, theoretically characters can be operated by more than one person: two or more people might represent themselves as the same character. Also, the online performance of a person in the midst of an offline audience might be informed or affected by the onlookers.

All of these potentials for identity ambiguity complicate relationships online. Maintaining group boundaries involves identifying group members and outsiders. Difficulties in such identification make groups vulnerable online. On a more personal level, forming close relationships usually involves disclosure of intimate information. While some people may be able to include detailed fictional information in the maintenance of a fictional character, few people can successfully carry off a long-term, detailed masquerade. Further, people expect consistency of identity in others and may need such consistency in order to build trust. Thus people seeking to form and maintain group and personal relationships online must find ways to deal with the potential for deception and ambiguity.

ROBOTS

From the perspective of the mud program, characters are objects like any other, producing and responding to text. People, on the other hand, generally assume that characters they encounter online represent people like themselves and thus treat them differently from other programmed objects. The ability to program objects that mimic characters and the existence of a sophisticated class of objects known as robots introduce potential confusion over which objects represent other human beings. Robots are characters that are controlled by programs rather than by human participants.[2] Some can be considered rudimentary artificial intelligence (AI) programs.[3] Others are different from the kinds of textually responsive objects described in chapter 3 only in that they show up as characters on the WHO list. While robots cannot long pass for human, they can fool people unfamiliar with them, particularly on first contact. More than other mud objects, robots blur the line between objects and people online.

Many BlueSky participants tell stories of being fooled by their first encounters with robots. Although these stories force some admission of naïveté, they are nonetheless exchanged with pleasure and amusement. Many expect that future development will produce more sophisticated AI programs. Robot encounters thus provide glimpses of a potential future, possibly highlighting the coolness of being an online "pioneer." Robots also provide amusement much the same way as pet antics do. Their almost-but-not-quite-human actions hold up a humorously imperfect mirror to the follies of human behavior.

While most objects on muds are written into the mud program itself, robots are actually separate programs, sometimes running on different computers. A robot connects to a mud character that represents it on the mud, just as such characters represent offline human participants. Robots frequently provide various types of assistance to participants, such as telling the time or how to get to a particular place on the mud. As such, they sometimes serve as "local guides."

For long-term mud participants such as the people on BlueSky, robots are an important part of the mud subculture. Although Julia, one of the first and most famous mud robots, does not connect to BlueSky, most BlueSky participants know her from previous mudding experience and can repeat the "song" she used to sing:

> Julia says, "Julia, Julia, she's our guide! She directs us far and wide!"
> Julia says, "If you're lost, can't find your way, Julia's here to save the day!"
> Julia says, "Julia, Julia, she's our spy! She's always logging on the sly!"
> Julia says, "Be careful what you say and do, 'Cause Julia's always watching you!"[4]

> (Foner 1993: 15)

Participant knowledge of Julia and Julia's song demonstrates membership in the mud subculture. BlueSky participants have written alternative versions of Julia's song, memorializing or making fun of her functions.

> henri chants, "Julia, Julia, where you been? / The town square's getting cluttered again / Whip out your hypo, book, or stick / And send these sleepers to limbo, quick!"

> Rostopovich says "julia, julia, she's our guide, she corrects us far and wide, the rod, the whip or just a shoe, mistress julia's over you"

On BlueSky, the robots Xena, Xavier, and Conductor provide both practical services and amusement similar to those of other toylike objects. Conductor, a very limited robot, runs on the same computer as BlueSky and mainly provides weather information. Xavier, based in part on Julia's program, and Xena, an original program, were both written by elflord and run on elflord's home machine. They can store messages for participants and give information about other characters, including quotes from those characters. As with objects such as the bartender, BlueSky's robots also have several joke-related responses to phrases people say to them.

> pez says "Xavier, thorazine"
> Xavier extrudes a thin crystalline needle and injects pez with 10cc of thorazine.

Participants also manipulate the robots' more "practical" functions for amusement value. In the following, McKenzie asks the robot Xena to quote the robot Xavier. Xavier picks up on his name and the word "quote" and responds as if he also were asked to quote, following which Xena again reacts to her name.

> McKenzie says "Xena, quote Xavier"
> Xena says "I once heard Xavier say 'Quote *whom*? Never heard of 'em, McKenzie.'"
> Xavier says "Quote *whom*? Never heard of 'em, Xena."
> Xena says "Never heard of 'em, Xavier."

Part of the enjoyment of this type of play with robots stems from their quasi-human status. Most robot responses follow relatively consistent and simple routines, making their status as machines apparent to knowledgeable regulars. Manipulating the robots to provoke unusual behavior can make them appear silly or broken or eerily more human. As with many forms of humor, these games highlight liminal conditions, in this case probing the boundaries between robots, computers, and the people who understand them.

A robot's ability to respond in human ways to certain prompts introduces identity ambiguity into mud interactions. In the following example, Vicious, a new character, has logged on to BlueSky at a time when almost no other participants are logged on. I came across him in a room inhabited only by one of BlueSky's robots, Xavier. Vicious has mistaken Xavier's robot description for an imaginative description presented by a human participant and is upset because the other "person" will not talk to him. Because Vicious is familiar with robots from other muds, once I demonstrate Xavier's capabilities, he recognizes Xavier as a robot. However, he then asks a question to which some robots will respond seriously but to which Xavier is programmed to respond jokingly.

> Vicious frowns.
> Copperhead says "why?"
> Vicious says "No rooms, and old tin-can here does not talk."
> Copperhead says "what Xavier?"
> Vicious nods.
> Copperhead says "Xavier, quote henri"
> Xavier says "I once heard henri say, 'spellcast Adrian'"
> Copperhead says "Xavier quote Copperhead"
> Xavier says "I once heard you say, 'hi allia'"

Vicious says "oh, god, a robot"
Vicious says "Xavier, tell me the time"
Xavier says "Why do you want to know the time, Vicious?"

Inability to recognize robots might mark him as a newbie, so, after mistaking Xavier for a participant's character, Vicious carefully demonstrates his knowledge of robots, although he fails to demonstrate knowledge of this particular robot.

Robots are generally too rudimentary in their response to pass as human for very long (although Foner [1993] describes several incidents of prolonged confusion). People can more easily pass as robots by making their own responses mechanistic or odd, and several BlueSky regulars tell stories of being mistaken for robots. Participants can also set preprogrammed "triggers" on their mud characters (which are, after all, merely another type of object on the mud). These triggers respond to specific bits of text with an automated response text. Because the participant does not have to type such responses each time, and the mud program processes them quickly, triggers can indeed make a human-controlled character seem more like a robot. Once they gain familiarity with robots and their functions, participants view robots more as utilitarian objects through which people maintain connections or gain information about each other. But initially, robots can add to identity confusion online.

QUESTIONS OF CHARACTER(S)

In the early days of muds, no mud had been up long enough, and no group together long enough, to develop social norms concerning identity. Then, as now, some newcomers to the net assumed that everybody was anonymous, and they considered that half the fun. Others decided early on that they owed people the same honesty and self-disclosure online as off. When these two different attitudes toward mud characters meet, confusion and disillusionment sometimes follow. Many of my interviewees told me stories of encounters during which they suddenly realized that others were taking what they said more seriously than they themselves had been, and most asserted that "from that moment on" they ceased "role playing" theatrically, instead using their character to represent themselves more or less "as themselves."

James started mudding on the original TinyMUD Classic. He left the Surly Gang group several years ago. Although he occasionally visits Blue-

Sky, he now participates mainly on a mud with almost no population overlap with BlueSky. James named his TinyMUD Classic character Velocity and created an entire fictional history for the character.

> JAMES: I sort of had this model of a character, and I started playing that, and about two weeks into it there was a conversation that suddenly made me realize, "Hey, this can be much more than a game." Part of this is acting things out, but there's also a part of it that's meeting other people and making friends, sharing, sharing experiences, and so on. At that point I just threw out the whole idea of role playing, and I haven't done any of that since.
>
> LORI: Do you remember what that conversation was about?
>
> JAMES: Yeah, it was . . . there were two other people there. . . . One of the things that I had in my character was he was a little more brooding than I am in real life and had had sort of a despairing life so far. And I think that might have been just when Alisa was talking about getting engaged to Corwin or something about that. My character made the comment about [in a mock-despairing voice], "Yes, I was engaged once." And Alisa interpreted it as a real thing that had happened for real and asked me about it. That's when it sort of clicked, and I said, "No no no, I just meant it as a character." I don't recall if it was online at that moment or in thinking about that conversation later on in the day that I realized what was happening.
>
> LORI: Did you change your name at that point?
>
> JAMES: No. I kept the name.
>
> LORI: Because a lot of people remembered you as Velocity?
>
> JAMES: Right. Yes.

James and Alisa had different understandings of the frames of their conversation. James initially assumed it to be within a framework of playacting, while Alisa assumed that she was conversing with someone who was revealing true personal information.

Many of my BlueSky interviewees experienced this form of frame confusion, and most resolved it in the same way as James did: they shaped their actions to a frame of normal social conversation, either completely abandoning role-playing frames online or relegating them to carefully designated separate spaces (on muds, usually distinct from spaces in which participants converse socially).[5] Many, like James, also retained their pseudonyms because of the histories and relationships attached to these names. (James, however, now uses the name "James" online, explaining when necessary that he used to be Velocity.)

Despite fanciful names, most BlueSky participants make little distinction between their online and offline personae. Rather than role-playing a character, they attempt to "be themselves" online. Barbie, a dino regular, is unusual in keeping a sharp distinction between her online and offline lives. While most BlueSky people eagerly avail themselves of opportunities to meet face-to-face, Barbie refuses to do so. In a whispered conversation online, she told me she had met online contacts in the past. Yet on BlueSky, where she has been a participant almost since the group's beginning, no one has met her.

Like others on BlueSky, Barbie does share information about her offline life, discussing her job, family, romantic involvements, and so forth. (Through their offline contacts, many BlueSky participants have gained information about each other that helps them judge the veracity of information divulged online, but most of the details about Barbie's life cannot be so verified.) However, somewhat contradictorily, she also distances herself from her online persona and does not claim it to be a representation of "herself." In an introductory message she sent to a mud-related e-mail list, she talked about her earlier mudding days and the difference she noticed between her view of mud relationships and that of others. She begins by indicating that she was introduced to mudding by her boyfriend:

> We decided to see if it was possible for the two of us to play the same character and have anybody else notice. As it turned out it was frightfully easy to do. Then we decided to "confess" (via the medmenham mailing list) that we were actually 2 people for a time, but that I had pretty much taken over the character. My boyfriend had pretty much given the whole thing up. Well, needless to say, the reaction was mixed. People expressed everything from feelings of betrayal to feelings of admiration. To be honest, I never fully understood the feelings of betrayal, since if they liked the output they were receiving from my character and felt a kinship with that person, what did it matter if I was one person, or two people or an entire committee. I heard second-hand a quote from someone who I felt was a pretty close friend something to the effect of "she's lucky anyone is even speaking to her now." Anyhow, when I heard that, I sort of laid low for awhile, not because it hurt me but because it became obvious to me that alot of mudders take their on-line "relationships" very seriously. Much more seriously than I did. Frankly I expected to hear a lot more

inquisition as to how I (we) had pulled it off rather than the chorus of "I FEEL SO BETRAYED." But I guess you live and learn. (June 4, 1996, e-mail list posting)

Despite Barbie's professed determination to keep her online and offline personae separate, some blending clearly occurs. For instance, although she refers to another online person as someone she felt was a pretty close friend, she later implies that taking online relationships very seriously is a mistake and claims not to do so. She further distances herself from her online persona by referring to her online communication with the mechanistic term "output."

The negative reaction to Barbie's revelation illustrates her breach of BlueSky norms and expectations regarding identity continuity. BlueSky participants expect people to bring their offline identities into the online realm. They viewed Barbie and her boyfriend's experiment not as a legitimate exploration of the potential of online media for identity multiplicity (or, in this case, conflation) but as a dishonest representation of a false identity. This reaction demonstrates not only their views on the proper use of computer-mediated communication but also their assumptions about the reality and continuity of offline identity. Significantly, no one appears to have doubted Barbie's revelation. Confronted with two conflicting online statements concerning Barbie's identity, they accepted the version that positioned her offline identity as true and her online identity as false.

Although the group expects a one-to-one correspondence between characters and participants, BlueSky participants by no means assume that others always represent themselves honestly online. Many have experienced several revelations such as Barbie's. Their stories about identity deception most often relate to gender masquerade.

Participants tell tales (usually about someone else) regarding romantic attachments online with people who turn out to be the "wrong" gender in real life. Barbie's quoting of "I FEEL SO BETRAYED" echoes the occasional ironic use of that phrase by other BlueSky members, who use it to refer jokingly to their earlier naïveté. For instance, in the following, Bilerific-Sid looks up a book reference for something the character Rockefeller wrote and finds a female name.

Bilerific-Sid says "So, how's the LARP biz, Rocky."
Rockefeller says "Not bad, got published; hit the shelves bout a month ago."
Rockefeller says "An Elder God's Return."

Bilerific-Sid looks for your name in the 1996 publications guide.

Bilerific-Sid looks at the guide, "hey, your name is Julia Johnson?"

Rockefeller says "Nope. jul's my co-author."

Bilerific-Sid aha

Bilerific-Sid was about to say I FEEL SO BETRAYED

Spontaneity grins.

Rockefeller chuckles.

On another day, Amnesia pretends to have assumed that Barbie is male. Since some people have suggested that Barbie *is* male despite her consistent female presentation online, this adds another layer to the "betrayal" joke. Adding even more irony is BlueSky participants' awareness that Amnesia's nominally female presentation online (consisting at this point of only a female description and use of female pronouns) thinly masks a known offline male.

Barbie says "I think I'm going to call the William Hurt Guy and see if he wants
    to dosomething"

Mender says "'do something'"

Barbie says "mender is very sharp"

McKenzie hasn't heard about the William Hurt Guy

Captin William Hurt Guy?

Barbie says "the guy I am dating currently looks like him"

McKenzie says "wow, I'm behind"

Amnesia says "BARBIE IS A WOMAN?"

Amnesia I FEEL SO BETRAYED

McKenzie is not as behind as Amnesia

In this convoluted *Victor/Victoria*-esque play, Amnesia pretends to mistake a suspected male portraying a female for a female playing a male. This highlights the use of the phrase "I FEEL SO BETRAYED" specifically for gender deception cases. Note also that Amnesia (mockingly) assumes Barbie's female gender from her description of a male date, demonstrating a normative assumption of heterosexuality.

MASQUERADES

The practice of deliberately misleading others online is well-known enough among mudders that the Frequently Asked Questions documents about muds contain the following warnings:

TinySex is the act of performing MUD actions to imitate having sex with another character, usually consensually, sometimes with one hand on the keyboard, sometimes with two. Basically, it's speed-writing interactive erotica. Realize that the other party is not obligated to be anything like he/she says, and in fact may be playing a joke on you. . . . A time-worn and somewhat unfriendly trick is to entice someone into having TinySex with you, log the proceedings, and post them to [a] rec.games.mud. [newsgroup] and have a good laugh at the other person's expense. (Smith 1998)

Smith's warning is based upon several incidents (some of which were perpetrated by members of the Surly Gang) in which people were embarrassed in the way described above. Most such incidents were perpetrated by males, usually against other males. The perpetrator thus often masqueraded as female in order to engage the victim in TinySex.

Issues of gender and sexuality relating to such masquerades can provoke particularly strong identity concerns. Some participants exploit the possibility of gender and sexual identity ambiguity for sexual enjoyment and adventure. One poster to a mud newsgroup said, "I think the rule should be: If you are a homophobe, don't have tinysex cuz that cute broad might be a guy in real life. If you aren't bothered by this, have fun." But others want to ensure that they are not interacting "inappropriately" with the "wrong" gender. The question "Are you male or female?" has gained legendary status among members of various online cultures and appears frequently in mud areas where newbies are likely to congregate. In such areas, it is often the first question asked of another participant.

In addition to masquerading in ways that conceal aspects of an offline identity, some participants deceive others by concealing previously known online identities. Aside from engaging in sexual adventure or exploration, participants may engage in such behavior to try out other personae (Turkle 1995). They may also seek to tease or test others. Or they may wish to engage in discrediting activity without attaching that activity to their known social identity.

This kind of masquerade is extremely rare on BlueSky, but it occurred more frequently on earlier Surly Gang muds. One participant, Cleo, was so notorious for creating multiple characters that BlueSky participants once assumed that any unknown female character was Cleo until proven otherwise. People still jokingly suggest that newbies must be Cleo, although she rarely participates nowadays. As one participant quipped, "There are plenty of girls on BlueSky, and all of them are Cleo." An earlier BlueSky robot named Larry even incorporated this running joke into a standard response. When asked "Who is" in conjunction with a character name, Larry would respond with a line referring to that character, as in this response concerning Jet's well-known (and oft-expressed) dissatisfaction with his job:

> Peg says "Larry who is Jet?"
>
> Larry says "HATE JOB HATE JOB HATE JOB HATE JOB"

When asked about a character it did not "know," Larry would respond with a reference to Cleo:

> Mike Adams says "Larry, who's Anguish?"
>
> Larry doesn't know who Anguish is. Probably Cleo.

The ability to masquerade and the subsequent potential for confusion influenced the development of BlueSky's culture. BlueSky participants discourage identity deception and encourage self-revelation and the trade of personal information. While other muds may tolerate masquerade or participants with multiple characters, such behaviors occur very infrequently on BlueSky. Most participants maintain a consistent identity that they consider more or less congruent with their offline identity. But because of the importance of masquerades to the historical development of BlueSky's stance toward identity, I provide an example here of my own experience with a masquerading participant. This incident did not occur on BlueSky, nor did it involve a BlueSky participant. However, it illustrates the potentially disruptive effects of masquerade on interpersonal relationships online. It also stands in for similar experiences in the Surly Gang's history, which influenced BlueSky's cultural development.

Dr.Morph's Masquerade

Early in my mudding experience, I had an encounter with an unexpected masquerader on ProphesyNet, a mud devoted to discussions of the occult. ProphesyNet does not require character registration; however, most participants on ProphesyNet know each other, and unexpected guests are rare. In the example below, I encounter Bud, a character previously unknown to me. Bud turns out to be a masquerade character created by a participant I had previously met as Dr.Morph. After a long and interesting conversation with Dr.Morph earlier in the day, I arranged to meet with him for further conversation that night. While waiting for Dr.Morph to show up for this arranged meeting, I met Bud, who presented himself as a newbie. After conversing with Bud for a while, I assumed that Dr.Morph had stood me up, and decided to go visit some other muds. (My character name here is hedgehog.)

> hedgehog says, "I'm going to logout for a bit and check on some other scenes.
>   I will probably be back in a little bit, if you're still here."
> Bud giggles. Dr.Morph sends his best, but don't tell anyone!
> hedgehog says, "what do you mean by that?"
> Bud says, "Which? Hey, I'm sorry if I've said anything wrong . . ."
> hedgehog says, "'sokay. Perhaps you have reasons for being cagey. I just
>   didn't expect it. Why did you say that Dr.Morph sends his best?"
> Bud smiles. "Shapeshifting. Part of the allure of the net is trying on other egos
>   for a little while and learning from them. Enchantress and I have a long
>   game of it."

After Bud revealed that he was indeed the same person I had spoken with earlier as Dr.Morph, Enchantress logged on to the mud. Enchantress had also participated in the earlier conversation with "Dr.Morph" and me and had not yet met "Bud." In the fifth line below, I indicate my discomfort at being part of Bud's deception.

> Bud says, "What's the deal? I thought you guys were up and running again"
> Enchantress looks around. "you talkin' to me?"
> Bud nods
> hedgehog rolls on the floor laughing!
> hedgehog says, "I don't think I can do this from the spectator position."
> In a page-pose to you, Bud laughs out loud![6]

After further discussion, Bud drops a hint to Enchantress:

> Bud says, "BTW speaking of grandmothers: do either of you know anyone in
>   Nebraska?"
> hedgehog says, "no."
> Enchantress snorts at you spoofer. duh, of course I do, dontcha know?
> Bud pouts. "Awww fooey
> Bud says "curses, foiled again. I didn't even get to give my speech about
>   Green Day's new album"
> Enchantress thinks you were REALLY convincing this time tho

Note that, here, Enchantress uses the term "spoofer" to indicate someone who hides his identity. Although "Bud's" name is attached to his text, it is not the name he is usually known by, making his entire performance as Bud a type of spoof.

Few people can convincingly hide a previous identity in face-to-face interaction. The limitations of online communication make this much easier. But for people who want to be part of a social group, such conduct is ultimately detrimental. Note that with both hedgehog and Enchantress, Bud dropped revealing hints concerning his previous identity. (He sent me regards from Dr.Morph and mentioned Nebraska to Enchantress, a point of reference they shared.) Bud's "hint" to me concerning his identity occurred as I was preparing to leave the mud in disappointment at not reconnecting with Dr.Morph. To continue our conversation, Bud had to reconnect to his former identity.

Accidental Masquerades

Bud's masquerade was intentional. Indeed, given our earlier conversation that day concerning life online, I believe he was specifically trying to teach me something about online interaction. Masquerades can also occur accidentally, however. Many mudders have characters on more than one mud, sometimes with the same name on each and sometimes not. People do not always intend deception or multiplicity in choosing different names on different muds. Sometimes they attempt to choose names that fit the themes of various muds. Therefore, when meeting someone for the first time on a mud, you cannot be completely sure it isn't someone you've previously met elsewhere.

For instance, in the following excerpt from a GammaMOO log, Previous, whom I had not met before, hailed me from afar while I was exploring GammaMOO. He then came to my location and started up a conversation with me.

> Previous asks, "are you really female or is that just your char?"
> hedgehog [to Previous]: that question kind of surprises me. Why do you want
>   to know?
> Previous smiles at you.
> Previous says, "just checking"
> Previous says, "best to catch these things early . . . people here tend to
>   switch sexes almost as often as clothing"
> hedgehog is female in real life.
> Previous says, "good :)"
> hedgehog still isn't sure why you need to know my RL gender, though.
> Previous says, "I don't like being switched genders on, so I make sure early on
>   so I don't inadvertently use the wrong social mores with anyone"

Previous's connection of gender switching with confusion of social mores indicates the degree to which all social interactions are gendered, particularly in arenas where sexual connections or activities occur. I also read his concern as indicating that he wished to flirt with me without fearing that I might "really" be male. Why he felt reassured by my simple statement about offline identity is unclear. He, like other long-term participants, would certainly be aware of mud lore indicating that gender switchers frequently will not admit their different offline gender identity.

Although I did not know it at the time, Previous was the GammaMOO character of a BlueSky participant I had met online under his BlueSky name. I discovered his dual identity much later on BlueSky. During a discussion of my research on BlueSky, he paged me with the suggestion that I visit GammaMOO.

> cipher whispers "hey, if you want to do research on some really sophisticated
>   environments, check out gamma.largeuniversity.edu 8888"
> Copperhead whispers "Yeah, I've a character on there too. What in particular
>   do you recommend?"
> cipher whispers "oh yeah? drop by and chat with me :) I'm Previous"
> cipher senses "Copperhead LAUGHS!"
> cipher senses "Copperhead is hedgehog, cipher!"
> cipher whispers "oh, you . . ."
> From afar, cipher waggles a finger
> cipher senses "Copperhead smiles."
> From afar, cipher grins.

Previous clearly felt embarrassed at having interacted with me without knowing my other identity on BlueSky, probably because his behavior on GammaMOO differs considerably from his behavior on BlueSky. Previous's arguably flirtatious approach to me would have stood out on BlueSky but did not on GammaMOO, where stranger interactions occur much more frequently. BlueSky participants, having mostly met face-to-face, feel no need to ask real-life gender designations, and I have heard neither Previous nor anyone else do so there. Unlike most BlueSky participants, who generally express contempt for GammaMOO, Previous preferred GammaMOO to BlueSky. He spent more time there and was much more gregarious in his interactions, whereas on BlueSky he tended to remain quiet. My discovery threatened the distance he maintained between these two worlds.

Fooling others through masquerades can be fun, and even being fooled occasionally may be pleasurable. However, for most people, extended and intimate relationships require a degree of consistency and reliability from other parties. To create and maintain a cohesive social group, BlueSky participants find ways to encourage such consistency and identity relia-

bility in each other. They also find ways to protect their group from outsiders who might wish to fool them. Their motivation and ability to develop such strategies stem from their knowledge of the conditions of online
participation and their familiarity with particular events that have demonstrated those conditions.

AUDIENCE PROBLEMS ONLINE:
EAVESDROPPERS AND INVASIONS

In addition to knowing the identities of those with whom they interact,
people in social settings have an interest in knowing the general composition of their audience. We tend to present differing messages and perform
different identities depending on audience (Gergen 1991; Goffman 1959).
Meyrowitz (1985), in his discussion of the effects of television on social
settings, suggests that electronic media, particularly television, blur and
combine different social audiences, making some types of backstage performances impossible and creating new forms of social interaction. Similarly, people participating in online communication usually have less information available about the composition of their audience than people
in face-to-face interactions have. The Internet contains thousands of different kinds of forums, many geared to particular, specialized audiences.
Hence it might seem that the forms of electronic media available over the
Internet counteract the tendency of television to create a generalized audience, all of whom have access to the same social facts. However, as with
television, specialized content may not indicate specialist audience members. Content in newsgroups on Usenet, for instance, may be geared toward people with particular interests, but this tells us little about the actual
audience for that newsgroup.[7]

Many forums on the Internet, unlike television, are interactive. That
is, anybody who can read messages can also respond to them. However,
people reading or posting messages cannot tell at any given moment who
their potential correspondents are. A newsgroup may be set up to function
as a "backstage" area, but participants on that newsgroup can never be
sure that the "audience" for whom they rehearse is not eavesdropping.
For instance, members of a particular political group may set up a newsgroup for the purpose of discussing strategy, but they can never be sure
that members of opposing political groups are not reading their messages.

Online groups in general are vulnerable to outsiders. A bully bent on
harassing a particular group is difficult to stop and can make the environ-

ment so unpleasant that it loses its value as a social space. A famous example of this is the "invasion" of the Usenet newsgroup rec.pets.cats by participants from several other Usenet groups, especially alt.bigfoot and alt.tasteless. The invaders posted inflammatory messages describing physical harm to cats in a newsgroup populated by cat lovers.[8] Given the historical male dominance of the net, harassing incidents like this frequently have an important gender component, although most net culture accounts of the rec.pets.cats incident do not acknowledge this. Despite numerous accounts of the invasion, I have seen none that point out that the invaders (and the groups they invaded from) were predominantly male and that the posters and readers of rec.pets.cats were predominantly female; nor do they point out that these demographics almost certainly contributed not only to the idea of staging an "invasion" of another newsgroup in the first place but also to the choice of that particular group for invasion.

John Quittner's account in *Wired* magazine comes closest to acknowledging the gendered aspect of the invasion.[9] Quittner calls the invasion "A Usenet panty raid!" and coyly adds, "If you were able to put all of humanity on a giant spectrum, cat lovers would undoubtedly occupy the frequency opposite people who are alternatively tasteless."[10] During the invasion, numerous readers of rec.pets.cats were driven off by the barrage of deliberately gross postings, often hidden behind innocuous titles.[11] Although there are safeguards against exposure to repeated offensive words on the Internet, including killfiles (on Usenet) and gag commands (on muds), a determined harasser, or in particular a group of harassers, can make most such solutions nearly useless.[12]

Depending on their purposes, groups on the Internet employ a variety of strategies to control membership and participation. Among muds, some freely advertise and attempt to attract a particular group through emphasis on a particular type of theme or activity. Others attempt to hide their existence completely from the Internet public, inviting participation solely through individual contacts. Part of the advantage in staying publicly accessible is illustrated by BlueSky's status as the latest in a long history of muds frequented by a particular group of people. Past participants sometimes reappear and reconnect with the group. However, this means that some of those who appear and attempt to participate may not share the cultural norms and expectations of the BlueSky group. BlueSky remains more or less publicly accessible, but participants dislike being widely publicized and have objected to the group's inclusion in several Internet guides.

BORDER PATROL: NEWBIES AND GUESTS ON BLUESKY

Participants liken BlueSky to a private club, in part because people must register with the wizards to receive a character (with a password) for participation on BlueSky. However, since BlueSky is openly available on the Internet, it isn't precisely private. This means that participants have to deal with newcomers and with the effect that such newcomers have on the culture and on people's enjoyment of the social space. BlueSky participants have a reputation among the mudder subculture for being intolerant, obnoxious "dinos." Although this obnoxiousness has gendered significance in the interrelationships among participants, it also serves a useful function for the group, forming a barrier to casual interlopers.

BlueSky does not share the vulnerability of rec.pets.cats. (In fact, some BlueSky participants may have participated in the rec.pets.cats invasion.) But its participants share a valued social space. Like many other long-term net participants, some on BlueSky worry about the effect of online population expansion and the discovery of the Internet by groups of people with different values and expectations. Many muds have experienced rapid increases in their population because of media exposure, sometimes to detrimental effect.[13]

Ulysses has been mudding for about five years. Before that he had been active on several newsgroups. In my interview with him, he connected BlueSky's hostility toward newbies to the similar impatience of net veterans with the influx of people previously unfamiliar with the Internet.

> The other thing is the sudden popularization of the net, and all of a sudden people outside . . . everybody knows about it, and there are lots and lots of really bad hack-job guides to the net, and they would have little articles about how BlueSky is the place where the smart people hang out: "Go and listen to them; they're really funny and they're really sharp." And people would just show up and expect to be one of the gang and to be accepted, and BlueSky people objected to being thought of as a public resource.

The factors Ulysses describes, added to a situation in which guests and newcomers can remain relatively anonymous, intensify an existing hostility to outsiders. BlueSky's defense against potential hostile obnoxiousness and grossness is preemptive obnoxiousness and grossness. This appears to have been relatively effective, since newcomers rarely last long.

Infrequent or previous BlueSky participants I interviewed indicated that other mudders perceive BlueSky as a hostile and cliquish group. These less frequent participants connected the BlueSky attitude toward newbies more specifically to elitism associated with BlueSky's "dino" status. James, who no longer muds much on BlueSky, describes it as elitist.

> There seems to be a real sense of elitism . . . as a social group they've probably been around on muds longer than any other social group, and that could be part of it. I don't like to judge other people, and you know probably when I was spending all my time on [a previous Surly Gang mud], I might have been a little bit cliquish and elitist too as being one of the in-group. But I sort of hate to see that happen. It doesn't feel . . . BlueSky doesn't feel to me like a friendly place for new people.

Atticus started mudding on Classic. Like James, he left the Surly Gang group and continued mudding elsewhere. He also categorized BlueSky participants as elitist and connected their attitudes toward outsiders to their status as dinos.

ATTICUS: The exclusionary attitude bothers me. [It] seems to me to give rise to a sort of stratification and rigidness. I don't think it's very often, from what I remember, that the accepted patterns of thought are ever challenged. Especially since newcomers are, again, as I remember it—unless you fit very well—ostracized, run off, berated, yelled at.

LORI: What do you think that's about? Why are they doing that?

ATTICUS: A very human desire to feel special. There seems to me to be a certain amount of . . . what they've got to base their elitism on is the fact they've been around a long time, and that may explain some of the dismissal of newbies.

In contrast with these two relative outsiders, only a few regulars agreed that being a dino conveys high social status. Most felt that humor and intelligence are more important. Several other muds also claim populations of people who have been around since the beginning of TinyMUDs. However, it seems likely that, as James and Atticus indicate, the status of BlueSky as "the dino mud" contributes to an attitude of suspicion toward newbies.

Most newcomers first appear on BlueSky using the guest character before registering a character name. Previous Surly Gang muds had not required registration, and several regulars at first objected to the new registration procedures. They refused to register a character, using the guest character instead. This made the anonymity of the guest character somewhat ambiguous. During that time period, Guest might be either a known person not immediately identifying himself or herself or a complete newbie. Hence, the first step for BlueSky regulars in determining a guest's identity was to attempt to determine if it was another regular, which they did by interrogating guests on their arrival.

In the following excerpts, a regular who previously had a character on Surly Gang muds logs on as Guest. In the first excerpt, Guest enters and greets henri using a drawn-out phonetic spelling of his name. When Guest refuses to self-identify, henri kills it.

> Guest onreeeee
> henri says "which Guest is this"
> Guest onreeeeeeeeeee
> henri killed Guest!
> Guest has left.
> Guest has arrived.
> Guest says "onreeee is on the rag, apparently."
> henri mutters "what guest is this" to everyone but Guest.

henri next makes a guess as to the identity of Guest, using a nickname form, "winger," of "RedWing," the name of a previous regular who was one of the registration resisters and logged on to BlueSky periodically as Guest. When Guest still does not reply, henri suspects Guest of being jeff, the offline name of the character shorthop, who, as described in chapter 3, is an ex-regular shunned by other BlueSky regulars.

> henri says "is this winger again"
> Guest whistles innocently.
> henri suspects it's jeff
> henri killed Guest!
> Guest has left.
> Ichi cackles at henri
> Guest has arrived.
> Guest says "onreeeeeeeee is mean"
> Guest says "Don't make me come out there and whup you, henri."
> henri killed Guest!
> Guest has left.
> Guest has arrived.
> Guest says "I mean it. I'll have Sam hold you while I give you indian burns."
> fnord says "RWGuest?"

At this time BlueSky had only one guest character; when a second person logged on as Guest it resulted in the message "Guest has reconnected." In this case, the "reconnection" below is henri. Each time a character connects, the mud displays the machine name from which that character last connected. By logging on as Guest (in a separate window, leaving his character henri logged on also), henri can find out what machine Guest logged on from, providing a clue to Guest's identity. (In all but the last line of this segment, Guest is henri.)

> Guest has reconnected.
> Guest says "hsm where is Butler.edu"
> fnord says "in Indianapolis"
> Guest says "that's who guest is"
> fnord has been there
> Guest has partially disconnected.
> Norman says "henri is sneeeky."
> Guest says "You wussies"

When the domain name fails to reveal Guest's identity (as the participants discuss in a section I have not included here), henri makes one more attempt to confirm Guest's identity as RedWing. henri initiates a ritualized joke sequence in which RedWing has previously participated. This gives Guest an opening line as an invitation to identify himself. After a brief pause, Guest supplies the appropriate follow-up line, thereby finally acknowledging his identity as RedWing.

> henri tests: "SUNDAY SUNDAY SUNDAY"
> henri watches guest carefully
> Guest says "TAG TEAM ACTION"
> henri says "ok it's winger"
> Guest says "okay, someone kill these people for me"
> henri says "get a real char and do it right, 'Wing"
> Guest has no email address, henri.
> henri says "ok, don't be so ornery next time and the detective work won't
>   happen"
> fnord could forge one
> fnord grins evilly
> henri says "maybe some nice sysadmin would give you an account"
> Guest says "I don't know any sysadmins, nice or not."
> henri says "you know a ton of sysadmins on here"
> Guest says "Oh well."

> Guest says "Laters"
> fnord says "baiRW"
> henri says "later 'wing"
> Guest says "Henri"
> Guest has disconnected.

As RedWing demonstrates in the above episode, several of the people who initially refused to register characters also highlighted their resistance to identity specificity by being cagey about their identity when they logged on as Guest. henri's "guest test" allows RedWing to identify himself without explicitly naming himself and thus not appear to have backed down on his refusal to self-identify. Once henri successfully identifies RedWing, conversation resumes normally, with a relatively mild request that RedWing get a character.

In the next example, Guest turns out to be a newbie rather than a regular. Beryl attempts to determine whether it might still be someone previously known from another mud.

> Guest has arrived.
> Nightcrawler says "speak of the devil."
> Guest says "eh?"
> Sparkle says "may not be the devil"
> Guest isn't the devil :)
> Nightcrawler says "Which guest would you be?"
> Guest says "I'm new here"
> Nightcrawler says "Oh. How depressing. We thought you might actually be
>   someone."
> Guest says "no . . . just exploring :-)"
> Beryl says "were you on tinymud, tinyfarm, tinytim, islandia, discord, sanctuary,
>   FlyingDutchman, mirage, or spammud, guest?"
> Guest says "I'm on MicroMUSE and EcoMUSE"
> Beryl says "ecomuse, never heard of that."
> Beryl hmms

After determining Guest to be a stranger, BlueSky participants harass Guest using two mud objects. Sparkle loms Guest. Then Beryl uses an object called a wormhole, which enables her to observe Guest's actions even though Guest is now in another room. (The numbers in the ninth line of the following exchange represent Guest's "coordinates" within the mud's spatial layout.)

Guest says "what's the point of this mud?"
Sparkle says "there is no point"
Sparkle pulls a large lever, and a trapdoor opens right underneath Guest!
Guest has left.
Beryl cheers sparkle
Sparkle smiels :)
Sparkle says "I'm learning :)"
Sparkle smiles, even
Beryl sends the other end of the wormhole to 0,−2,14.
Beryl chases guest
Sparkle giggles at Beryl
Mike Adams says "hounded by a wormhole"

The behavior of these regular participants toward the guest also reveals aspects of group hierarchy and newcomer education. Beryl, as one of the earliest BlueSky participants, enjoys considerable respect among the group. Sparkle's more recent arrival in the group, combined with a "bubbly" interactive style somewhat different from BlueSky norms, endows her with lower status. This provides context for Sparkle's assertion that she is "learning" the norm of guest harassment. Sparkle also demonstrates her understanding of BlueSky expectations of accuracy in written expression by quickly correcting her typo in "smiels." BlueSky participants almost always correct typos in order to show them as mere finger slips and thus represent themselves as interactively competent. This approach treats written text as similar to speech and subject to similar expectations of competence (Goffman 1981). BlueSky participants pride themselves in being literate and well educated.[14]

By treating guests with suspicion and harassing people who fail to identify themselves meaningfully, BlueSky participants engage in a "border patrol" of their group's boundaries. As these episodes illustrate, anonymity goes against BlueSky social norms, and participants tolerate it only temporarily. Refusals by old or new participants to identify themselves either with a known name or with pertinent offline information (type of job, geographical location, etc.) incur hostility from regulars. (The above instance of newbie harassment was, in fact, relatively mild for BlueSky.)

BlueSky regulars whom I interviewed held varied opinions concerning what sort of newbie behavior constitutes justification for harassment, but most felt that some harassment of newbies is always appropriate. Some even spoke of this treatment as a form of hazing, necessary to ensure the compatibility of group members.

RAVEMAGE: [People will lom a guest for] any excuse. Hey, guest, you know what, you don't smell so good, you need a bath!

LORI: Well, that's the way Jet is. Jet'll do 'em like within the first minute.

RAVEMAGE: The way that Jet does it, it's less an attempt to eject them. It's almost a form of hazing. It's like: "You have to be able to take this. If you can take it, that's great, then hang with us. But if you can't take it . . ."

Hazing provides a ritual barrier. People have to make it through the initial harassment in order to become part of the group. However, it also demonstrates some of the standards for behavior on BlueSky. Hazing of newcomers doesn't differ significantly from the kinds of behavior directed on occasion by regulars toward each other. Thus hazing presents a message to newcomers that they must be able to tolerate a certain level of grossness, obnoxiousness, and aggressiveness.

This treatment sometimes results in a misapprehension by newcomers that they should adopt an obnoxious demeanor at all times. Newcomers see the surface level of belligerence without knowing the history of relationships and the underlying affections and connections among participants. In the following excerpt, Beryl and Ulysses attempt to explain to a guest why politeness demands that the guest identify itself. In doing so, they evoke offline analogs for the type of social group BlueSky represents.

Guest1 arrives from the south.

Copperhead waves to Guest1

Beryl eyes guest1

Guest1 waves.

Beryl says "speak up, guest, who are you?"

Guest1 says "Guest1."

Ulysses says "specify"

Guest1 says "What do you mean?"

Beryl says "who are you? do you not speak english?"

Copperhead grins at Beryl

Guest1 says "In what sense?"

Beryl says "if i were to walk up to you in a bar and say "Hi" and asked who you were, what would you say?"

Guest1 smiles. . . . then I would say I'm a stranger . . . looking around for something interesting . . .

Beryl says "yikes"

Copperhead says "well that wouldn't get you very far, would it."

Beryl says "nothing interesting here"

Guest1 says "Interesting description, btw, Beryl."

Guest1 chuckles.

Ulysses says "or, more to the point, if you walked up to a group of friends
   talking amongst themselves at a bar and tried to join their conversation,
   what would you say if they wanted to know why you wanted to join their
   conversation"

Beryl nods to Uly

Beryl says "Uly has it exactly"

By evoking the analogy of friends in a bar, Ulysses and Beryl describe BlueSky regulars as people who know each other's identities. They contrast this with Guest1, whose anonymity and cagey behavior they consider rude and suspicious. Even Guest1 would probably acknowledge that such behavior would be unconscionably rude in a similar setting offline.

Some newcomers to the net appreciate the freedom of online anonymity and mistakenly believe this to be one of the main features of all social groups on the net. BlueSky's insistence on immediate identification may be startling to such people, while the reluctance of newcomers to identify themselves further irritates BlueSky regulars. BlueSky may differ from other groups in its attitude toward anonymity. However, other descriptions of relatively stable social groups on muds have reported that people in such groups also have an interest in the offline identities of other participants (Allen 1996a; Cherny 1999; Rheingold 1993).

Hostility toward guests is neither universal nor consistent on BlueSky. Guest reception can depend on who is around, the mood of the participants, what conversation has been going on before, how the guest behaves when it enters the space, and whether the guest can claim friendship with a known person or history on known muds. People occasionally help guests with mud commands or suggestions regarding social norms.

Nevertheless, a group whose membership is protected by obnoxiousness tends to limit participation to people who are themselves obnoxious, as seen in particular by RedWing's behavior and henri's recognition of that behavior as congruent with that of a regular. This attitude sets a particular tone for group interactions. Some participants on BlueSky indicated that they dislike the harassment of newcomers for these reasons.

Alisa, one of BlueSky's wizards, speaks in an almost motherly way about trying to reform BlueSky's treatment of newbies.

ALISA: Lately on BlueSky we've made a concerted effort to [get people to] try to be less harsh on new people.

LORI: Why?

ALISA: Because it's irritating. You introduce somebody new that you deliberately think will get along with this group and they walk in and say something and the whole group turns to you and [makes an aggression sound kind of like a cat spitting]. And of course that person feels bad, and they didn't know what they were doing, and they may not come back, and we get a bad name.

Alisa's attempt at reform does not necessarily extend to random newbies wandering in from the net. In the hypothetical situation she describes, the new person has been introduced to the group *after* being evaluated as somebody who would get along with the group. This highlights the importance of known identity to BlueSky. Newcomers stand a much better chance of successfully integrating into the group if they are already known by a BlueSky regular from another context or if a regular "adopts" them early on.

Alisa's distinction between complete newcomers and invited guests points again to the difficulties stemming from the normalization of obnoxious behavior. Free-ranging obnoxiousness deters potentially desirable newcomers as well as undesirable ones. Several BlueSky regulars identified this as a problem on BlueSky. When I asked Peg, a dino and regular, about her least favorite aspect of BlueSky, she replied that the treatment of newbies bothers her.

> I don't like it when they pick on newbies that don't deserve to be picked on. I'm not going to say that [mock nicey-nice voice] "I'm nice and caring to newbies." If I wasn't known for having some sort of dry wit, I don't think I would have survived this long on that mud. If someone logs on and they're a moron, I'm going to treat them like a moron. But if somebody logs on there [and I'm] trying to help them, then [other BlueSky participants] get mad. . . . If I was coming on now [new], I think it would be kind of cold. Sometimes I feel like we've exhausted all the things there are to talk about. Everybody knows how everyone feels about politics, about abortion. Everybody knows what everybody does, they know who they've slept with. There isn't anything like that [left] to talk about.

Both Alisa and Peg distinguish between newbies who fit into the BlueSky group and those who do not, indicating that some harassment helps keep out the latter. Peg also specifically connects wit (a valued quality on

BlueSky) to aggressive treatment of newbies. Her mockery of being overly nice further connects this form of wit to masculinity, illustrating that BlueSky favors certain types of intelligence over others.

Even BlueSky participants who consider newbie harassment appropriate sometimes expressed concern regarding the balance between protecting the group and its resources and enabling it to grow and change in positive ways. In the conversation below, Corwin and Alisa discuss these competing concerns. Corwin felt there might be reason to limit newcomers even further through technical means:

CORWIN: I have a temptation to make the thing invitation-only.

LORI: So what would that mean, there would be no guest character?

CORWIN: That would be one of the things it would mean, probably. I don't know. There might still be a guest character, I'm not sure.

ALISA: The only problem that I have with an invitation-only mud is that you're severely limiting the amount of new blood you're going to get.

CORWIN: And we do get a certain amount of new blood. It's a slow trickle, but it's still there. Which is why I've been hesitant to do it all along. The main reason it came up was to keep shorthop from applying for a new character from [different] e-mail accounts.

As Corwin indicates, his temptation to close BlueSky to newcomers stems from concerns raised by activities shorthop engaged in that threatened the operation of the mud as well as shorthop's renowned tendency to thwart exile by masquerading as a newbie, sometimes by applying for a character from someone else's e-mail account to hide his true identity. As in all of these discussions regarding how to treat newbies, Corwin specifically connects anonymity with threats to the mud database and to the group.

BlueSky participant identity strategies illustrate important aspects of identity both online and off, highlighting connections between identity and power. Commentators such as Gergen (1991), Meyrowitz (1985), Poster (1995), and Turkle (1995) suggest that technological changes, along with resulting or concomitant changes in social arrangements, are producing increasingly fractured and multiple selves. However, other postmodern theorists of identity argue instead that identities have always been contin-

gent, performed, and multiple and that only our perceptions and understandings of identity are changing (Butler 1990, 1993; Fuss 1989; Garber
1992). This latter argument also emphasizes the political nature of identity,
including its exclusionary ("we're not like them") and normative ("people
in *our* group never do X") aspects. BlueSky's treatment of newbies provides ample evidence of these exclusionary and normative identity strategies. These tactics illustrate not just small group protective strategies but
also the larger hierarchical social structures these strategies also uphold.
Online identity practices demonstrate how particular race, gender, and
class identities wield greater power and receive more benefits than others.
My research on BlueSky thus provides support for theories of identity that
emphasize connections to relations of power. This further suggests that
technological changes, whether or not they change people's understandings
of identity, are already embedded in such power relations.

Yet BlueSky participants, unlike postmodern theorists and researchers,
interpret their own and others' identities as consistent and singular. They
resist conceptions of identity that acknowledge either power or multiplicity, suggesting in part the awful intractability of identity hierarchies.
BlueSky participants' discussions of identity reveal that, while some en-
durance of structures of power relates to people's desire not to lose ground
(or their attempts to gain further advantage), some stems from more mundane concerns. For instance, confusion regarding a participant's identity
disrupts the social interaction and relationships within the group. People's
continued view of selves as consistent and integral wholes thus may stem
in part from the perceived necessity of consistency for trust in relationships, as I discuss in the next chapter.

6 Computer-Mediated Relationships

On a pleasant fall afternoon, I drive through a suburban neighborhood in a medium-sized midwestern town. Midcentury houses alternate with newer apartment and condominium complexes. Two of my BlueSky interviewees live in one of these newer complexes, in a large, pleasant set of townhouses, where winding tree-lined paths link four-unit buildings. Faust, a long-term participant on BlueSky, and Aurora, a mudder who participated for many years mainly on muds other than BlueSky, met online, fell in love, and became engaged before ever meeting offline. Married now for several years, neither currently spends much time on muds. But when they were younger, muds provided a forum that allowed them to explore various ways of relating to other people.

During my first year on BlueSky, Faust participated frequently, but since graduating from college and acquiring a programming job at a company with no Internet access, he rarely logs on. Aurora mudded frequently while in college, although mostly not on Corwin and Alisa muds. Now she rarely muds. She says, "Everyone's polite to me when I log on. You know, like, 'Aurora, we never see you on here; you should get on more often!' But, I don't know—it's not really very interesting. I guess my mind moves faster than that."

Faust, a stocky young white man with blond hair, has lived most of his life near where he grew up. Both of his parents have a Ph.D. and jointly own a consulting business. Faust majored in computer science in college. He avoided muds at first, because he had a friend who "was, I guess, your typical addict," and Faust was concerned about the amount of time mudding would involve. But curiosity finally led him to try it out. "The idea of interacting with a lot of people at the same time over a network was very appealing to me."

Faust met Aurora online while both were still in college. Aurora, a petite

Chinese Australian, lived in Australia at that time. Aurora says about her first online meeting with Faust: "He had a lot of problems. And I kind of wanted to keep tabs on him to make sure that he was okay." Aurora often took this caretaking role in her mud interactions: "Both on the mud and off the mud I tend to be kind of a listener. I'll listen to people's problems, because I feel everyone needs someone to talk to. On the muds people tend to talk to me more because of that, but when I meet them in real life they just kind of—they don't want to talk to me as much. I don't know if they're surprised."

These listening abilities and Aurora's online sociability appealed to Faust. Faust describes his reaction to her: "She was the most popular person online. She was extremely friendly, happy all the time, and very social. Mostly [at first] I just got to know her. At one point I have to admit I decided that I wanted to get to know her *really* well. Which is kind of strange. It sort of took me by surprise. I knew she was from Australia, which made it completely absurd."

Faust and Aurora's relationship proceeded from mud interactions to other media, including letters, phone calls, and cassette tapes.

FAUST: At one point we were having a phone conversation and something happened and we both admitted our feelings for each other, which completely changed everything. During that time she'd gotten my photo and I'd gotten some footage of her. And things were going on at a very rapid pace at this point. And we decided to get engaged.

LORI: So you got engaged before you met, before she came out here.

FAUST: Yeah. Not quite before I knew what she looked like, but [almost].

Faust's comments highlight the importance of physical attraction to romance and the problem this presents for online relationships. Aurora remarks: "I know Faust was surprised when he first met me, because he envisioned this kind of short, fat, Chinese woman." Faust confirms this version of his premeeting expectations of Aurora: "I did have a mental picture. I knew she worked at Kmart, and she had asthma problems. So what I really imagined was this short, fat, Chinese girl with asthma problems, sucking on an inhaler the whole time." Faust laughs at his exaggerated and erroneous image of Aurora, which did not match his idea of an attractive woman.

Both Aurora and Faust thus take pains to laugh off their initial attraction, portraying each other in unflattering, gender-specific terms. Aurora characterizes Faust as emotionally impaired. Faust portrays Aurora as (potentially) physically undesirable. (The aspect of his negative image of her that probably concerned him most—her weight—turned out to be the most mistaken; Aurora is quite thin.) In this way, they rely on the perceived unsuitability of computer media for emotional connection and represent online romance as an unlikely event, evidencing both the luck and distinctiveness of their relationship.

In fact, despite having been married for several years now—a happy ending to their fairy tale of virtual romance—Aurora doesn't advise others to look for love online. "I think romance found over the Internet is pretty rare. I mean people always ask me and Faust for tips, and we always tell them, 'Well, don't do it; it doesn't work. Us, we're just a fluke!' "

. . .

Before predation and danger became the popular themes of media stories regarding online encounters, articles frequently described couples who met and fell in love online. Aurora's doubt echoes the tone of these articles, which paint such romances as remarkable. Our ideal of human interaction, especially romantic and sexual interaction, holds that such contact should not be mediated. Thus, stories about online relationships frequently portray computers as unlikely matchmakers.

Few if any reports of online life focus on friendship rather than romance or aggression. But while BlueSky has its share of romances like that of Faust and Aurora, most of the relationships among participants range between acquaintanceship and friendship. Participants point to these friendships as a primary benefit of online participation.

Although an important part of social life, friendships have not been widely studied. Considered primary and passionate in other times and places (Hansen 1992; Faderman 1989), friendships are portrayed by current norms as less passionate, primary, and central to people's lives than relationships with family members and romantic loved ones, and less socially important than political or economic connections. The paucity of studies of offline friendship groups makes it difficult to compare BlueSky's friendships with similar offline relationships. In addition, as the few existing studies of friendship point out, the very term "friendship" is both vague and symbolically charged and may denote many different types of relationship (see Allan 1989; Rubin 1985). Further, people's statements about the importance of particular friendships do not necessarily match their involvement in the relationship. Rubin's (1985) interviewees sometimes defined as "best friends" people whom they had not seen in years. In some cases when she interviewed two people involved in a relationship, each defined the relationship differently, with one defining it as an important friendship and the other declaring it to be little more than an acquaintanceship. However, the relationships among BlueSky participants, and both the benefits and disadvantages of online participation to those relationships, do suggest some interesting paradoxes of online friendship and some fruitful directions for future research on friendship, both online and off.

BlueSky participants enjoy connections with others that may weather life changes better than offline friendships do, allowing them continuity in a time when people, especially those in the middle class, are becoming increasingly mobile. But some of the trade-off for this continuity may be the depth or importance of the connection. Similarly, while online friendships sometimes become quickly intimate, that intimacy occurs within the constraints of text-based, online communication. The lack of physical presence can make verbal and emotional intimacy feel easier and less threatening. When participants attempt to expand such relationships into the offline realm, they often encounter discomfort and uncertainty when the rules and expectations for the relationship change.

ONLINE CONNECTIONS

As the metaphor of the pub suggests, BlueSky resembles the types of social settings Oldenburg (1997) describes as "third places." Neither work nor home, such public and quasi-public spaces provide forums for sociability and interconnection with others. Offline people use such places for sociability and to keep up with neighborhood doings. Such hangouts can also provide economic benefits for accepted regulars and may be integral to daily work and economic activities (Anderson 1978; Liebow 1967; Whyte 1955).

As in the cafes and bars that Oldenburg (1997) describes, topics of conversation on BlueSky include personal events and stories, exchanges of information, political debates, and discussions of news of the day. People sometimes pop in for brief visits to make announcements of life events, such as the birth of children or receipt of academic degrees. Sometimes such announcements appear quasi-officially, as part of the "message of the day" seen upon first entering the mud. Conventionally, the message of the day provides information on technical changes or other mundane mud business. Because it is displayed to everyone upon connecting to the mud, it has become a place to announce events deemed of sufficient magnitude to be of interest to all. The events that qualify for highlighting in this nongeographical space are the same as those that might in a similar offline forum: births, marriages, graduations, and similar changes in status and rites of passage. Following are several examples, the first from December 1994:

> MESSAGE OF THE DAY
>
> WELCOME TO BlueSky MUSH. Read +help. Read news. Read help. Read it all! Learn it. Live it. Love it. // Backups are done at 5am every day. The mud will be down for an hour at that time. // ANNOUNCEMENT: Phase 1 of BlueSky Renovation is done! The Dynamic Sky is gone, replaced by conventional building. All references to xcoord, ycoord, and zcoord should be removed. Watch this space for more bulletins. // IMPORTANT ANNOUNCEMENT: evariste and Peg are ENGAGED! Congratulate them both!

From October 1996:

> MESSAGE OF THE DAY
>
> WELCOME TO BlueSky MUSH. Read +help. Read news. Read help. Read it all! Learn it. Live it. Love it. // Backups are done at 5am every day. The mud will be down for an hour at that time. New command: +where. It's rough, but it works.
>
> THE COUNSELOR IS *IN*
>
> Congrats to evariste for passing the bar and becoming a LEGAL STUDBOY!

And from November 1996:

> WHEN MUDDERS SPAWN
>
> Lisa reports that she's expecting, and due July 8. Congratulations to her (oh yeah, and Frodo, who had something to do with it).

Like message boards in physical locations where people congregate, announcements like these can promote group identity and feelings of involvement in one another's lives. They mark important passages, making these individual attainments part of the group's history, lore, and interpersonal connections. BlueSky participants also use the e-mail list medmenham to communicate similar information. Several ex-members of the Surly Gang who no longer mud, or mud only very infrequently, keep in touch solely through the mailing list.

BLUESKY AS A SOCIAL SAFETY NET(WORK)

Participants compare BlueSky to a variety of analogous "real world" spaces, including bars, clubs, and other types of quasi-private social spaces. But unlike these real life analogs, BlueSky has no geographical locale. People connect from all over the United States (mostly from major cities) and in a few cases from other countries.

Some people emphasize the opportunities BlueSky has given them to meet people they might not otherwise have met. In a face-to-face interview, elford recounted his history of online participation, beginning on bulletin board systems (BBSs) in his home town. Several BlueSky people participated on BBSs prior to their mudding experience, including both of the other wizards, Corwin and Alisa. BBSs offer information, connections, and services similar to those available over the Internet, but participants connect to them directly by modem (rather than through a separate service provider), and they therefore usually attract people from the local area. The ease of holding face-to-face gatherings of these geographically local groups may have influenced many mudders' later expectations that online relationships should include such offline contact. (Currently, many BBSs also connect to the Internet, but in the early to mid-1980s, when these BlueSky mudders began exploring the possibilities of connecting with others through computers, most were isolated, single-computer systems.)

elford describes the difference that the broader geographical connections of the Internet make to him.

> One of the neat things about mudding that's even neater than BBSing is the geographic distribution of the people. When I log on, generally I'm in touch with people—at the very least—in Utah, California, and on the East Coast. And this sort of expands my perception. It gives me some awareness of what's going on in these places. And particularly if Bistro is on from the Netherlands or Emily from Australia, there's an outreach that gives me a little bit more of a feel that I'm in touch with distant places.

henri, another long-term participant, concurs:

> I think one of the best things about muds is, if you look at the list of people that I know, they're people that I would never know. There's no way I would ever have known them. Barbie is one example. She's someplace in Bakersfield that I never would have gone and never will in all likelihood. But I'm glad I've met her.

elford and henri both talk about the minimization of the importance of geographic distance and their ability to meet people at some remove.

Statements like these concerning the value of such meetings tend to exaggerate the differences between distant people who meet online. Most of the people on BlueSky, for instance, come from relatively similar cultural, class, and race backgrounds. Although henri states that he has never been to Barbie's town and thus would never have met her, nothing about Barbie's identity or life history makes it unlikely that henri could have met someone *like* her in his own town.

The real advantage of this "spaceless place" becomes apparent when people move. As Corwin points out below, most people started on the Surly Gang muds when they were in college or professional school. Many of them moved after graduation, and others have moved since then for a variety of reasons. Throughout these moves, BlueSky participants can maintain at least one of their social groups without significant disruption.

CORWIN: With the BlueSky crowd I think, almost always at least one point in time since they started muds, they have had a major life change and/or move. Okay. Now, let's take henri as an example. (I'm willing to put motives into henri's head.) henri got his Ph.D. Then, he moves to California where he knows nobody. But he had net access at work, so he stayed on the mud. You know. No jarring discontinuity. That's the great thing.

LORI: You've got people who start this in college, and there's always going to be some sort of disjuncture after that, but they've made this social connection, and you can keep that, unlike the friends they make in college, sometimes. You keep some of your friends, but you lose touch.

CORWIN: I think about how few people I know from college, much less high school, or whatever. But while you're making this breach move across the country in the case of many people, you've got this connection still. I think it really softens the impact of that. That was true for me. The first opportunity I had after we moved, I got back online.

henri expressed similar sentiments and confirmed Corwin's description of his move to California: "Over time, your best friends move. [But] it doesn't matter where they move as long as they have net access. I've brought them with me in some sense when I moved to California."

In addition to being able to maintain relationships with people on BlueSky, participants may find people in their new locale whom they already know from online connections. Lisa describes her experience of moving to a new city: "Actually Mender was the person who [got me to move to Madison]. I went up and visited him, and he was great; he sent me the yellow pages listings for environmental engineers, and that's how I got my job. I cold-called out of the yellow pages, found a job in Madison, and moved up there. And he was the only person that I knew up there when I moved." Mender also later moved from Madison to a city on the West Coast in which half a dozen other BlueSky people live, and he currently works for the same company as several other BlueSky participants.

Beryl and fnord used BlueSky to help maintain their romantic relationship when fnord moved out of their shared apartment to take a job (which Corwin helped him obtain) in another state, several hundred miles away. Both were much happier when fnord found a new job in his original city and they were able to resume living together. However, BlueSky (along with e-mail) helped them stay in touch without relying on expensive phone calls.

People also make use of their BlueSky contacts when visiting other cities. Corwin describes such a trip: "One of the fascinations to it is that if you go somewhere you may have somebody already there. We took our honeymoon in Boston and knew that there were mudders there. The whole point was we had people volunteer to take us to see the sights in Boston." Some have even taken mudder "grand tours," traveling from city to city throughout the United States, stopping to stay with and visit BlueSky mudders along the way. People use the medmenham e-mail list to let others know their itineraries or to solicit places to stay. elflord posted the following message to the list:

> From: elflord
>
> Date: Tue, 9 May 1995 11:22:35 +0000
>
> To: Medmenham@machine.university.edu
>
> Subject: The Great Elflord and Carla Road Trip
>
> Carla and I are in the planning stages of a road trip, nominally from Cheyenne to Charlotte, North Carolina, and back. We would probably be on the road for between two and three weeks, falling between June 15 and July 13.
>
> If you are somewhere along our route (likely to follow I-80 on one leg and I-40 on the other, roughly speaking), and would like to meet up with us, please let me know (including best/worst times) to help our planning!
>
> Offers of crash space would be Most Welcome, as well.
>
> —elflord

elflord also mentioned this trip to me in his interview, counting the ability to make remote contacts as one of the major benefits of mudding:

> Having contact with all these people in different places makes it possible to have acquaintances in distant places that we visit. The nominal point of our road trip was to visit Carla's family and friends in North Carolina. But all the way there and all the way back we stayed with and met up with people that I knew. And that would not have been possible. The same sort of thing if we ever do a West Coast tour. I know a lot of people out there, just by virtue of muds. I not only know their names and a little about them, I know the person from having actively spoken with them online.

Work-related trips can also be opportunities to meet other BlueSky participants and may similarly be announced on medmenham.

> To: Medmenham@machine.university.edu
>
> Subject: trip to bay area
>
> Date: Tue, 09 May 95 18:25:56-0400
>
> From: allia
>
> i'll be 1.5 hours north of sanfran from may 15 until may 21.
>
> i should be free from that friday night until saturday afternoon.
>
> crash space in town is welcome, but not required. i would like
> to meet mudders and hang out and stuff.
>
> allia

The success of such solicitations for meetings varies depending on people's schedules and also on the status of the person seeking to meet others. allia began mudding on TinyMUD and has thus known several BlueSky participants for many years, but she now participates online only infrequently. Several more regular participants consider her "whiny" or are disturbed by her openness about her sexual practices. Thus only a few people responded to her medmenham posting. By contrast, when Alisa, one of BlueSky's wizards and a highly respected member of the group, similarly visited northern California on a work trip, her spare time was easily filled with meals and get-togethers with other participants.

McKenzie recently moved cross-country. His destination and even his reasons for moving were influenced by his mud participation. McKenzie decided to leave his job to return to graduate school, influenced in part by experiences of mudders currently in graduate school. He also chose his school on the basis of recommendations from other mudders.

LORI: You've just recently moved?

MCKENZIE: Right. And mainly did because of people I'd met on the mud.

LORI: That brought you out here particularly?

MCKENZIE: Yeah, to NorthernU. Partly because I found out about NorthernU and found out about projects that are interesting to me, but also just partly because I knew people. I was friends with them. . . . So, as far as my social life out here, it's been virtually everybody that I know in the real life social situation is someone that I know online. That's just because I . . .

LORI: Came out here because . . .

MCKENZIE: Right. My uncle lives here, so that's the only person I don't know from the net. It's just because I haven't met people. [laughs] I'm assuming I'll [eventually] meet people who are not mudders!

In addition to choosing his destination on the basis of the recommendation of mudders, McKenzie met up with several mudders from both BlueSky and ElseMOO (a mud with some overlapping membership with BlueSky) during his cross-country trip out to his new school.

DISAPPEARANCES AND THE FRAGILITY OF ONLINE RELATIONSHIPS

Mud relationships can be more easily maintained through various life changes than face-to-face relationships. They can also quickly become intense and intimate. However, they are also vulnerable. Disruptions due to loss of net access or other similar changes can occur suddenly, sometimes leaving friends to wonder forever. As henri says:

> You have these friends, but maybe the worst thing is knowing that the last time you see somebody may be the last time you *ever* see them. There's no guarantee that they're ever coming back. This happened with Barbie last year. She just disappeared. If I hadn't had her snail-mail address, we never would have [seen her again]. . . . I have other friends that I have never seen again. . . . There's also the sense that if something happens to me, I may never see them again and they'll never know what happened. It's not like my parents will even know how to contact them if they want to tell them, well, he's in the hospital or he's dead.

henri mentioned several people who lost net access and thereby disappeared from the group. In one case, a college student dropped out of school (reputedly for "mudding too much") and lost his school-provided computer account. In another, a mudder lost his job, losing both work-provided access and the economic wherewithal to attain private access. In these cases, the participants made the effort to log on and let others know what was happening. Others have simply disappeared for reasons unknown. These examples highlight the requisites for online participation. Although the cost of online access may be low, it is not nil. Even people from middle-class backgrounds, like most BlueSky participants, who have multiple connections to computers and computer-related networks, can find their online connections disrupted by offline events.

On BlueSky, people manage some of the uncertainty of online participation by making connections outside the mud. They exchange e-mail addresses and in some cases snail-mail addresses and phone numbers. Some people who live near each other get together regularly or semiregularly face-to-face. But you know only what people tell you. When someone goes offline without notice, there may be no way to find him or her. Because muds are not geographic-based communities, it's easy for someone to disappear, "move" to a different online space, or leave the online world entirely.

On one occasion, I left the mud for nearly two weeks without notice. Knowledge of my ongoing research project probably made this an even more troubling event for other participants. People assumed that I wouldn't disappear unless something was wrong. henri lived nearby and tried to call me but had written down my phone number incorrectly. Although most likely nobody really thought I was dead, the response I got on return was surprisingly intense, not to mention gratifying.

> fnord says "COPPERHEAD ltns"[1]
> henri says "COPPERHEAD"
> henri says "where you been"
> Copperhead says "fnord, henri"
> Florin COPPERHEAD
> henri says "we've been worried"
> Copperhead FLORIN
> Copperhead !
> henri says "and I don't have your new phone #"
> Copperhead says "same phone number"
> henri got a "boo-WEEE" error

Copperhead is okay

Corwin has arrived.

henri says "CORWIN"

Copperhead says "Corwin"

Corwin says "Copp"

Corwin says "look henri it's Copp"

henri says "I was just commenting on that"

Mender says "SHE AIN'T DEAD"

Copperhead grins unconvincingly

henri says "we were worried"

Copperhead :(

Corwin wasn't worried, Copp is indestructible

henri says "it's been WEEKS"

henri says "well almost 2 weeks"

Copperhead says "it has been awhile; I didn't really realize how long"

Corwin says "we were worried you got a life or something"

Corwin says "THE HORROR"

henri nods at Corwin

Copperhead got less of a life, actually

henri says "work + school?"

Copperhead nods

You whisper "it was nice of you to try to call" to henri.

henri whispers "well that and we were wondering where you went"

Bilerific-Sid says "We thought you were dead CH."

Copperhead says "rumors of my demise, etc."

Phillipe says "CHHHHHHHHH"

Phillipe says "yay, we missed you"

The comments that greeted my return make it clear that my absence was discussed. As in other networks of friends, unexplained absences are noted and discussed, with strategies devised to get information about the missing member. In addition, the greetings of others upon return help reinforce ties between the prodigal mudder and the remaining group. My own absence had been motivated by distress and anger regarding the sexism I perceived on BlueSky. But I rarely felt more warmly connected to the people on BlueSky than when I returned and discovered my absence had worried them.

Sometimes people leave the mud not because of specific discomfort but because they come to believe mudding to be a waste of time. Online socializing carries some stigma, and people sometimes worry that they're mudding too much. Some decide that other things in their lives are more important. Barbie has left the group periodically, usually returning after several months' absence. On one occasion, a discussion on a mud newsgroup apparently caused her to reflect negatively on her mudding experience. She posted the following as part of an ongoing discussion of dinos.

> All the dinos I know are, for all intents and purposes, "dead." That is to say creatively "dead." We all have everybody's schticks memorized and the on-line interaction is basically empty. Other than the occasional good record recommendation and occasionally funny one-liners, nothing new ever seems to happen. If the interesting discourse among people from different backgrounds (that originally attracted me to muds) is still going on, it must be entirely in whisper.
> So I don't know. I guess what I am saying is that maybe it is time for most of us to hang it up. I am woman enough to admit that my online persona is now hackneyed and non-entertaining, and what's worse is that I no longer have the desire to attempt to remake myself. Believe me I have tried, never with any success. If you make up a new character you will instantly be hounded to reveal who you "really" are or else shunned entirely.

As in the previous chapter, Barbie's assertions here concerning online personae reveal a slightly different take on mudding from the views many BlueSky people express. She talks about her persona as a separate entity that she created and that now bores her. Barbie also connects her inability to get out of her mud-persona rut to the insularity of BlueSky culture. Once you've created an accepted identity within the group, you may feel locked into that presentation of self. Changing one's self-presentation can be difficult when people link their memories of others specifically to the way they "talk" on the mud rather than to physical characteristics. Add to this the facts that new people are not readily accepted and that Barbie distances herself from her online identity, and one can imagine why she may feel constrained.

Barbie's online persona may bore her, but others on BlueSky do not share her self-evaluation. Her wit and flamboyant personality make her a favorite, and people miss her during her occasional self-imposed exiles. In 1996 she announced she was leaving for good (although she later returned), but during late 1994 and early 1995 she disappeared without warning or explanation, provoking periodic speculation concerning her whereabouts and lamentation over her absence. The following conversation occurred after a quote fest during which someone used a Barbie quote, reminding others how long it had been since they'd seen her.

Corwin says "BARBIE COME BACK"

henri says "BARBIE"

Kay shouts into a microphone, "BAAAAAARBIE"

henri thinks she's dead or something

fnord shouts into a microphone, "BARBIE COME HOME"

henri says "she could have at least sent a postcard"

Kay shouts into a microphone, "BARBIE COME HOME STOP ALL IS FORGIVEN
    STOP"

Corwin says "maybe she moved somewhere with no access"

Corwin says "i mean she barely had access as it was"

Copperhead says "did Barbie move?"

henri says "we don't know, c-head"

henri says "she just stopped logging in, and won't answer my physical mail"

Copperhead ohs

henri says "and nobody has her phone # and she's not listed"

Ulysses says "baaaaaarbie"

Her return provoked a reaction similar to the one I received after my brief
absence, although Barbie's was even more effusive because of her high
standing in the group and her longer absence.

Jet says "BARBIE"

Jet says "good lord"

Barbie says "Jet"

Jet says "You return from the DEAD"

Corwin has arrived.

henri points at Barbie

elflord says "LOOK IT'S BARBIE"

Corwin says "BAR-FREAKIN-BIE"

Announcement: Corwin shouts "Barbie is HONORARY QUEEN OF ALL SHE
    SURVEYS for today"

Jet says "QUEEN BARBIE"

elflord applauds

Copperhead bows low

henri . o O (I thought she was Queen of the Universe every day)

henri says "Barbie tell us what you've been doing with all your time"

Barbie says "AIEE, I can't read this fast"

henri says "just gag some people, Barbie"

Barbie hard to say

Barbie has been spending her time doing basically nothing . . . nothing exciting
    anyhow . . .

Rimmer has arrived.
Rimmer says "BARBIE"
Rimmer says "Welcome back."
Barbie says "Rimmer!"
Ulysses proclaims today Official Prodigal Barbie Day

Barbie's earlier betrayal of expectations regarding offline and online identities, the persistent rumors that offline Barbie is "really" male, her refusal to meet others offline, and her occasional disparaging remarks about the value of her online participation—all would suggest that Barbie ought to be marginalized by the group. Yet instead she holds high status, and many consider her one of their favorite people on BlueSky.

In part, this apparent contradiction relates to the features of BlueSky sociability that participants value. Humor in particular is important to the interrelations of many small interacting groups (Fine 1987b). For boys and men it likely provides a particularly important form of pleasurable interaction, since expressions of affection may violate expectations of masculinity. Several interviewees indicated that they participated on BlueSky primarily for its entertainment and humor value. This forms such an important part of BlueSky that one participant, asked by another to describe BlueSky in a single sentence, asserted that "Wit is King," and several others present agreed with this characterization.

Barbie enjoys a reputation as a humorous participant and excellent storyteller. Others enjoy her sarcastic depictions of coworkers, frank tales about dating disasters, and sometimes poignant depictions of her family. (In an excerpt in chapter 3, henri says he has eighty Barbie quotes in his quote file, an unusually high measure of perceived wit.) The richness of Barbie's descriptions of her offline life probably compensate somewhat for her unwillingness to allow her online contacts into that life. In addition, her reputed wit and overall online friendliness lead others to ignore the insult implied in that refusal.

Barbie's status on BlueSky also reflects assumptions and understandings about women's experiences both on and offline. Barbie's gender allows participants to interpret her unwillingness to meet online contacts face-to-face as stemming from fears regarding encountering strangers. Barbie herself relied on this rationalization in her explanation to me regarding her unwillingness to be interviewed offline.

Barbie whispers "I have this rule about meeting computer people. I don't do it anymore."
Copperhead whispers "hmmm, that's interesting. Why is that?"

> Barbie whispers "well, after a number of psychopathic people met me in
>   person (one guy showed up at my doorstep from Michigan after only talking
>   to him once on the phone) I just don't do it anymore."

Whether or not this is Barbie's real reason for not meeting BlueSky people, its plausibility deflects criticism of her reclusiveness.

Awareness of the gender imbalance on BlueSky also makes participants willing to forgive Barbie's lack of adherence to some of BlueSky's norms. Most participants like to think of BlueSky as diverse and tolerant. As a woman who, when she does log on, participates often in conversations, Barbie helps support this view. Barbie's reputation for raunchiness also supports the male participants' view that their style of talk constitutes normal, friendly conversation rather than gender-specific discourse.

Participants may in fact have some investment in *not* meeting Barbie face-to-face. They know that many people cannot maintain the same level of outspokenness offline as they do online. Barbie may not display offline the aspects of her online presentation of self that others enjoy. In addition, while rumors concerning a possible discrepancy between Barbie's offline and online gender identities probably stem precisely from her unwillingness to meet others, these rumors may also strengthen people's acceptance of her reclusiveness. Many would probably rather take her female gender presentation at face value than have to risk a reconsideration of whether females can indeed fit into BlueSky's culture as well as Barbie does.

MEETING OFFLINE

Most BlueSky participants do not share Barbie's insistence upon separating online and offline contacts. Although most interactions among BlueSky participants occur online, their relationships extend offline as well in various ways, as we've seen. In some cases, BlueSky participants exchange information that enables them to contact each other through other media. Particularly for people geographically close to each other, this allows for phone calls concerning events of mutual interest or in cases where someone has gone missing from the mud for a period of time, as I did. People have mailed care packages to members of the group who have recently moved, and some participants have regularly exchanged music recordings through the mail.

A small but important portion of BlueSky interactions also occur face-to-face. One feature of the longevity and insularity of the Surly Gang group is that most participants have met each other in person at some time. Almost every participant has met several others, including people at some geographic remove. In earlier years, when most participants were students, there were large group gatherings, usually connected with science fiction fan conventions. Now that most work full-time, these get-togethers tend to take the form of one person traveling around the country, making contact with several other participants, many of whom will drive several hours to connect with the cross-country traveler. During my travels for interviewing people, I was frequently asked whom I had met and whom I was going to meet. I was also treated to verbal lists of group members my interviewees had already met. Such lists also periodically form the topic for roll calls, like the following:

Obtuse BLUESKY DENIZENS MET IN REAL LIFE ROLL CALL
Obtuse Perry, devnull, Captin, allia
David Mender, Sparkle, luke if he counts
fnord too many to list off the top of his head. over 50, he knows, approaching 100
henri too many to list
Copperhead oh gads many many
Obtuse fnord and Beryl, yes
fnord says "just off biglist I've met: Elektra, Pez, Rockefeller, RaveMage, NightBird, evariste, Mu, Bemer, QueenMab, Pyramid, Beryl, symmetry, weasel, Riverrun, Copperhead, dozer, allia, BlackBeauty, Peg, BJ, Gambol, Cleo, McKenzie, Corwin, Sparkle, Mike Adam, henri, Obtuse, Brine, Phillipe, Ulysses, Rostopovich"
Scrounge hsm biglist as a reference
fnord counts, that's 32
RaveMage says "THIRTY SEVEN"
fnord knows there's as many not on that list
fnord says "there used to be 20 mudders just at Dartmouth"
Scrounge Alisa, Corwin, Othello, henri, Perry, Farron, zombie, elflord, Starfish, Dot, Rimmer, Locutus, Stingray
Scrounge says "but not fnord"
Phillipe has met like 5 whole people from here not counting the ones who live in New Jersey
David says "You got me beat, Phil"
RaveMage says "twerp dilemma rockefeller mu queenmab chipper beryl weasel riverrun ch susanah locutus fnord devnull dozer allia peg rimmer gambol cleo anguish corwin cauda ME henri madmonk perry"

Because having met many people suggests longevity within the group as well as closer connections with those people, participants notice who has met more and fewer people and acknowledge the status implications.

I asked people about the difference it made to their relationships to have met other people face-to-face. Most of my BlueSky interviewees stated that some people they had never met were nevertheless considered friends. However, meeting face-to-face did make a difference to their relationships.

ATTICUS: People I've met I feel that I'm more willing to put my trust in them.

LORI: When you meet people, you've got more of a solid base?

ATTICUS: Right. You know something's actually there. It's more solid. [For instance], there's someone I trust a lot [but haven't met face-to-face] and who I try my best to be very open with. As far as I can tell—and I am pretty good at reading people online, because I've been doing it for awhile—as far as I can tell, she's said things that she wouldn't say if she was trying to [hide herself], but I'm still conscious that I'm not going to know what she's like until I've met her.

Some of this question of trust has to do with people's representation of their identity online. On BlueSky, as previously discussed, participants expect that people will represent themselves in accordance with their off-line identity. However, they are aware that in other online spaces, people frequently masquerade, particularly with regard to gender.

In my interview with Mu, one of the earliest BlueSky mudders, we discussed the percentage of women on BlueSky compared with other muds. Mu pointed out that it is hard to get a sense of how many women participate on other muds. But on BlueSky, the longevity of relationships and the offline connections among participants prevent people from hiding their offline identities. As Mu says: "I know everybody by this time. There may be a few exceptions, [but I] have either met them or someone who I've met who I trust has met them."

Meyrowitz suggests that textual representations always remain in some sense impersonal; however, "after thirty seconds of face-to-face interaction between us (or after seeing me on television), . . . you would know things about my *personal* being that you could not discover from reading everything I have ever written" (1985: 99, emphasis in original). BlueSky participants would apparently agree. They privilege information about others gained during face-to-face meetings over information received online.

Note, for instance, that Mu associates "knowing" somebody with meeting him or her face-to-face.

Several people brought up the issue of trust when asked about the difference face-to-face meetings have made to their relationships. Trust can relate to issues of identity representation, as in Mu's discussion of gender identities. But trust also relates to forms of behavior that cannot occur online. Some people told me stories of meeting other mudders for the first time when these mudders dropped into town and stayed in their homes. In a few cases, people felt taken advantage of when their house guests failed to pay for meals or stole items from their homes. Such incidents made people warier of those they had not yet met face-to-face. This reinforced their belief that you can't really know someone, for bad or good, until you meet them face-to-face.

Another possible explanation for the connection between face-to-face meetings and trust relates again to the features we consider important to identity (at least in U.S. and similar cultures). We rely on several kinds of information to evaluate people. We expect that people have limited control over "given-off," or expressive, information, and we read such information for clues as to the other person's "true" feelings or personality. On text-based forums such as muds, all information is transmitted through text; thus all information is intentionally presented, what Goffman (1959) terms communicative information. Participants understand that others choose what information they present in this way and could be lying or misleading them. Although emotions and the facial expressions and tones of voice that are connected with them can certainly be controlled or manipulated, we expect that some amount of given-off information is uncontrollable and thus remains to be read by others. To the extent that people rely on "gut feelings" about others based on evaluations of such given-off information, they are unlikely to fully trust someone they have not met face-to-face.

Allen (1996a), in her mud research, states that people she interviewed were interested in gathering information about others' offline identities. On the basis of some of her own meetings with people, she concluded that meeting face-to-face could change the way people feel about each other. I experienced my meetings with interviewees similarly. Sometimes I found myself uncomfortable with a person in a face-to-face meeting—for reasons I couldn't always clearly identify—even though I'd been quite comfortable with that person online. After the face-to-face meeting, I found I could return to our previous level of comfort online. However, I now noticed things I had not noticed previously, and I reinterpreted some aspects of the other's communication style. (The reverse experience—being more comfortable face-to-face with someone than I had been online—was rarer and seemed to have less effect on my experience of people online.) Face-to-face meetings thus enable people to interpret and reinterpret online texts.

Most BlueSky regulars indicated that early on in their experience with muds, meeting people surprised them, often in negative ways. But after years of experience with online communication, they said they either learned what kinds of things they could expect to translate from online to offline, or they learned to hold all expectations in abeyance.

> BERYL: At first I was really bad at meeting people. I guess I had real expectations or something. But I learned.
>
> LORI: So what kind of things would happen? Were there people that you liked online and you'd meet them and you wouldn't like them?
>
> BERYL: Yes. Like Cap turned out . . . he's not bad online . . . but he's never mastered being social. So he was a totally different person in real life. In general, though, I've gotten pretty good about it now, in the past few years. You can tell if somebody's rude online, they're going to be rude off. If you genuinely like someone online you're probably going to genuinely like them when you meet them. You have to be careful not to mistake having hung out with someone for years with liking them.
>
> LORI: So you kind of get more experience with how to read online so you know what's going to translate online and what isn't.
>
> BERYL: Yeah.

Beryl's comments about Cap illustrate that sociability online doesn't carry the same status as the ability to socialize offline. Other participants mentioned similar discrepancies between online and offline social skills. Some felt that mudding could serve as a sort of training ground for people with inadequate social skills. RaveMage borrows terminology from his professional psychiatric experience:

> RAVEMAGE: It's almost like a day hospital for people who have social difficulty. First you interact in a literally faceless and completely defended way with people that if anything upsets you, you just disconnect, no big deal. And you can do it without having to worry about,

unfortunately, things like personal hygiene and stuff
like that. [In the early days] we were going around
yelling, "mud naked, mud naked," because you can! So
after all that, what comes out next is that then you
try to go to a [face-to-face] get-together.

LORI: [So] it's sort of a training [ground].

RAVEMAGE: Exactly.

LORI: And then you can use those same skills with other
people.

RAVEMAGE: First you learn to do it on the muds, and then often
[when] you try to do it in person, the first time you get
a really rude shock. But that's okay because that also
is educational, and they learn that and then after that
they move [on]. [He mentions two BlueSky participants.]
They are just terribly nice people, great to be around,
[but] if we hadn't had the chance to talk to them [online]
first and realized that, we wouldn't have put up with
[them face-to-face].

As RaveMage suggests, some people come across better online than off.
Other BlueSky participants also report that face-to-face meetings sometimes negatively affect relationships, especially where gross violations of
standard U.S. manners occur. Some people mention factors such as body
odor or strange physical mannerisms. Also important are issues of politeness, such as being turned off by someone's tendency to interrupt others'
speech. Interrupting a speaker is impossible on muds, since each utterance
is discretely typed and entered into the mud program. Also, although some
people clearly talk more than others, and some can also type faster than
others, monopolizing a conversation can be more difficult online. These
kinds of speech habits, which can be offensive in face-to-face encounters,
do not arise to the same degree in online communication. Face-to-face
interactions can actually disadvantage relationships. Particularly for people
who have mannerisms or habits that they find difficult to break despite
their offensiveness to others, online interactions can enable better relationships with others than face-to-face interactions.

FROM SPACELESS PLACE TO FACE-TO-FACE:
RELATIONSHIPS IN TRANSITION

While most BlueSky relationships are conducted online, some geographically close participants also enjoy offline relationships. Some people have

introduced offline friends to BlueSky. Others began socializing offline after getting to know each other online. Several BlueSky participants are involved in romantic relationships with each other.

The transition from a solely online relationship to an active offline one can be uncomfortable. The most acute difficulties between online and offline social presence arise in romantic relationships. Online romances can engender strong hopes and expectations, freighting the eventual offline meetings with anxiety. Many also find issues of physical presence and compatibility more problematic in romantic or potentially sexual relationships that move offline.

Peg has had two romantic relationships with other BlueSky participants, each of which began online. Atticus moved across the country primarily to change his relationship with Peg from an online to a face-to-face romantic relationship. The relationship with Atticus ended after about a year.

evariste also moved across the country after becoming romantically involved with Peg online, although he insists that his move was motivated primarily by the desire to attend a good law school near where Peg lived. He characterized as foolish and even pathetic the willingness to make such a move solely for romantic reasons (as he knew Atticus had done). Peg and evariste eventually married and have been married for several years.

Peg talked about the difficulty involved in shifting the relationships from online to offline and about how the things she learned from meeting Atticus helped her to handle her first meeting better with evariste.

PEG: When I met Atticus the first time, it was a big shock, because we had very high expectations for how it was going to go, because we were already very enamored of each other from letter writing and from talking on the phone and from being online.

LORI: So letters and phone calls?

PEG: Yeah. Oh yeah. And then when I met him it was very hard to put the online person and the person in the same room with me together. It took . . . he stayed with me for a week. . . .
He came out with a whole bunch of people. I was very overwhelmed, because not only was I meeting Atticus for the first time, but a whole bunch of people: fnord, Rockefeller, Calvin, RaveMage. I met a lot of people that weekend. It was very disconcerting.
To contrast, when I met Jim [evariste], we had talked on the phone the same, we had done letters the same, we had sent pictures; I hadn't sent him a videotape, but I had thought of it. When I went to see Jim, we looked at each other for a

while and then we stopped looking at each other. And it was enough to be close to each other. So we waited for my luggage in the airport, and we sat next to each other and didn't look at each other, and we held hands. I remember thinking that

was very strained, and I wasn't sure if it was just me, and so I went to touch his face to turn him to me, and he said, "I can't look at you right now." And I said, "okay." And then it was almost like sort of an accustoming. We talked without looking at each other, and it was getting used to his voice.

LORI: Because you had the voice before, so this was sort of a little more presence, [then] a little more presence?

PEG: Right. And we kind of oozed into it. Very slowly. Then later we looked at each other more, and we did a lot [of things together]. I was more comfortable with the way it happened with Jim, but I know a lot of people that it's happened the way it happened with Atticus. I've got the two different experiences. I got used to Atticus, and then we looked at each other all the time, so it wasn't like it ruined our relationship. But it was . . . he was one of the first people, whereas by the time I met Jim, I was much more used to meeting people online.

In the early stages of romantic attraction, people often idealize the object of their affection. This is especially easy to do when you can't see the other person. Thus, looking for the first time at someone to whom you consider yourself attracted can be threatening, both to the relationship itself and to the participants' views of how realistic they've been about each other. Peg illustrates this in her emphasis on the great difficulty of *looking* at people previously met only in mediated encounters.

These experiences tend to reinforce the expectation that face-to-face communications give a greater sense of presence. Berger and Luckmann state that "the most important experience of others takes place in the face-to-face situation, which is the prototypical case of social interaction. All other cases are derivations of it" (1966: 28). Similarly, Schutz discussed the "We-relationship," in which two (or more) participants share the same space and time and "are aware of each other and sympathetically partici-pate in each other's lives" (1967: 163–64). He emphasizes the greater level of information that is available through a variety of senses to each of the participants about the other in a face-to-face setting. "As I watch his face and his gestures and listen to the tone of his voice, I become aware of much more than what he is deliberately trying to communicate to me" (169). Online interactions can sometimes provide this sense of shared presence, but like Peg, most people I spoke with described face-to-face encounters as more intense.[2]

This intensity means that even when people want ideally to de-emphasize the importance of looks, the first face-to-face meeting with someone they considered attractive online can be a shock. Beryl became romantically involved with Cap online. But when she met him face-to-face, she did not find him attractive. "Ew, he was so gross! When we met in person, I discovered I had no desire at all for him. But it took a little bit of convincing him." The effect of previously unperceived given-off information can be particularly intense in a romantic relationship, especially in cases where bodily responses to and arousal for the other person have already been evoked through online discourse.

Meeting people face-to-face with whom you've had only an online friendship can also be uncomfortable. For one thing, people often say things online that they would feel uncomfortable saying face-to-face. RaveMage finds this a negative feature of online interactions, because the tendency of people to reveal very personal details of their lives sometimes reminds him too much of his professional psychiatric activities.

> LORI: It almost sounds like it's possible to have very strong friendships with people online, but it's always sort of a maybe until you've met them.
>
> RAVEMAGE: Yes, it is.
>
> LORI: And then that cements it or doesn't.
>
> RAVEMAGE: Sometimes they can be pretty decent friendships, and then the problem is that I notice people are a lot more willing to talk about some things on the muds than they are other places. . . . When people are talking about certain things, "it's too much like work. You're telling me too much about a problem that is too specific to my profession."

RaveMage uses BlueSky in part as an escape from his relatively sober and responsible offline life. Although he does sometimes give limited advice and assistance to online friends (particularly on general medical topics not connected specifically to his psychiatric practice), he finds online communication's facilitation of personal revelation distressing.

henri, on the other hand, finds it advantageous to discuss topics online that could provoke discomfort offline.

> HENRI: One thing I find easy to do on muds is to talk about virtually any topic that's bothering me. I don't know how much

other people do that. But it's easier for me to be totally
honest.

LORI: Is that just because you don't see facial expressions? You get
reactions, but it's not quite that visceral?

HENRI: I think maybe it's partially that, but what occurs to me is
the syndrome of people being able to talk to total strangers.
These people [aren't quite] strangers, but there's that
element, because you don't know what I look like, or if
you've only met me once or twice, you're not going to
show up at my house. . . . [It's] safe because you're never
going to go down and meet any of these people. You don't
know anybody they know. You don't know their coworkers,
you don't know their family, or anything. That's part of
the stranger-confession thing. It's also one way that people
can be totally anonymous. You're not going to mention
something to her mother that she doesn't want her mother
to know. I mean this has happened too, but it's the exception.

henri's suggestion that these people will never meet each other contradicts
the actual experiences of BlueSky participants, who *do* in fact meet each
other. It is true that most BlueSky mudders have met neither henri's parents nor his coworkers. (He did introduce one coworker to the mud, and
some BlueSky participants have met that coworker offline as well.) However, they know where he works and know enough about him that they
could probably even locate his parents. Concern about this level of exposure of his offline life in fact fueled much of henri's anger at shorthop
when shorthop wrote about the BlueSky group in a popular net guide
using their real mud names.

henri's emphasis on anonymity and the experience of strangerlike relationships, which seemingly contradicts the reality of the routine revelation of personal and identifying information among BlueSky participants, highlights two important considerations. The first concerns the
qualities of online relationships, which often appear to combine degrees of
both intimacy and aloofness. BlueSky friendships suggest the extent to
which online relationships can combine a willingness to reveal very personal information quickly with an acceptance of the casualness and con-
tingency of online connections.

The second important consideration highlighted by henri's remarks
concerns research into the nature of online relationships. If a researcher
were merely to interview henri without actively participating on BlueSky,

he or she might gain a misleading picture of the relationships among BlueSky participants. Even participants such as henri, who knows much about his fellow participants and about whom much is known by them, may represent online life as generally anonymous. henri, like Faust and Aurora, treats deeply felt connections as the exception in computer-mediated relationships.

While BlueSky relationships are far from anonymous, the tendency of people such as henri to emphasize their anonymity suggests that the connections fostered by online interaction, even over many years, may never feel as deep or as close as those enabled by face-to-face contact. This accords with Virnoche's (1997) analysis of the Internet as a "strange making technology," which can introduce distance even into offline relationships experienced as quite close.

This distance, although it may impart a feeling of anonymity even to close and long-term relationships, can facilitate certain types of disclosure. Because of this, as several participants explained to me, online relationships sometimes quickly become verbally intimate, making the transition to an offline friendship particularly difficult. Toni, a relative newcomer to BlueSky, recently changed careers and moved from the South to a large East Coast city where several other BlueSky participants live. As was true for McKenzie, these mudder contacts helped her during a potentially difficult transition. However, Toni had not yet met her BlueSky contacts in the new city face-to-face. She explained that she had previously allowed her online relationship with Jonathan to become very personal, in part because she *didn't* expect to meet him in person. This complicated the already difficult circumstances of a cross-country move and first meetings with online friends.

TONI: Jonathan and I just, you know, we were kind of always around and kind of always [talked] together and talked about important stuff and unimportant stuff and just kind of [hung out]. So when I met him, it was really really weird. He and I both moved here almost the same day, and we were both staying at Kay's house. So I get here with two cats, and I haven't so much as sat behind the wheel of anything in four or five years, and I've got this fourteen-foot truck, and I've just driven it through snow and ice and fog. You name it—if it sucks to drive through it, I was doing it. So Jonathan's at Kay's house already, and here's this person that . . .

LORI: And you're completely exhausted . . .

TONI: Yeah, I'm freaked out. I've got two freaked out cats, you

know, and I'm kind of nervous, because here's this person
that, in some sense of the word "close," I've been very very
close to. And now he's going to be . . . and it's like, oh god,
what if we hate each other?
So it was just so overwhelming for me. It was the first time
that I met somebody under those circumstances . . . that I'd
known him really well online. I never thought I'd actually
meet him in person, and so we were pretty free with each
other. [laughs] Here, it was so overwhelming that I [left and]
went with Kay to NorthernU. Well, of course, immediately
I logged in and start talking with Jonathan. But I just . . .
I couldn't just meet him and sit there and talk to him. It was
too much.

Toni echoes henri's analysis of online communication as similar to
"stranger interaction." As with Peg and evariste's slow physical acclimation to each other, Toni's flight back to online communication helped her
ease the transition from a fully online relationship with Jonathan to one
which now includes relatively frequent offline meetings, because they currently live in the same city and share many of the same friends.

The discomfort people feel when making the transition from an online
to an offline relationship suggests that although online relationships may
not feel as close as offline relationships, they inspire the kinds of disclosure
usually reserved for closer relationships. Some of the ability to disclose
may stem not just from physical distance (including the absence of physical
communication cues) but also from a certain kind of disinterest. Online
friendships often carry fewer expectations and responsibilities than offline
relationships. As henri says, "One of the things that happens in real life
that stresses friendships is people imposing themselves on you in some
way. . . . It's much easier to pick and choose who and when you interact
with on muds."

henri points out that offline relationships often require greater responsibility and interdependence than relationships conducted solely online.
Many of the kinds of things friends do for each other offline cannot occur
in primarily online relationships. Favors such as babysitting or housesit-
ting, helping people move, and so forth contribute to the depth of offline
relationships. However, when such activities are not reciprocated or the
reciprocity is perceived as unbalanced, people can feel imposed upon. As
henri points out, this can stress friendships. Thus online relationships often do not have the opportunity to deepen through these forms of mutual
support, but they also escape the potential friction that interdependence
can generate.

Online, people can also easily forget the exact composition of the group with whom they are conversing. That group may be much larger than a face-to-face conversing group could be. For instance, there may be twenty or more active people in the Falcon at any one time, all of whom may be part of the same conversation. Not only would such a large group conversation be difficult offline (my experience facilitating student discussion groups of this size convinces me of this!), it is unlikely that all members of that twenty-person group would feel equally friendly toward each other. When conversing online, the size and composition of the group are less obvious. This led henri to point out to me that on muds, it's "easy to forget you're not among friends." It can be easy to reveal things you would otherwise say only to friends.

The limited nature of online communication can sometimes also facilitate friendships that might not have formed in an offline setting. henri describes this phenomenon as well:

> I think it's very easy to misinterpret what people say or interpret it in a way that [they didn't intend]. Which I think leads to a lot of [BlueSky's] group cohesiveness. If you really understood, there'd be a lot more friction in our group. People will say something, and you can choose to take it as sarcastic or deadpan or serious or whatever. You don't see people [on BlueSky] saying, "What do you mean by that?" a lot. They laugh or whatever.
>
> By the same thing, it's hard to convince somebody you really don't like them and don't like anything about them and don't want to have anything to do with them.
>
> The good side of that is you can say things that maybe you'd regret later and say, "Oh I didn't mean that." [The other person has] the choice of being mortally offended or just taking it as a joke.

Online interactions can make some forms of relationship repair and face-saving work easier. The inaccessibility of facial expressions, tone of voice, and other aspects that add nuance to communication gives people greater latitude in their interpretations of others' intent. This, combined with a desire to remain part of the group, can lead people to ignore slights. For instance, in my field notes from June 2, 1994, I wrote: "I find it *much* easier [online] to ignore the sexism and other things that are obnoxious. When Larry was telling me about his class and being friendly and low key, I could almost forget what a pain in the ass he can be sometimes." This ability to let things go has contributed significantly to my ability to stay online in an environment that I sometimes find hostile. It also has implications for the continuation of social norms online. As henri suggests, when all communication is through text, you have more latitude in choosing an interpretation. You can choose to read a statement as hostile and respond with even greater hostility (flaming), or you can choose to read the same statement in a light that allows you to ignore its offensiveness. When it's easier for me to ignore sexism, it's easier for me not to try to change it and to go along with the existing social norms. It's also easier for other participants to ignore my critiques if I do try to change those norms. Relationships and group boundaries may take longer to form online, but once formed, they may be more resistant to change than those of offline groups.

Researchers of computer-mediated communication have tied the lack of cues available in online communication to increased aggressiveness. Specifically, some have suggested that the phenomenon of flaming stems from disinhibition related to this lack of cues (Kiesler, Siegal, and McGuire 1984; Kiesler et al. 1985; cf. Cherny 1999; Lea et al. 1992). However, the ability to misinterpret or reinterpret communications because of lack of cues such as tone of voice can also enhance rather than threaten social connections. In addition, in both friendly and romantic mediated relationships, fantasizing features of the other person and fitting him or her to an ideal is easier than it would be with the greater number of social cues available in face-to-face situations. As henri points out, this can smooth over social conflicts and contribute to group cohesiveness.

MASCULINITIES AND FRIENDSHIP

BlueSky participants' efforts toward group cohesiveness involve not just interpersonal relationships but also group and individual identity work. Acts of forging and maintaining bonds with others involve assertions of our own identity as well as recognition of the identities of our friends. On BlueSky, the predominance of men means that the friendships formed there relate specifically to masculine identities. BlueSky participants relate to each other in ways that importantly recognize, reinforce, or reconstruct their identities as men.

Both popular anecdotes and scholarly work reveal conflicting information about men's friendships. Rubin, for instance, comments that current descriptions of men's friendships are likely to include "laments about men's problems with intimacy and vulnerability, about the impoverishment of their relationships with each other" (1985: 60). Similarly, Reid and Fine found that their male interviewees were "willing to discuss intimate topics but [were] prevented from doing so by the behavior of their friends" (1992: 140). Swain states that "men's closeness is more restricted than women's in that weaknesses and fears that may be construed as dependency may be more difficult to express to other men" (1989: 162). Yet he also found that "a majority of men said that they were more comfortable disclosing personal problems to close men friends" than to women, and he quotes one respondent as saying, "I'm more at ease talking about my personal problems with men" (160).

While BlueSky interactions clearly reinforce some stereotypical expectations about group relationships among men involving, as they do, horseplay, friendly insults, and derogatory remarks about women, these interactions also provide evidence of mutual support and intimacy. In the following example, several participants give Mender emotional support and advice about asking someone out on a date. The group quoted below includes both male (Roger Pollack, bodkin, Mender) and female (Ronald Ann and myself as Copperhead) participants, but conversations like this also occur among all-male or mostly-male groups on BlueSky.

> Mender says "speaking of which maybe I should call the blind date babe"
>
> Copperhead says "do it Mender."
>
> Mender says "should I ask if she wants to go to dinner or start with something smaller"
>
> Copperhead says "start smaller"
>
> Mender says "with what, lunch? :)"
>
> Ronald Ann says "how about lunch"
>
> Mender could ask if she wants to go to lunch next week
>
> Copperhead says "coffee or drink sounds good. Give a choice."
>
> Ronald Ann says "drink sounds too scary"
>
> Copperhead says "I don't like first dates where people eat. coffee would be okay though."
>
> Roger Pollack says "adopt the salesman approach: only give her 2 choices, neither of which is 'no'; would you like to go for coffee, or would a drink be better?"
>
> Roger Pollack says "okay maybe not"
>
> Ronald Ann says "if someone asked me out for a drink I'd think 'Hmm, he wants to get me drunk'"
>
> Copperhead nods @ RA
>
> bodkin says "Well I think food is a good way to start, unlike Ron"
>
> Ronald Ann thinks food is good
>
> bodkin says "when you don't have anything to say, you can always chew"
>
> Mender says "I like the lunch idea"

Copperhead says "yeah, but I wouldn't digest well if I was nervous (which I
   would be)."
Mender says "of course that means it won't happen until next week"
Roger Pollack STOP PROCRASTINATING

Mender's shyness and timidity were well-known, and Mender employed
this knowledge to poke fun at himself, often in ways so formulaic that
they became his online "shtick." Yet other BlueSky males also spoke of
offline personal relationships in similarly vulnerable and open ways.

While some of the participants' willingness to risk disclosure of very
personal information to each other may stem from the distancing effects
of online textual connection, the scholarly record provides very little evidence concerning offline male friendships with which to compare
BlueSky's norms. In particular, studies of offline men's friendships are
limited in that they consist solely of interviews with men about their
friendships, not direct studies of the interactions. Interview respondents,
familiar with societal expectations and stereotypes about masculinity, may
interpret their experiences in light of those expectations. Walker points
out that "when men and women discuss friendship they emphasize the
behavior that corresponds to their cultural notions of what men and
women are like" (1994: 246–47), but their descriptions of *particular* friendships show more variation and less conformity to stereotypes. BlueSky's
conversations thus may not differ much from those occurring in similar
face-to-face groups.

Comparison with one of the very few ethnographic works depicting
participant-observation of a group of male friends proves instructive in
this regard. In *Slim's Table*, Mitchell Duneier (1992) studied a group of
working-class black men who hung out at a local restaurant. Their quasi-
public meeting place thus resembled BlueSky except for its existence in
physical space and the group's face-to-face meetings. But the men themselves differed so much from those on BlueSky—older, working-class black
men as opposed to young, mostly white, mostly middle-class men—that
the reported similarity of their conversations startles.

Duneier reports that "a willingness to disclose personal weaknesses is
not unique to Slim. Most of the black men here opened up in some significant way. This is most evident in discussions about personal life, when
rather than viewing themselves as lovers and exploiters, men often com-
miserate as victims" (40). The friends Duneier describes thus sound re-
markably similar to the BlueSky men discussing heterosexual relationships in chapter 4, especially considering Duneier's assertion that "such

discussions place the blame on the women rather than on the narrators" (45). Both groups identify themselves as victims and lay the blame on women, and both derive support for their view of themselves as wronged men through their friendly conversations.

We have too few studies like *Slim's Table* to allow us to draw significant conclusions about men's behavior in groups or about self-disclosure in men's friendships. But the very different social circumstances and life histories of Duneier's group compared with those of the BlueSky group, in conjunction with the similarities in the two group's discussions, suggest that some types of vulnerability may be more commonly expressed among men than popular anecdotes indicate.

CONSTRUCTING GENDERED IDENTITIES THROUGH TALK

Conversations among friends reflect and reinforce gendered identities. Talk specifically about gender demonstrates particularly clearly the connections among gender, identity, and friendship. In addition to interpreting such cues as dress and mannerisms, people read gender identities through expressed beliefs about gender. Talk about gender can thus connect friends through acknowledgment of shared understandings or create rifts when differences are discovered.

In the following excerpt from an exceptional day on BlueSky, a disagreement among several participants revolves around these issues. In this conversation, BlueSky participants strengthen and sever alliances, opine on the nature of men and women, and puzzle over their relationships with each other. It took place over several hours (and the aftermath continued for several days). Because of the complexities of these issues, I have included a substantial portion of the dialogue, interspersed with my own commentary.

At the beginning of the conversation, Obtuse, a frequent participant with a moderate to low social standing in the group, poses a question about women to the group. Unlike Mender's question about a personal issue, Obtuse's question concerns third parties not known to the group, from which he wishes to generalize about gender relations. For this reason, his query does not meet with as sympathetic a response as Mender's did. Several people respond without necessarily answering Obtuse's question or even agreeing with the assumptions on which the question was predicated.

> Obtuse wonders if anyone wants to take a stab at explaining (to me, a male) a mysterious aspect of feminine psychology.

Obtuse says "I have an old friend who married a 16-year-old girl approximately three years ago. Just recently she left him and moved in with a guy who is known to beat up on his girlfriends. So my question is a) why would she DO that? and b) why do women in general seem to be attracted to men that treat them like dirt?"

Bilerific-Sid says "A) imaginary relationships with real life. b) they don't."

Obtuse is afraid he doesn't understand BS's answer to a). "Do you mean that she is confusing fantasy relationships with real life?"

Bilerific-Sid says "No, I mean that there is a reality out there that we all experience, but we interpret the experience through a huge bunch of conceptual errors, nonsensical rules and silly assumptions."

Obtuse says "OK, try this one: why would it appear to guys like me who tried to be nice to women that they could care less about me and run around with jerks?"

Bilerific-Sid says "Maybe you're a jerk but can't bring yourself to say it."

Obtuse says "could be, that or nobody convinced me of it at the time"

Bilerific-Sid says "Maybe you subconsciously eliminate women who aren't with jerks from your sample."

Corwin says "because it's easier to derive 'women are all insane' from 'a woman dumped me' than getting a grip"

Bilerific-Sid says "Man, there's an oprah book title in that somewhere."

Obtuse says "so that explains why she's threatening to sue her husband for abuse when she's living with this woman-beater?"

Bilerific-Sid says "yes."

Obtuse's initial question depends on an understanding of men and women as substantially different. He holds that women do something (move in with jerks) that he (as a male) cannot understand. However, most of his audience is also male and, within the terms of his own question, would theoretically know no more than he. Furthermore, he is one of the few married men present. Obtuse's audience and his status as a person who lives with a member of the supposedly mysterious gender suggest that his inquiry serves more to open a "gripe session" than as a serious request for information. Such conversations constitute both identity work and group bonding. Complaining about others "not like us" serves to reinforce the identity of those present (in this case, men and a few women deemed savvy enough not to be included in the "women in general" referred to in Obtuse's question). This kind of group identity work can also foster feelings of warmth and belonging, thereby reinforcing friendships within the group.

Unfortunately for Obtuse, those present failed to pick up on his theme, rejecting the identity premises around which another group of guys might bond. This conversation thus contrasts with the one among Stomp, BJ, and Ulysses discussed in chapter 4. In that conversation, three men bonded together through a common understanding of men and women and their own identities as rejected, nonjerk males. Here, Obtuse puts forth a similar interpretation of "feminine psychology," which is summarily rejected by the other men present. They even imply that his own issues about rejection may underlie his assumptions, although both Corwin and Bilerific-Sid know that Obtuse is married.

Obtuse continues to puzzle over the issue, drawing others into the conversation. Meanwhile PAL, a very active but not very well-liked participant, arrives and joins in after consulting the magic recording device to see what has been said so far.

> PAL has arrived.
> Levi says "An important consideration is whether or not this new guy beats her."
> PAL . o O (would his beating her be considered good or bad by her ?)
> Obtuse says "maybe she considers NOT being beaten abuse"
> Farron peers at Obtuse
> Farron says "Possible, but unlikely."
> Obtuse would peer at allia if she were here
> Bilerific-Sid says "Whoops, and there they go, flying from vulgar objectivism to extreme relativism in three short sentences."

Obtuse, and now PAL also, continue to present women as so outlandishly unfathomable that they might actually enjoy and seek abuse. Obtuse also references connections between gender identity and sexuality, as indicated by his reference to allia. BlueSky participants know allia to be interested in sadomasochism, and therefore he assumes that she would understand Obtuse's implication that women might be seeking beatings as a form of sexual pleasure. Bilerific-Sid, however, rejects this connection between abuse and sadomasochistic sexual practices.

In the next segment, PAL and Obtuse continue to press the point, and participants begin to align themselves on two sides of the argument.

> PAL says "I don't think it's so much that any woman wants to be *injured*, as it is that many women are attracted to men who "overpower" them . . ."
> Obtuse nods to PAL. "Could we perhaps learn something from canine behavior— 'powerful' men appear as the alpha-male?"

Bilerific-Sid says "Oh, that's epiphenomenal horse shit, Obtuse."

Corwin says "Obtuse and PAL, I am forced to inform you that I wouldn't pay
10 cents for your dime-store psychology"

Bilerific-Sid stands next to Corwin, crosses his arms and nods solemnly.

Obtuse says "would you pay 5 cents for my nickle-store psychology?"

fnord says "face it, Obtuse, you're not even going to get a penny for your
thoughts"

Corwin will pay you 5 doubloons to stop trying to apply your bogus theories to
people

PAL says "I'll pay you 10 doubloons to tell me accurately which of my theories
is bogus. :-)"

Bilerific-Sid says "Women enjoy men who 'overpower' them."

PAL says "*SOME* women do, they've told me so in exactly those words."

Corwin says "some shoes are brown."

Corwin says "shoes are brown."

Corwin says "See any improper logic leap?"

PAL says "I didn't make a universal statement, I made an existential one. Learn
some logic ya smeg."

Bilerific-Sid scrolls back, "many women like men that 'overpower' them."

Obtuse and PAL indicate agreement with each other, as Bilerific-Sid and Corwin do. Bilerific-Sid even pantomimes a physical alliance with Corwin, suggesting an image of the two of them as a physical barrier, arms crossed against what they perceive as Obtuse and PAL's illogic. As the conversation continues, logic becomes an important focus. Corwin and Bilerific-Sid express their disagreement and distaste in the terms of formal logic, thus distancing themselves from the more emotional and personal facets of the confrontation. PAL initially accepts the challenge on those terms and suggests instead that Corwin's logic is faulty. Bilerific-Sid's "scrolling back" indicates that he is reviewing the recorded log of the conversation for PAL's exact words, highlighting one difference between this online textual argument and similar discussions offline. The existence of a record prevents participants from denying something they said or subtly altering the terms of the argument, as people sometimes attempt to do offline.

In the next segment, Corwin continues to speak in terms of logic, but now in a specifically personal rather than an abstract way. He criticizes PAL and PAL's relationships rather than just the logic of his statements.

Corwin says "from 'some women PAL knows tell him goofy stories about how
they want dominating men' we can derive one thing, and one thing only: some

women PAL knows tell him goofy stories about how they want dominating
men"

Corwin says "and possibly the corollary that PAL believes things women tell
him about the nature of women and is therefore nuts, but I digress"

Bilerific-Sid says "No you didn't say every single woman that ever lived, but
your statement was pretty cut and dried."

PAL says "By the time *you* dried it, it was jerky."

Bilerific-Sid says "Write that yourself, or is Joey Bishop helping you out, PAL."

Corwin and Bilerific-Sid may undertake their critique of Obtuse and PAL's logic partly to allow PAL and Obtuse to distance themselves similarly from their potentially socially damaging statements. Their strategy attempts to construct the conversation as a debate or contest rather than as an argument or disagreement. This turn from the personal to the (supposedly) abstract fits with standard expectations of hegemonic masculinity, and the format of a logical debate conforms particularly well to ideas of desirable masculine identity among these college-educated males who pride themselves on intelligence and wit. However, PAL rejects their strategy, returning the conversation to a more personal level:

PAL says "Well Corwin, you can learn from other people's experiences, or you
can learn from your own. I can see you prefer the latter."

Corwin says "God help me if I start learning things by gross unwarranted
generalization."

PAL says "FUCK OFF *I* DIDN'T OVERGENERALIZE *YOU* DID ASSHOLE!"

Copperhead blinks

Captin blinx

pez says "wow"

mu says "however PAL you *are* guilty of overcapitalization"

Obtuse says "are we sure? maybe his capslock key just got stuck for a
moment"

Calvin says "Someone did something over . . . I'm just not quite sure it was
generalization."

pez says "well I'm convinced! it was that controlling male thing that convinced
me!"

PAL waits for capital punishment.

Bilerific-Sid sentences PAL to exile.

Bilerific-Sid pulls a large lever, and a trapdoor opens right underneath PAL!

PAL SHOOTs out into the sky!

PAL has left.

PAL's sudden explosion into all-caps and profanity startles all present, drawing reactions from several participants who had remained silent through most of the conversation. PAL clearly expects Corwin to exercise the wizard's prerogative of character disconnection or termination, but instead, Bilerific-Sid resorts to the less severe and more traditional rebuke, lomming PAL.

While PAL is out of the room, the others discuss him. In keeping with his own personalization of the issues, they continue to connect his position on gender relations to his own gender and sexual identity.

> Corwin says "have to say I admire his debate methods, though"
> pez says "I think he just wanted to be spanked by a dominating woman"
> Corwin laughs at pez
> Bilerific-Sid wonders if PAL was counting all those times where women
>   approached him and said, "Oh, you're so big and strong! take me!"
> henri LAUGHS at BS

pez and Bilerific-Sid suggest opposing interpretations of PAL's sexual activities, with pez relying on standard sexual lore that men dominant in other areas of life like to be dominated sexually and Bilerific-Sid suggesting instead that PAL's stance stems from an overly literal and naive belief in statements uttered by potential sexual partners. The ironic and sarcastic tone of the group's comments reflect their understanding that PAL's reaction was excessive.

In most cases, after a disagreement like this, the lommed person would return to the room, lom the other person in retaliation, and the conversation would be defused, lapsing into horseplay or being supplanted by other conversations. More rarely, the argument might continue, or one of the participants might log off to show disgust. But in this case, when PAL returns, he announces his intention of leaving the group permanently.

> PAL has arrived.
> PAL says "Alright, how does one un-join this cesspool?"
> henri says " 'quit' "
> PAL says "No, I mean permanently."
> henri says "quit and don't login again?"
> PAL says "I wish to erase all traces of my existence here. Am I being unclear or
>   what?"
> Corwin says "this is nostalgic. it's been years since I've had to tell someone
>   that I have no intention of assisting a tantrum."
> PAL says "I've already @destroyed everything I own except me."

Corwin says "so rename yourself. repassword yourself. do whatever."
fnord says "@password yourpassword =
    8yhg9oiuejhg89sug8y9swe8we4t.li9er5"
PAL says "Ah, screw it"
PAL goes home.
PAL has left.

Over the years, the frequency with which people have made dramatic "I'm never coming back" exits has inspired the term "mud suicide" to refer to people who accompany their departures (not always as permanent as apparently intended) with melodramatic denunciations of mudding or of the particular group. Mud suicides also usually destroy all objects they have created on the mud, as PAL indicates he did, and sometimes change their password to an impossible-to-remember string of garbage so that they will not be tempted to return, as fnord suggests PAL do. However, mud suicides happen very rarely on BlueSky.

The extremity of PAL's reaction causes confusion and some consternation among the other participants. Most consider PAL's personality abrasive (a significant judgment, given the overall level of obnoxiousness tolerated on BlueSky). Some, especially Corwin, still have concerns about PAL's mental state and about their own potential complicity in his virtual "demise."

Corwin says "he wasn't, IMO[3], being ridiculed much to speak of"
Corwin says "either he will get over it and log back on later, or he will not, but I
    don't know that I could do much about it"
Jet says "is PAL committing suicide or something"
henri says "mud suicide"
henri says "he dest'd all his stuff and logged out after trying to get toaded"
Corwin says "he wanted me to @dest[4] him, but I refused, as always"
Obtuse says "he tried but Corwin wouldn't play Kevorkian"
Corwin always hates this part, where he sits around and figures out whether or
    not he accidentally said something he should've known better than to say
henri says "regardless of what you said, it wasn't even ad hominem it was
    just an argument"
henri says "it's like tapping the back bumper of a Pinto and having it explode"
Locutus has arrived.
henri says "Locutus you missed the major Pal freak out"
Locutus says "really? what did he do this time"
henri says "he dest'd all his stuff and vowed never to return"

Locutus says "yess no more PAL"

henri HOWLS

henri says "don't try to conceal your feelings"

Locutus says "Xena, quote PAL"

Xena says "I once heard PAL say 'I wish to erase all traces of my existence
here. Am I being unclear or what?'"

henri says "erase all trace of his existence? TOO LATE BUDDY YOU'RE IN CH'S
THESIS NOW"

Many, like Locutus, did not like PAL and were happy to see him leave. Yet any departure, especially a rancorous one, disturbs the harmony of the group and reminds people of the fragility of online relationships. Most continued to evaluate PAL's reaction as unreasonable and to reassure Corwin that he was not at fault for PAL's blowup. However, the length of the discussion, which continued off and on for the next several days, indicates the concern that such an extreme action generates. The rehashings and evaluations of the event helped people repair the breach in the group and reassure themselves of the group's continuation.

As participants puzzled over the issues, they also continued to discuss the original gender issues, reiterating their own disagreement with PAL's position and attributing that position to PAL's own identity flaws.

henri says "could someone coherently explain what that was about, I'm unable
to pick it out of scrollback"

elflord says "ohe[5] is gone"

henri says "yes but why"

Corwin says "because I said his conclusion was a bogus over-generalization, I
guess, henri"

Bilerific-Sid says "Because we didn't buy his pop-fascist psychology about
women wanting to de dominated by men."

Copperhead says "I don't think it's explainable on this end"

Copperhead says "because I've certainly seen him get in as heated an argument"

Tempest says "wow, i missed PAL losing it. too bad."

Obtuse offers to email Tempest what happened

Tempest says "yes please"

Tempest looks at the log of PAL going nutso . . . ahhh, the Why women Like
Jerks discussion again

Corwin says "PAL put forth that many women want someone to knock them
around, and backed this up by saying some women he knew told him
that they want a dominating male"

Corwin says "we said 'get real'"

henri says "I think PAL got offended because he pictures himself as one of the
   guys who obliges"

Corwin nods at henri

Corwin says "perhaps; although, again, I am loathe to assume"

Tempest says "women like jerks because jerks are interesting or seem to be
   interesting"

Jet says "women hate me: I must not be a jerk!"

Corwin says "I fall back on my original thesis: 'women only like jerks' follows
   directly from 'a woman didn't like me' 'a woman liked someone I think
   is a jerk' 'I don't think I am a jerk' 'women like jerks'"

Tempest recognizes the entire theme as a common one on BlueSky. However, while his comment seems dismissive, he also seems to agree somewhat with PAL when he later provides the first real answer to Obtuse's
original question, saying, "Women like jerks because jerks are interesting
or seem to be interesting." The others continue to suggest that PAL believes women like jerks simply because this enables him to translate his
rejection by women as proof that he is not a jerk.

Yet this interpretation of PAL's motives does not fit with known facts
about PAL's life. In previous conversations, PAL was not shy to remind
them that he lived with and shared sexual relationships with two women
simultaneously. Whether or not they envied him this, most were annoyed
at what they perceived as bragging. Although his current apparently successful relationships with women would not preclude previous rejections,
his living situation does not resemble that of other BlueSky participants,
such as Stomp, BJ, and Ulysses, who also have put forth the "women like
jerks" thesis. Therefore, the portrayal of his warped logic presented by
Corwin and Jet constitutes less a description of PAL than a rejection of
that particular masculine identity.

Corwin, Bilerific-Sid, and Jet represent themselves as being able to handle sexual rejection by women maturely, without assuming that all women
are somehow flawed. They reject the identity, earlier suggested by Stomp,
BJ, and Ulysses, of nice guys victimized by the inexplicable realities of
heterosexual relations and the concomitant view of women as puzzlingly
attracted to abusive men. Yet their statements also continue to support
aspects of hegemonic masculinity, particularly the version of it practiced
on BlueSky. The conversation constructs a male identity that emphasizes
logic, intelligence, and the ability to dish out and take verbal criticism. Not
only does gender then constitute a "hot topic" that can either threaten or

strengthen relationships, but also friendships provide a forum that can either threaten or strengthen particular gendered identities. In and through the verbal acts that construct (and destroy) friendships, BlueSky participants, like other friends both online and off, construct, reinforce, and reinterpret gender identities and beliefs about men and women.

7   Class, Race, and Online Participation

On a warm September afternoon in 1995, I'm interviewing Perry in the suburban tract house he shares with three others in southern California. His roommates, two men and one woman, all work for computer-related businesses. One of them, devnull, is also a BlueSky participant. In his early twenties, Perry is a white graduate student in computer science. His round face reveals a friendly, easy-going demeanor. In a voice so quiet I have trouble picking it up off the tape later, he answers my questions about his family and his introduction to computers and later to mudding.

After the interview, Perry takes me on a tour of the house. As in most mudders' houses I encountered during my research, decor here is minimal and haphazard, giving the ambience of a college student house, although most of the inhabitants now work outside academia. The furniture appears to be mainly castoffs or hand-me-downs, and there are very few wall decorations. The refrigerator contains almost no food. Most of Perry's roommates make good middle-class salaries as computer professionals, but the only visible signs of that income are in the form of electronics. The complex stereo system is sleek and up-to-date. Next to the television are shelves and shelves of videos, mostly of Japanese animation.

The house also contains seven computers of assorted ages and capabilities. As in many business settings, these computers (owned by the various house members) connect to each other, forming an in-house network. They also connect to the Internet through an outside phone line (and Internet service provider). Perry demonstrates the network for me, explaining which functions the different computers perform and pointing out where the in-house muds reside. To maintain the Internet connection and the availability of the in-house muds, several of these computers are always on, providing a constant background hum that some would find annoying or too reminiscent of the workplace but that the residents of this household take for granted.

Perry explains that he and his roommates use one of the in-house muds to contact each other during the day, especially to coordinate dinner plans. Often, he will be logged on to several muds all day without using them much. It's a way of being present to various groups of people—a more convenient, and in some ways more familiar, way of communicating than the telephone. In an earlier conversation I had with him on BlueSky, Perry explained the different muds he uses:

> Perry whispers "Well, I believe in one mud per function, and so we have a mud
>> in our house for talking about who's going to make dinner and who's
>> hogging the slip line, I have one in my lab for talking about what we're
>> doing, there's a couple muds I sit on and idle because one or two other
>> people occasionally page me . . ."
>
> Copperhead whispers "what, are you serious? a mud for dinner discussion?"
> Perry whispers "sure, small muds take almost no resources, we've got 3
>> or 4 in the house"
> Copperhead whispers "that's funny; muds as a household convenience"

A month later, I'm outside a national government lab, getting my visitor's badge from the guard. At the visitor center reception desk, I stumble over the unfamiliar name of a person I regularly converse with. I narrowly avoid giving the receptionist his mud name, Obtuse. I finally make it through the large lab campus to the correct building and locate Obtuse's office. Lanky and pale, Obtuse shakes my hand and takes me immediately into the virtual reality lab where he spends most of his workday. We've hardly said anything to each other when he startles me by putting a visual display headset on my head. Up until now, I've avoided virtual reality (VR) demonstrations, disliking the look of the graphics and fearing the oft-reported disorienting and nauseating effects. I'm a bit put off by the technophilic assumption in Obtuse's action, but I gamely wait in the VR chamber's default 3-D starfield for the demonstration to begin. It proves less physically disorienting than I expected, and I find the exhibition of potential scientific applications for VR mildly interesting. Obtuse's responsibilities are peripheral to the actual design and operation of the VR system, but he exhibits considerable pride in his role as part of the team on this project.

Although I'm in a work environment, not a house, the rest of the lab that Obtuse shows me resembles what I saw on Perry's tour. The buildings, like Perry's suburban tract home, are architecturally uninteresting. Decor is minimal and the furniture worn, but the electronic equipment is high-tech and up-to-date. Obtuse too shows me a local mud, this time a work-place mud. He and his coworkers use it like interactive e-mail, asking and answering questions during the day, and occasionally chatting online. Obtuse says:

> If I want to ask somebody a question and I don't want to try to pick up the phone and call, it's easier than sending e-mail when you know he gets two hundred pieces of e-mail a day. I'll just poke him and say, "Bob, what happened to this executable?" And later in the day or the next day, he'll get back to me, and he'll quote it, and he'll say, "This is what happened to it," and I may not be on, so that conversation can go on in a time-shifted way.

Like Perry, Obtuse tends to have several mud windows open at once, with most of those sitting idle. These open communication channels signal a willingness to talk but can also be easily ignored if other things become more pressing.

Both Perry and Obtuse are computer programmers and comfortably use computer technology at home and at work. The spareness of their home and work environments relates to the predominance of men in computer-related occupations and the resultant emphasis on instrumental, technology-related activities. But although materialistic display is anathema to the aesthetic of both these mudders' lives, they are by no means nonconsumers or opposed to consumer culture. As Pred points out, consumption occurs "through situated practice" of daily life and "cannot be severed from the power relations associated with the practice of everyday life." Such power relations "permeate nonconsumption as well as everyday consumption" (1996: 13). While, by "nonconsumption," Pred meant the "inability to purchase" desired goods due to class and other power relations, his insight applies equally to practices of consumption that studiously seek to avoid the appearance of consumption.

Perry, his (mostly male) house mates, and many of the other participants on BlueSky avoid consumption practices associated with femininity, such as following fashion in their choice of clothing or purchasing items to beautify the home. These choices connect also to their relative youth and, for some, their single status. Their home and work environments nevertheless reflect their middle-class status and their ability to purchase those consumer items that support their particular male, young, white, technologically savvy identities. The ability of Perry's household to eat out or order take-out frequently (indicated by the empty refrigerator), the suburban locales of their homes and workplaces, and their ease of access and acclimation to technology all point to a particular type of middle-class background and status.

Most BlueSky participants share similar middle-class backgrounds. Many work and live in environments similar to those of Perry and Obtuse. Their online interactions reflect this background, as the culture of BlueSky, the cultures of other muds, and the cultures common on the Internet do. BlueSky functions for BlueSky participants as another arena within which they negotiate the intertwined facets of identity and consumption.

Class background may be the single most important factor influencing online participation. Over 60 percent of Internet participants (63 to 75 percent, depending upon the data source) hold some form of professional, technical, managerial, or other white-collar job, with reported incomes consistently clustering in the thirty thousand to ninety thousand dollar range (approximately 60 percent of participants fall within this range).[1] Yet, in their depictions of interactive forums such as muds, online researchers rarely discuss class, usually focusing instead on gender. This tendency reflects online culture itself, where gender and sexuality are much more frequent topics of discussion than class or race identity. Turkle does, however, discuss the possibility that muds can provide participants with "the sense of a middle-class peer group" (1995: 240). She connects the appeal of muds with the economic difficulties experienced by many young people from middle-class families whose job prospects have not met their expectations. Although Turkle does not specifically examine this issue, the fact that these mud participants can feel more "themselves" online than in their downwardly mobile "day jobs" suggests the extent to which muds, and online culture in general, are shaped by middle-class cultural understandings. Online social spaces would not function as an escape from perceived or feared lower-class existence offline without somehow conveying a sense of middle-class culture to participants.

For the most part, BlueSky participants do not fit the portrait of downward mobility that Turkle's interviewees present. Most have jobs that appear to give them economic status similar to that of their parents. I gathered information about their own and parents' occupations and education from thirty-eight participants. Of those, twenty-four have levels of education and occupational status similar to their parents (allowing for their relative youth). Two of the highest BlueSky income earners, for instance, have fathers who hold high-level corporate positions (vice president and CEO), and both of these participants have jobs that include some management responsibilities in addition to programming. Another participant who is a medical doctor comes from a family in which both parents and all of his siblings are also medical doctors.

Nine participants have improved their economic status, including three participants from working-class families who entered the middle class primarily through their educational attainments and/or computer skills. Only five appear to have fallen from their parents' class status. Three of those work in computer-related industries and appear to be gradually improving their status. One has recently obtained a better-paying job, in part through the efforts of a fellow BlueSky participant. Thus only two of these thirty-eight participants appear to be caught in marginal and uncertain economic situations, working odd jobs and barely getting by.

Further reflecting the relative affluence of the group, several participants have found themselves able to buy homes before reaching the age of thirty, a goal few can attain, particularly in competitive real estate markets such as California. During the main period of my research, few BlueSky participants owned their own homes, but within a short period recently, several have started buying houses. As of 1998, at least thirteen regulars owned homes, including some people living in areas with very high median home prices.

The BlueSky group thus represents, if anything, an upwardly mobile group, although many are following career paths somewhat different from those of their parents. For instance, several participants with parents who are professors completed bachelor's degrees only after several years in and out of college. Their work as system administrators or programmers gives them slightly less prestige than their parents but at least as much income. BlueSky participants' computer skills enabled them to negotiate the potentially treacherous job market of the 1990s and maintain an income level similar to that of their parents.

CLASS BACKGROUNDS AND COMPUTER USE

The most obvious class issue regarding online access concerns the cost of equipment. Many online participants, speaking as people familiar with the range of computer equipment available, point out the extremely low cost of minimal computer systems and Internet accounts as evidence that the Internet does not limit participation by class. However, this exaggerates the accessibility of computer equipment. It fails to take into consideration cultural aspects that affect both perceptions of online interactions and their accessibility, not to mention perceptions of computers and computer use

generally. The bias toward individualism in U.S. political discourse exhibits itself in this view of the computer as an accessible commodity that any individual can purchase and use. But interest in computers does not "just happen." Access to computer equipment matters little without various kinds of social support for learning about and interacting with computers. Furthermore, the ability to gain online access says nothing about what one finds once one arrives online. Although there is no single "net culture," the demographics and history of the Internet have fostered certain cultural tendencies over others.

Most BlueSky participants began using computers fairly early in life. Although they report levels of computer use that were higher than those of most of their childhood peers, they found their access to technology unremarkable and often took computer use for granted. Some of this ease stemmed from the fact that others close to them also used computers.

Of the thirty-two people I interviewed, over half were exposed to computers by a family member. Some were given computers directly, some had fathers who tinkered with computers, others learned about computers from cousins or other family members they visited. Only ten of my interviewees were initially exposed to computers in school, usually between the fifth and seventh grades. They often described the school's equipment as minimal. Few were given formal training in school, but they tinkered with the computers on their own, in some cases teaching themselves rudimentary programming. Two of my interviewees learned about computers from their friends and then wanted them also. Three didn't use computers at all until college.

The computer interest of many of my interviewees derived in part from their parents' use of computers. The experiences of this group of interviewees point out the importance of family practice to computer literacy. Haddon (1992) found that family belief in the importance of computer use for children's futures significantly increases the likelihood of further use. Livingstone (1992) and Wheelock (1992) also found that gender dynamics within the home affect which children are more likely to use computers. In most cases, boys were more likely to be the heaviest computer users in the household (even in families in which the computer had been purchased mainly for a parent's use), and boys used the computer for a wider range of activities. It is interesting to note in this regard that several of BlueSky's most active female participants have no siblings.

A relative newcomer to BlueSky, BlueJean is eighteen years old and thus one of its youngest participants. Her savvy, confident style of speech, and an air of greater emotional sophistication than is typical for her age

facilitated her transition from complete newcomer to accepted (albeit somewhat infrequent) participant on BlueSky. I interviewed her during a break between classes at the private midwestern university she attends. She described her introduction to computer technology:

> LORI: When did you start using computers? How did you get into that?
>
> BLUEJEAN: I've been raised with computers, essentially. My father brought home the first computer when I was five. It was like a Kaypro, ancient, dinosaur.
>
> LORI: That's surprising to me, because he's not in the computer industry.
>
> BLUEJEAN: It's always been a hobby of his. The X rays [he works with] are controlled by digital imaging, so they were computerized. The first computer that we got was from his company for his use. So he brought it home and sort of got me oriented on it, and I would type up my little journals on the computer, and you know . . . starting in kindergarten. So computers have always been a part of my life.

Seven of my interviewees mentioned that, like BlueJean's, their fathers worked with computers and/or had a hobby of tinkering with computers at home.

RaveMage specifically tied his class background to his childhood use of computers:

> LORI: So how did you start getting into computers and using computers and stuff?
>
> RAVEMAGE: Actually one of the good things about having two doctor parents around, it was possible to . . . because people . . . I've always been amused when people tell me, "Jeez, I've only been using these for a couple of years." I've had 'em since, uh . . . I had one of the original Radio Shack Trash-80 Model ones. I've had 'em ever since then.

Several BlueSky participants whose parents had much less disposable income than RaveMage's family were nevertheless able to obtain computers at an early age. McKenzie, for instance, indicated that he saved up his own money from odd jobs to purchase a computer in the seventh grade. However, as RaveMage indicates, having "two doctor parents" certainly makes obtaining computers easier.

Even among families who were not specifically interested in computers, their educational backgrounds most likely predisposed them to accept computers as a useful home schooling tool or as a reasonable toy for a preadolescent. Of the thirty-eight participants for whom I obtained parents' educational data, thirty-three had at least one parent who had attended college, and twenty had one parent with graduate school education. While fathers' education levels were almost always higher than mothers', seven mothers had at least some graduate school experience. A frequent pattern among mothers was to stop higher education for child raising, then return to school as children got older or left home. Thus, several people had mothers who had recently completed a Ph.D. or other degree.

The number of interviewees who come from families in which *both* parents have graduate degrees (six of thirty-eight respondents) suggests that computer use may be fostered by a home environment in which family members take for granted the value of higher education and expect that all family members will obtain at least an undergraduate degree and enter a profession or a technical career. This was the case for most regulars on BlueSky. BlueSky patterns also suggest that the support for computer use may be particularly strong when parental professions involve some use of computers.

PERFORMING MIDDLE-CLASS IDENTITIES

That participants experience online interactions as culturally middle-class reflects in part the fact that they *are* middle-class. In order for these participants to create a middle-class cultural online space, however, they must enact middle-class identities there. While we can readily identify what it means to perform a "female" or "male" identity, most mudders (like other people within U.S. culture) would not consider themselves to be *performing* middle-classness. Yet as West and Fenstermaker (1995) point out, class meanings and identities are created and expressed through interaction. (See also Collins et al. 1995 for a critique of this article.) Given that muds are limited to textual communication, participants must convey their class status through verbal exchange of information about their lives and backgrounds, along with patterns of speech, and so forth.

Mudders rarely discuss class directly. In this they differ little from people in the United States in general. What does get said reveals important ways in which people view, or try not to view, class distinctions. Sherry Ortner points out that in the United States, we have an "impoverished language for thinking and speaking about" class (1993: 410–11). In her research, she found that people tended to change the subject from class, often to "related but subtly different categories" (416) such as success and money, or that they identified specific class positions "with specific ethnic or racial groups" (418). For my younger group of interviewees, all of whom have some college education, class distinctions emerge most clearly in discussions of education. How much education one has and where it was obtained can serve as status markers in and of themselves, but they can also serve as indicators of class background.

Most BlueSky participants learned about mudding through friends at college, graduate or professional school, or from newsgroups or e-mail lists they accessed at that time. Since they all went to college, it is not surprising that most of their parents did as well. In this group of sophisticated, long-term computer users, higher education forms an important part of their background and experience. BlueSky participants greatly value education along with the knowledge and skills derived from it. Level of education provides one aspect of status on BlueSky, and the types of knowledge and skills acquired in college contribute to the conversations held there.

The prominence of college education as a marker of status and a valued facet of identity contributes to the middle-class ambience Turkle described as appealing to her interviewees. When asked to characterize the group of people on BlueSky, many regulars mentioned the high levels of education, often with some pride. During my interview with Corwin, we discussed how participants use BlueSky as a resource for work-related questions. Corwin noted the high level of expertise among BlueSky participants and began listing educational degrees held by various people on BlueSky:

> I think BlueSky has an amazing concentration of degrees. . . . Let's see Ph.D. holders: henri, Captain, domehead, and Ulysses. There was Tom before he stopped logging on to most muds. [He lists several other non-Ph.D. degree-holders.] It's quite a list. It was so bad that in the Nebula Cafe the bartender had a response to probably about ten people; when they walked in the room, he would immediately say, "Go work on your thesis."

As Corwin indicates, pride in education was written into an automatic response of an object in one of the hangouts. Here is the description of that hangout, with the automaton's response to my entrance, and then to the entrance of several other participants, also working on theses.

Nebula Cafe Bar

This is the bar of the fantabulous Nebula Cafe, where patrons wait for a table to become available. The entrance is through a firehouse-type sliding pole

> that enters through a hole in the ceiling. On one wall is a large viewscreen;
> opposite the bar is a doorway.
> the automaton says "Copperhead, stop mudding and finish your thesis!"
> zombie has arrived.
> the automaton says "zombie, stop mudding and finish your thesis!"
> Starfish has arrived.
> the automaton says "Starfish, stop mudding and finish your thesis!"

The automaton's response makes a joke about the perceived dangers of mudding to educational pursuits but also identifies those people working on higher degrees, thereby marking their educational status.

My own reactions to comments about education during some of my interviews highlighted for me connections between class and education and the ways in which people use discussions of education to mark their class identity. Focusing on my own discomfort in some of the face-to-face interviews helped me see class issues being brought up. I wasn't expecting such discomfort over class issues, since I initially assumed my middle-class background was similar to that of most BlueSky participants. As with many regulars on BlueSky, my father is a computer programmer, and both he and my mother have college degrees. Also like most of my interviewees, I grew up in middle-class, mostly white suburbs. Yet, in many of my conversations with my interviewees, I suddenly felt "put in my place" in regard to class. Often these moments occurred during discussions of education.

Mu is a dino whose participation on BlueSky has decreased in recent years as work responsibilities in his programming career have taken more of his time. He startled me with his nonchalant statement that he had chosen to go to Harvard because he "liked Boston." Similarly, I felt a twinge of envy when talking with Donatello, who is in his early twenties and a graduate student in biology.

LORI: Did you have jobs using computers along this time?

DONATELLO: I've always been a student. I've never had a job that involved using computers.

My jealousy stemmed from my confrontation with someone who, unlike me, was apparently able to complete his education without outside employment. Yet, as I learned later in our conversation, Donatello *has* in fact held several jobs, all of them in academic settings. Despite his disavowal, most of these jobs—including his current research assistantship—have involved the use of computers. His characterization of himself as only a student reclassifies these jobs as part of his student experience and lays claim to the class privilege of not working until after graduation. In this depiction of a "proper" upper-middle-class career trajectory, Donatello won't have a "real" job until after he obtains his graduate degree and embarks on his career as a biologist.

RaveMage, on the other hand, signaled both recognition of and discomfort with the class cachet evoked by going to a school like Harvard.

> LORI: So where did you go to medical school?
>
> RAVEMAGE: Um, let's see, Riverview State University. It's in [town].
>
> LORI: And where were you in college before that?
>
> RAVEMAGE: I always hate to tell people.
>
> LORI: [laughing somewhat incredulously] You hate to tell people?
>
> RAVEMAGE: [soberly] Yes. [pause] Harvard.
>
> LORI: Oh; okay, I understand.

RaveMage readily informed me that his parents were both doctors and did not hesitate to name his state-funded medical school, but he almost refused to say that he'd done his undergraduate work at Harvard. Thus not only does having a college education become a class marker, but where that education was obtained and under what circumstances further differentiate members of that broad category of the "middle class" in America. The ability of people to make these kinds of fine distinctions and the importance of them to people's identity further highlights the importance of class to identity, despite our denial of significant class differences in the United States and our unwillingness to discuss class directly. My interviews also demonstrate some of the ways in which people perform class identities in ongoing social interactions. Although I have used examples from interviews in the above discussion, clearly these same kinds of conversations can occur online and become part of the performance of classed identities online.

Understandings of class also inform the meanings of occupations. When Beryl referred to her father as an executive, I found the term vague and attempted to find out what kind of work he did. Beryl seemed affronted at my suggestion that he was "just management" (my clumsy attempt to find out what *kind* of work he did as an "executive"), stressing that to her being an executive meant something different.

BERYL: But my dad's an executive and has money. He has this beautiful place down in [a wealthy midwestern suburb]. Anyway, he's very wealthy.

LORI: He's just management, kind of?

BERYL: [somewhat offended] No, he has his own company. He *is* an executive. It basically sells insurance.

Beryl resists placing her father in either the category of "management" or that of "sales." Her father is not an insurance salesman; rather, "it"—the company—sells insurance. She defines her father, as owner and chief executive, in terms of leadership and equates the term "executive" solely with the top level of company management. These kinds of distinctions demonstrate the fine-grained analysis that Americans are able to make concerning class, despite the supposed lack of class distinctions in U.S. society.

ONLINE TALK ABOUT CLASS

BlueSky participants bring these class backgrounds and attitudes toward class to their online interactions, but group discussions rarely refer specifically to class. Class instead emerges in discussions of other topics, including, in addition to education, income, lifestyle, and discussions of U.S. politics, especially economic issues such as welfare. Because class and race are inextricably connected, such discussions (especially those about welfare) also express racial identities and attitudes and, indeed, address issues of class *through* discussions obliquely referring to race (Ortner 1993; Bettie 1995; Stacey 1996).

As in Ortner's interviews, one topic on BlueSky that substitutes for class is income. The following excerpt demonstrates that income has meaning beyond the expectation that people "of course" prefer to have more money. Participants first answered a salary roll call, which itself had a particularly individualistic tone, given the antitax sentiment expressed in the phrase "paycheck leeches."

Corwin ANNUAL SALARY BEFORE THE PAYCHECK LEECHES GET TO IT ROLL
   CALL
Corwin roughly $27k
McKenzie $42k
Faust $32k currently, $35k soon
Copperhead roughly $24K
Bidle $20k before he quit.

Barbie 29K

Corwin believes Alisa's is $30k or so

Starfish $36K

bodkin $n/a

Mender $40k

elflord $40k

Ulysses $53k

Following this, Perry called a roll call on monthly rent. Starfish next supplemented this with a roll call on "what you get for your monthly rent," and then Corwin came up with the ratio of annual rent to salary, to come up with a rough index of buying power:

Corwin's is 1/9, for the record

elflord .198

Corwin says "aka .111111"

Jet is .15

Mender's is .245

Starfish .19

Half Life's is 2.4. sigh. go go gadget parent's money

Faust hms. potentiall .17?

McKenzie is .214

Mender says "half has the still-in-school exemption from the roll call"

Half Life phew

Faust says "current .0937, unless you count Aurora in this, in which case halve
    it"

fnord 0.18, for the record

Captain .33 but General makes lots

Barbie says ".161"

Obtuse is .13 in the rent/salary

Given U.S. cultural attitudes toward work and success, income represents not only purchasing power but also an index of social standing, that is, class. By factoring in considerations such as cost of living, BlueSky participants illustrate their understanding of the inadequacy of looking solely at income levels to determine class position. Although language concerning class does not appear in the discussion, class status clearly underlies the import of what is said. For instance, Mender's comment about "exempting" Half Life from the roll call because of her student status suggests the understanding that student status affects income but should not be held to disrupt continuing middle-class status.

Similarly, in these excerpts, Corwin, Captain, and Faust refer to their wives' salaries. (They use online names for their wives: Alisa, Aurora, and General.) In doing so, they move from an emphasis on personal income toward a recognition of the effect of total household income on class standing. This also reflects changing economic realities in the U.S. middle class, in which the majority of households require two incomes to maintain their middle-class status and lifestyle.

Overt recognition of class differences in the United States would bring participants to the uncomfortable recognition of power imbalances in society. Concern with power and autonomy fuel anxiety about income, but the cultural predominance of individualistic explanations for class differences channels that anxiety into worry about personal attainment. The following discussion concerning henri's salary demonstrates these connections between personal attainment (of high salaries) and class and an implicit understanding of the power implications involved in different class positions.

> McKenzie says "henri answered out of order"
> Mender says "henri was sparing us the horror of his salary"
> henri didn't see the salary roll call
> Corwin says "henri doesn't answer salary roll calls"
> elflord says "We all know the answer :)"
> McKenzie says "if henri doesn't answer then I end up with the highest salary"
> henri says "my salary is public knowledge on here anyhow"
> Corwin says "smash McKenzie utterly, henri"
> henri $90k
> Corwin says "henri crushes everyone anyway"
> henri says "Shub makes more than I do"

The participants hold salary to be a measure of success and therefore a source of pride. However, Corwin's violent metaphor in suggesting that henri's salary information will "smash McKenzie utterly" and henri's apparent discomfort with being at the top of the salary hierarchy demonstrate that that this pride is mixed with ambivalence. The ambivalence may merely reflect envy or feelings of guilt over making less or more money than many others do. However, even when individuals do not actively recognize the power relations involved in class differences, their ambivalence about monetary "success" points to their awareness that such success does not necessarily stem from merit or hard work.

The competitive, "mine is bigger" tone of much of this conversation also points to interconnections between gender and class identities. People view class issues through gendered lenses (and gender issues through class-based understandings). As many feminists have pointed out, "Race, gender and class are not distinct realms of experience. . . . Rather they come into existence *in and through* relation to each other" (McClintock 1995: 5, emphasis in original; see also Connell 1995: 74–76; Spelman 1988). Here, the BlueSky participants express a middle-class identity tied to the traditionally male public space of competitive economic enterprise. Successful performance of masculinity involves successful economic performance and the achievement of a middle-class lifestyle. Similarly, performing a middle-class identity entails adopting particular gendered behaviors recognizable as middle-class, in this case the behaviors and demeanor associated with the competent, competitive male breadwinner.

As a consequence of the focus on individual attainment rather than social class structure, even people with relatively privileged class positions worry about their personal success and may perceive themselves as disadvantaged. Although he attempts to separate salary from class by explicitly emphasizing differences in cost of living in different parts of the United States, Corwin leaves the discussion still concerned that others regard him unfavorably because of his comparatively low salary.

> Corwin says "keep watching these fractions, MadMonk, and consider cost of
>   living differences"
> MadMonk says "True, Oklahoma, like NM, has a pretty low cost of living."
> Corwin has the smallest resulting ratio so far. See? He makes plenty of money.
> BJ makes less than McKenzie, ulysses, mender, etc but more than some
>   others
> Corwin says "TIME TO GO"
> henri says "bye Cor"
> Corwin says "you may all make fun of my salary behind my back now"
> Faust HAHAHAHAH oh he hasn't left
> Mender is too busy wallowing in self-pity over no recent raises
> Corwin has disconnected.

These discussions demonstrate both the importance of class and class positioning and the difficulties Americans have in discussing class. Salaries provide a source of pride, reflecting beliefs in individual merit and effort. But they are also a source of ambivalent feelings, reflecting an underlying perception of the inability to depend on continued good fortune. Corwin in particular exhibits anxieties about income, engendered in part by the individualistic language common in the United States. Corwin's anxiety suggests that despite seeing class attainment as an internal quality, as a matter of will and effort, BlueSky participants may still be vulnerable to a lingering "fear of falling" (Ehrenreich 1989).

However, most BlueSky participants have few fears regarding their earning potential. In discussions of the job market for people with computer programming and system administration skills, most express the belief that there are more jobs than skilled workers. California participants, in particular, frequently advise temporarily out-of-work colleagues in other states to come take advantage of the many openings for system administrators in the Silicon Valley and surrounding areas.

BLUESKY AS PROFESSIONAL NETWORK

In addition to providing a middle-class social space for participants, BlueSky also serves as a resource through which participants can consolidate or secure their middle-class status. Like professional organizations and private clubs, BlueSky provides a network of similarly situated others from whom to obtain job-related information of various types. Many participants report that they owe the job they currently have to expertise gained on BlueSky and/or continuing assistance from other BlueSky participants.

For instance, although she had some exposure to computers as a child and began mudding in college, Peg's degree in broadcasting and film production did not prepare her for a job in computing.

PEG: If I wasn't online, I wouldn't have the job I have now. And the stuff that I've learned—enough to get me this job—I learned from people online.

LORI: So you find BlueSky useful that way?

PEG: Oh yes. In fact a lot of times I feel bad because the only time I'm logging on is to ask somebody a question. But it's like the consultant's dream. We have so many people who have experience, or if they don't they can tell you who to talk to.

Most (although not all) of the programmers on BlueSky majored in computer science in college. However, many of the BlueSky sysadmins did not major in computer science. Rather, they either parleyed their previous computer skills into part-time work while in college or learned computer skills, often through friends, while pursuing other studies in college. After graduation, computers provided the easiest-to-find or most lucrative employment available to them. As in Peg's case, finding out about and getting into the group on BlueSky require a previous level of computer competence. However, once there, participants can find support and encouragement for increasing their computer skills and experience.

Once BlueSky participants have the requisite skills for sysadmin or programming work, they sometimes also obtain jobs through their contacts on BlueSky. Some have hired other BlueSky people or have made recommendations regarding a fellow BlueSky participant to their boss. In addition, people share job openings they know about with the group.

A job listing object built in one of the main hangouts acts as a bulletin board for job opening announcements. Following is a list of the jobs posted on this object on May 5, 1995. The list includes the name of the person posting the job, the date of the posting, and a brief description. After viewing this index, participants can access longer descriptions and contact information for each job. (I have changed some identifying details in the following.)

0 henri	Jun 29	CareerMosaic—many jobs on line!
1 Mender	Jan 6	OSF/1/Ultrix system administrator, MI
2 Felicia	May 20	Systems programmer opening (NJ)
3 Gamer	May 20	Omnis hacking in Pittsburgh
4 Felicia	May 20	Sysadmin opening (NJ)
5 Captin	Jan 31	Sysadmin at Mouseworks
6 Beryl	Aug 17	full-time mud admin in the bay area
7 carnival	Jul 14	Part time internet hacker
8 Gravity	Jan 22	MIS and CS jobs in DC—Interviews Easy to get!
9 Shub	Jan 29	Senior SysAdmin (NYC/NJ)
10 henri	Mar 6	Lots of Jobs, Northern CA
11 Corwin	Feb 17	UNIX Sysadmin/Netadmin
12 henri	Mar 6	Receptionist, Northern CA
13 henri	Mar 6	Programmer Analyst, Northern CA
14 henri	Mar 6	Electronic Connectivity, sr. Programmer Analyst, Northern CA
15 henri	Mar 6	Senior Programmer Analyst, Northern CA
16 henri	Mar 8	Production Assistant (Northern CA)
17 henri	Apr 18	Sr. Programmer Analyst, Northern CA
18 henri	Apr 27	Fearless C++ Hackers (Northern CA)
19 henri	May 5	Mailing List Maintenance, SF

While the list above does include some nontechnical clerical positions (job numbers 12 and 19), most jobs require computer knowledge and experience. Job number 1, for instance, requires knowledge of specific computer operating systems and equipment; job number 18 requires proficiency in a specific programming language; and job numbers 14, 15, and 17 require a significant level of programming experience and ability. This list demonstrates both the kinds of jobs that BlueSky participants hear about and the kinds of jobs they expect people on BlueSky would want or could qualify for.

People also solicit each other directly concerning employment. In the following conversation, Farron, who works for Shub, another BlueSky participant, attempts to recruit someone for a system administration position at his company.

> Farron sidles over to elflord. "Would you be interested in pr'aps doubling your salary by a quick job change?"
>
> elflord says "Do I have to move (back) to Bahston?"
>
> Farron says "You just have to work in Bahston."
>
> Bilerific-Sid says "Shub will be your boss!"
>
> elflord says "Double my current salary would be a substantial sum, but not enough to uproot me at this time"
>
> Farron nods at elflord. "Alas."
>
> Dave idly asks Farron if he needs a decently good sendmail hacker.
>
> elflord says "Try again in a year, when Carla is through with sch00l"
>
> Corwin says "Don't look at me, Farron. You'd have to double mine and Alisa's together, for one thing."
>
> Farron grins at Corwin. "That could be arranged."
>
> Corwin says "That may be more than you think. What were you intending to offer?"
>
> Farron notes that senior unix sysadmins make between 60 and 90k, senior DOS/win people probably between 50 and 75k, depending.
>
> Jet says "I believe the cost of living of Boston is about 2x that of WY"
>
> Corwin says "Which is why doubling would be the minimum"
>
> Dave says "How do they define 'senior' in this context?"
>
> Farron says "Well, currently I'm a senior sysadmin, and I've been doing this professionally for, what 3 years?"
>
> Dave only has somewhere between four and six years of sysadmin experience, depending on how you define it.
>
> Farron says "Which gives you more than anyone else except possibly Shub, in our dept at least."
>
> Dave says "So do you need a sendmail guy, Farron?"
>
> Farron says "What's more, you're competent."
>
> Farron says "What we need: Competent people. Doing anything."
>
> Dave says "Ah. Okay."

Dave makes a little mental note.

Obtuse sighs. "Do they need people in, say, Seattle?"

In these kinds of conversations, BlueSky resembles a professional club or association, through which members can network and make professional contacts. Like many such clubs, it allows its members to augment whatever local job resources they have, giving them countrywide connections and opportunities. Farron attempts to interest elflord, Corwin, and Dave—who live in Utah, Wyoming, and New York, respectively—in employment in Boston.

The advantages of technical connections formed on BlueSky can also last beyond active participation in the group. Atticus, although still a mudder, left the BlueSky group many years ago over various personal differences. He got his current job through contact with another ex-BlueSky mudder. "I was actually doing tape transcription at [a state university] part-time when Bernie gave me a call and said, 'Hey, we need tech support people over at [a large internet service provider] right now; can you start working next Sunday?'" Atticus went on to get jobs at that company for various other people he knew from muds, most of whom did not live in the state but moved to take the jobs. This both provided employment for people he knew and expanded his own social circle in the state.

The connections between BlueSky participation and participant job status follow a somewhat circular logic. Not only does participation help people get computer-related jobs, but these are in fact the types of jobs that allow them to continue their participation on BlueSky. This relates partly to the computer-oriented culture on BlueSky but also to some basic requirements for participation in online groups.

VIRTUALLY WHITE: RACE ONLINE

Many BlueSky participants acknowledge that BlueSky can be characterized as a male space or is at least male dominated. However, despite the fact that the class and race demographics of BlueSky are even more uniform than gender, many were perplexed when I tried to talk with them about ways in which BlueSky might also be characterized as a "white" space. Their unwillingness to think of BlueSky's culture in this way reflects the general taboo in U.S. culture against speaking of race as well as the tendency to view "white" culture as generic, with no racial content (Frankenburg 1993; Pfeil 1995).

The absence in text-based online interaction of physical cues associated with race strengthens the prevailing U.S. cultural tendency toward "colorblindness" (Omi and Winant 1994), in which race's effects on interaction and on power differences in society go unacknowledged. Yet, despite social taboos on the acknowledgment of race, people do talk about race and racial issues. Bernardi (1998), for instance, demonstrates the intricate and complex language with which fans discuss the meaning of racial aspects of *Star Trek*. Similarly, while racial topics occur much less frequently than topics concerning gender on BlueSky, participants do occasionally discuss issues of race, ethnicity, and identity.

Most BlueSky participants live in the United States, where a discourse of "color blindness" predominates, making direct references to race more or less taboo (Frankenberg 1993: 14). Further, over 90 percent of BlueSky participants are white. As members of this racially "unmarked" category, very few think of their identities in racial terms. White BlueSky participants think of themselves not in terms of race—fraught as that concept is with issues of dominance, oppression, and violence—but in terms of ethnicity. Like many in the United States, they know their family background and history and can identify the (usually mixed) ethnicities from which family members originated. Whereas thinking about race requires people to think in terms of groups, ethnicity allows them to focus on unique individual heritages.

For instance, in the following conversation, several white BlueSky participants discuss their ethnic backgrounds. This conversation began as a discussion of immigration policies, which were in the news at the time. The topic of immigration led participants to reflect on their own families' arrivals to the United States.

> elflord has one parent whose ancestors have been on this continent for nigh
>   on 400 years, and another who is an immigrant. Provides an interesting
>   perspective.
> Farron nods @ elflord. "Same here."
> Farron's grandfather immigrated, but he had relatives on both sides of the Civil
>   War, back into the 1600s.
> Ulysses' grandparents were all born here, and he has pre-revolutionary
>   ancestors
> Bilerific-Sid's father is an immigrant and his mother's folks are immigrants.
> Pyramid is like unto Ulysses ancestorally
> Bilerific-Sid is surrounded by honkies.
> Ulysses says "and since I'm a tiny part Seneca, I have ancestors who were here
>   long before all you WHITE PEOPLE"

elflord has aunts, uncles, and first cousins scattered through Europe and
    southern Africa.
elflord is 0% Native American, but Diana has some Injun blood
Corwin is a bit Cherokee
Corwin says "or so I'm told"
Farron has no native american blood.
Farron is so white that he disappears against snowbanks.
Pyramid is a bit Jewish, that's the only thing keeping her from utter WASP-
    hood
Corwin says "Farron looks exactly like he should be in an Irish pub getting
    plastered"
Farron nods @ Corwin.
Farron says "all my traceable ancestors are Irish, Scots, or English."
elflord's ancestors are German, Scots, English, and Norvegian
Bilerific-Sid's ancestors are greek and Rom.
Ulysses' ancestors are English, Irish, Scottish, Welsh, French, Dutch, German
    and Seneca

Several aspects of dominant United States discourses of race emerge in participants' expressions of their own heritage. The focus on ethnicity, rather than race, reflects dominant U.S. discourse regarding difference (Omi and Winant 1994: 14–23). Lists of mixed ancestry evoke "melting-pot" assimilationist models of U.S. culture. Sleeter has pointed out that "equating ethnicity with race is a . . . strategy for evading racism. When whites conceptualize cultural diversity within the U.S., . . . we usually subdivide Euro-American groups by ethnic origins, placing groups such as Germans, Poles, and Scots within the same conceptual plane as African Americans and Native Americans. This conceptual plane highlights cultural heritage; it denies whiteness as a phenomenon worth scrutiny and with it, white racism" (1996: 260). I would add that the evocation of the national origin of one's ancestors as a "cultural heritage" in itself is disingenuous for most white Americans. Most of the participants quoted above do not strongly identify with the cultures they name, nor do they engage in particular practices that reflect those cultures.

To use myself as an example, the legacy of my mother's Czechoslovakian ancestry for me has consisted mainly of knowledge of approximately twenty Czech words that my grandfather retaught me on each annual visit (and that, since his death, I've mostly forgotten); an appreciation for a type of Czech pastry; knowledge of a card game called Pitch and general enjoyment of large familial card games; and the ability to polka. While all of these things evoke considerable personal meaning and feelings of affection for me, that meaning and affection resides mainly in memories of my grandparents and hence embodies familial, rather than broadly cultural, meaning. Without a community of practice and the continuing reinforcement of recurring performance, such customs cannot be read as an ethnic identity. Further, while many with European ethnic heritages can point to instances of discrimination in their families' pasts, most with white ethnic identities no longer experience discrimination based on their ethnic heritage.

Not all BlueSky participants have the same relationship to their ethnic backgrounds that I have. Itchy, born in Armenia, maintains active connections with and participation in his Armenian immigrant community. The historical oppression of Armenians by the Turks, their relatively recent arrival in the United States, and continued prejudice within this country against people from the Middle East and nearby regions give Itchy's Armenian identity meaning quite different from that of my own Czechoslovakian background.

Similarly, BJ's Jewish family left the Soviet Union during its 1980s loosening of emigration restrictions. Knowledge by participants that BJ emigrated from Russia at the age of eleven gives his self-identification as Russian a different meaning from, for instance, that of elflord's identification as part German. White relationships to ethnicity thus vary, particularly according to distance from time of immigration and connection to ethnic communities within the United States. But even the stronger meaning of some ethnic identities for white Americans doesn't erase the benefits they receive from white privilege. Race remains salient in the lives of white people, despite their disavowal of an identity termed "white."

In the above discussion, participants recognize their connection to racial as well as ethnic identities through several references to whiteness. However, in most of their discussion they differentiate themselves from each other rather than recognize this common white identity. Frankenberg has identified lists of ethnic heritages such as those the BlueSky participants above cite as "belonging names" (1993: 205), demarcating an absence of identity that many white Americans perceive in themselves. Because of U.S. perceptions of whiteness as bland, empty, and normative, white people often name more specific "bounded" heritages. The need to evoke such boundaries relates specifically to commentaries concerning online "community," which suggests that the need for community and perceptions of a lack of community in modern, urban U.S. culture drive people to create new kinds of community online. Such claims regarding the lack of community can be read as specifically white perceptions of a loss or an absence of identity.

As Frankenberg has pointed out, the strategy of identifying with bounded "belonging names" risks "romanticizing the experience of being oppressed" (1993: 230). This romanticization combines with guilt avoidance in the above discussion of Native American ancestry. Many white American families point to a single "Native American ancestor" in near-mythical fashion. Often the exact history of these ancestors is vague and unknown, as demonstrated by Corwin's assertion that he is "a bit Cherokee . . . or so I am told." Whites who can point to this ancestry can lay claim to being "good whites" who presumably married rather than killed the Native Americans they encountered upon immigration. (This practice fails to consider, among other things, the ways in which social constructions of gender and race intertwine and the ways in which oppression occurs in and through sex and marriage.)

Conjuring the mythical nonwhite ancestor also serves to disavow white status, further reinforcing "melting pot" theories of U.S. ethnic experience and continuing to reproduce whiteness as empty and null. Pyramid's statement that she is "saved from utter WASP-hood" by virtue of being "a bit Jewish" enacts a similar strategy and presents whiteness as a negative identity to be "saved from." Similarly, Bilerific-Sid's use of the pejorative term "honkies" and Ulysses' ironic distancing from "all you WHITE PEO-PLE" demonstrate continuing uneasiness toward white identity. Pyramid, Bilerific-Sid, and Ulysses use these ironic statements to distance themselves from the implied privilege of white identity. Such statements, like RaveMage's earlier hesitation to admit his Harvard background, take on the appearance of modesty or disavowal while actually highlighting the claim to status, in this case whiteness. Few if any of these participants would likely actually give up the white identity they verbally disavow.

WHITE FLIGHT: AVOIDING RACIAL LABELING

BlueSky participants' responses to direct questions about their racial identities reflect the different experiences they bring to their online interactions as well as the charged nature of discussions of race. No one objected to my questions or refused outright to label themselves racially, but most asserted that their race made little difference online. Some also felt race made little difference in their offline lives. For instance, many white mudders said they didn't think about race much.

fnord whispers "um, just sort of generic caucasian mix, I suppose, never really
     think about it much"

HalfLife whispers "hmm . . . It's not something I think about. When asked I
     usually say Jewish; though I don't know if that's a race"

Alisa pages: I rarely give race thought at all—this may be mainly due to my
     upbringing more than a conscious effort on my part

Whiteness as an unmarked, empty category allows white people the luxury
of not thinking about race. They fail to see the ways in which race and
racialized understandings shape their view of the world and their move-
ments within it. As Feagin and Vera note, "Most white respondents in
research conducted by Robert Terry in the 1970s said that they had rarely
or never thought about being white" (1995: 139).

As demonstrated in the conversation concerning ethnicity above, white
BlueSky participants prefer to refer to themselves in ethnic terms. In this
strategy, the term "Caucasian" sometimes substitutes for white. Others
use more specific ethnic identifiers.

elflord whispers "I don't tend to think of myself as 'a white boy' so much as in
     terms of being 'German/Norwegian/English/Scots,' though—I think
     more in terms of nationality than race"

elflord's desire not to think of himself as "a white boy" saddles him with
a complicated string of European referents. His labeling of these as na-
tionalities exhibits the ambiguity of their meaning as identity terms. If
asked his nationality in a context other than a discussion of race, elflord
would likely label himself American or of United States nationality. But
like the term "national origin" on census forms, here nationality stands
in for the important but forbidden term "race."

Other terms that participants substitute for white also indicate the difficulty whites sometimes have in finding terms that avoid the pitfalls of
identifying as the upper term in a relationship of dominance, yet retain
meaning in defining personal identity.

Ulysses whispers "yankee"
Ulysses senses "Copperhead laughs; 'yankee?'"
Ulysses whispers "well, that's more of a culture than a race. race is white"
Alisa pages: My racial identity is 'me'. I think if any physical characteristics have
     something to do with interactions, more often it's gender and cultural
     background more than 'race'. ie, New Englanders vs native Californians vs
     midwesterners vs Them Dang Foreigners.

In these responses, the categories of race, ethnicity, place, and culture become conflated and confused. Alisa lumps three very different terms—"gender," "cultural background," and "race"—under the same rubric of "physical characteristics" that "have something to do with interactions." This naturalizes racism as something having to do with the way people look. It also highlights the way in which "cultural background" substitutes for "race." How else can one explain cultural background as something having to do with physical characteristics? As Bernardi (1998) notes in his analysis of online *Star Trek* fans' discussion of race, people consider race in terms both of physiognomy and social and cultural characteristics of groups, often in contradictory ways.

Talking about regional U.S. cultural differences also elides the question of power and displaces questions of difference into a less charged arena. For Alisa, as for a woman Frankenberg interviewed, "the assertion of differences that she can live with . . . stood in as quasi substitutes for race" (1993: 38). Interestingly, Alisa holds that differences between, for instance, New Englanders and Californians—often identified by accent and speech patterns in face-to-face interactions—can carry over to the electronic forum, where such speech patterns cannot be heard, while racial differences—usually equated with skin color and other similar phenotypical signs—supposedly do not carry over.

Similarly, Ulysses' response of "yankee" replaces race with a quasi-ethnic regional identity, while Alisa's definition of her racial identity as "me" attempts to elude group classification altogether. The endeavor to elude racial classification may stem in part from a dissatisfaction with broad categories and the perceived lack of agency that such categorization imposes. Such dissatisfaction occurred in responses from both white and non-white respondents. However, coming from white respondents, the attempt to elude racial classification also serves to escape from a categorization that implies despotic power over others. Such responses seek distance from the term "white" and thereby retain whiteness as a null space.

White respondents sometimes implicitly indicated embarrassment or discomfort with white identity through use of derogatory terms for whiteness.

> You sense Peg is pretty white, but not wonder-bread, her father's family are
>   eastern europeans

In addition to referring to "real" whiteness as Wonder Bread (bland, non-nutritious, overprocessed), Peg sets up a hierarchy of whiteness in which presumably only full-blooded WASPs would qualify as really white. Those who, like her, have other European ancestry, are only "pretty" white.

Asian American respondents also talked about racial identity in ways that mixed references to race and to ethnicity. Their distancing strategies from racial identity evidenced complex relationships to both their perceived ethnic heritages and communities and to the predominantly white spaces in which they worked and socialized. In their discussions, they sometimes associated whiteness with Americanization.

> Tempest whispers "filipino. i'm not your typical flip, tho', i've been too
>   americanized; the vast majority [of filipinos] are much calmer than i am :)"
> Tempest whispers "that translates to: no tazers or 2x4s :)"

Tempest identifies as Filipino, yet distances himself from other Filipinos. His mention of tasers and two-by-fours refers to his BlueSky shtick of implied participation in indiscriminate violence. (Tempest's answers to roll calls and doing polls often mention the violent use of such weapons.) Thus, his distancing of himself from Filipino identity in the above statement refers directly to his BlueSky identity, implicitly recognizing the ways in which BlueSky exists as a white space in which white identities are performed.

Two other Asian American respondents' responses to racial categorization highlight the inaccuracy or insufficiency of categories imposed on them by others.

> Spontaneity whispers "I'm in that 'Asian and Pacific Islander' bin the Federal
>   Government uses, yup."

> RaveMage says "hmmm, well, as you probably know i call myself the 'asian
>   punkboy' :)"
> Copperhead grins
> RaveMage says "which is funny 'cos i'm actually filipino, which is actually a
>   pacific islander; but bodkin and i have fun with the look :)"

RaveMage's reference to "the look" of Asian punkboy, as opposed to the "actual" identity of Filipino, highlights the artificiality of racial categories. His ability to "pass" as Asian relies on American racial categorizations, which take little notice of cultural differences.

Elektra similarly noted that people's perception of her racial identity did not necessarily match her understanding of her own identity. In the following discussion, she respond to my question regarding her racial identity.

Elektra pages: mexican, though i've been told i can pass for anything from
 white to asian to indian.
Copperhead whispers "I thought you were Filipina, although I don't know where
 i got that from."
Elektra pages: you know, i heard that same thing from someone in louisville
 last month. of course, some of my cow-orkers thought i was white, so . . .
Copperhead whispers "what do you think about that? about being seen
 different ways by different people?"
Elektra pages: i think it's pretty damn funny.

As with other participants, I also asked Elektra whether race matters on-line:

Copperhead whispers "how much do you think race matters online, esp. here?"
Elektra pages: i don't think it matters here at all. maybe if i met/hung with
 more of the people here RL but since i don't it's not an issue with me.
Copperhead whispers "well, given that race doesn't matter much here, maybe
 you can give me a better idea of how it matters offline?"
Elektra pages: here in [town], it really doesn't. i think i got more reaction from
 people when i dyed my hair blue.
Copperhead whispers "do you think it has made a difference with people from
 here that you've met offline?"
Elektra pages: no, not that i've seen.
Copperhead whispers "ah. I was wondering because you said race didn't
 matter online but that it might if you saw these people more offline"
Elektra pages: hmmm.

Elektra's inconsistent responses point to the dilemma engendered by U.S. culture's "color-blind" stance toward race. Race isn't supposed to matter, and members of subordinated racial groups may hope it doesn't have much impact on their lives. Hence, Elektra insists it doesn't matter much either online or off, despite indications in her discussion that it does.

Her ability to pass as "anything from white to asian to indian" may allow her some flexibility in negotiating her identity in her small, predominantly white, midwestern town. Her reports of multiple interpretations of her appearance reveal the persistent attempts of people to categorize her racially. While avowedly amused by these multiple interpretations, her knowledge of others' confusion suggests that the subject of her racial identity comes up repeatedly in interactions with others.

"HOW WHITE ARE YOU?"

While many respondents distance themselves from racial categories in a variety of ways, one BlueSky participant attempts instead to *re*categorize himself. Jet complicates his Chinese American identity by referring to himself in online discussions as white. As evidenced by other participants' reactions below to Jet's statement that he is white, most know that his parents emigrated from China.

> Jet rather enjoyed the LA riots in a sick way
> Jet went to Canter's 3 days afterwards, and there was us, 4 white guys, and
>   12 cops
> Jet says "That's it."
> Jet says "(we were the 4 white guys)"
> Mender . o O (Jet's a white guy!)
> Ichi giggles at Jet
> Jet . o O (oh i am)
> Jet says "You've met me, you know I'm white"
> Mender says "not as white as I am, bucko"
> Pyramid says "HOW WHITE ARE YOU?"
> McKenzie says "Mender gets waspy"
> Jet says "I'm pretty white"
> Jet says "no joke"

Jet's positioning himself as white in a discussion that related at least in part to the Los Angeles uprisings may represent a distancing from other people of color, particularly African Americans. (Notice also that Mender's claim to be whiter than Jet provokes an accusation of WASPiness from McKenzie, again reproducing the hierarchy of whiteness in which white Anglo-Saxon Protestants represent real whiteness. However, Jet also refers to himself as white on numerous other occasions.)

When I asked Jet about self-defining as white, he talked about the ways in which "whiteness" marks a cultural identity as well as a racial distinction.

> Copperhead whispers "several times when questions of ethnicity or race have
>   come up you've made the statement that you're white; I'm wondering
>   what you mean by that."
> Jet whispers "I mean that I am essentially an american clothed in a chinese
>   body. I hardly know how to speak chinese, I hardly know anything about the

culture, and I don't associate with orientals a lot by choice, unlike many immigrant children. So I feel 'white', i.e. american"

Copperhead whispers "so if 'american' = 'white' is BlueSky a white space? And what does that mean for people who aren't white here?"

Jet whispers "mudding transcends ethnicity"

Jet whispers "i don't consider blue sky 'white' or 'american' or any ethnicity, i just consider it a place to hang out. if you were all asian and had the same personalities, so be it"

Jet whispers "no no, american ! = white" [the "! =" formulation is programming shorthand for "does not equal"]

Jet whispers "i use 'white' in the sense of the martin mull stereotype; very bland, whitebread; obviously i'm not. it's a sort of irony"

Jet connects racial identity to language use and non-American customs. Yet he refers to his own "cultural whiteness" and simultaneously denies cultural effects of race or ethnicity through his suggestion that it would be possible for BlueSky participants to be all Asian and yet have the same personalities. This elision of the cultural aspects of race, which is high-lighted by his ironic labeling of himself as white, enables him nevertheless to claim that mudding transcends ethnicity.

Thus, Jet suggests that the physical characteristics associated with race do not determine his identity. Although acknowledging his ethnic heritage in some ways (at another point in the conversation he stated, for instance, that he would prefer to marry another Asian American) and labeling his *body* Chinese, Jet labels himself white on the basis of the cultural affinities that seem to him more salient for his identity. However, he still gives that identity a racial label. Also, although he denies that American equals white, the race label he gives his American identity is "white." Jet's representation of himself as white serves as a "racial project," which, in Omi and Winant's words, forms both "an interpretation, representation, or explanation of racial dynamics, and an effort to reorganize and redistribute resources along particular racial lines" (1994: 56). In Jet's case, his representation of himself as white reinforces the dominant order in which benefits accrue to those who are white. But he also attempts to reposition himself as entitled to those benefits, because, beneath the "clothing" of his Chinese body, he is "really" white.

In recognition of the ironic contradictions involved in his self-identity, Jet, like Peg, associates true whiteness with "bland, whitebread." Like Peg, Jet can thereby be white but not *really* white. Both participants mark themselves with an ironically detached white-but-not-white identity. But they arrive at this identity formulation from very different offline positions. For me, having met both Jet and Peg face-to-face, the irony of their similar self-definitions is heightened by their extreme difference physically. Peg is short and petite, with very pale skin and light reddish brown hair. Jet is over six feet tall and thin with medium brown skin and almost black hair. That I can so describe them and experience their similar self-identification as ironic points to assumptions concerning racial identity that I, like Jet and Peg, have internalized from the surrounding culture.

This emphasizes both the absence and the presence of race online. Gilroy argues that race and racism are *processes* and that the meanings of race "are unfixed and subject to the outcomes of struggle" (1987: 24). We are taught to classify people by skin color and other identifiers that we learn to associate with race. Hence, I can easily point to Peg and label her white and to Jet and label him Asian. But the meanings of these designations vary and are sites of struggle, as both Jet and Peg indicate in their self-identifications. When these struggles are brought online, some of their parameters change. (However, note that Jet's self-identification of white is challenged by others who have met him.) The assertion that race doesn't matter online essentializes the connection between race and physical appearance, but it also points out the potential unavailability of that connection in online interactions. While participants bring their assumptions about race with them to online interactions, they perform racial identities under slightly different rules.

As with Jet's statement that mudding transcends ethnicity, most BlueSky participants believe that race has no effect on their online interactions. However, their most common reply to my questions concerning the effects of race on online interaction highlights the ways in which racial assumptions nevertheless form a backdrop for those interactions. When I asked white participants whether race matters online or not, they often mentioned one of the few black mudders they know.

> Corwin is a white boy, and hasn't seen as how people have any clue what race
>   anyone is; he's pretty sure nobody realized for ages that a few black
>   MUSHers were black, for instance
> elflord whispers "I rarely see race playing a major factor in BlueSky discussion—
>   like many other forms of online interaction, one's race isn't glaringly
>   obvious. It was years before I even knew Sand was black, for instance.
> Peg whispers "well, i don't know unless someone mentions it, obviously, but
>   people don't seem to act any differently. there was one girl (katrina?) who
>   was black but it never came up in conversation"

These white participants associate race and racial relations specifically with the question of blackness. In these statements, the ultimate test of whether race matters online is the ability of black people to pass unnoticed as black. This emphasizes both the presumed desirability of hiding blackness and the assumption that people online are white. While the latter assumption is not unreasonable, given the current demographics of online participants, it demonstrates the extent to which anonymity cannot be classified as an absence of identity characteristics. When black participants must state that they are black in order to be recognized as such, anonymity carries with it a presumptive identity of whiteness.

That white mudders reference blackness also highlights the polarization of discourse about race in the United States into a question of whiteness versus blackness. While people certainly use racial language in references to mudders of other groups, my evocation of the "race question" through my questions about race online elicits responses that rely on this dualism. Rather than considering the many active Asian American regulars on BlueSky, these responses instead refer to the very few African American mudders participants have known. This may also allow them to distance themselves from potential racial conflicts "out there" rather than considering the racial differences in their own day-to-day lives.

Nonwhite BlueSky participants recognize the default assumption of whiteness online and consider its implications for their own identities.

> Copperhead says "one of the things I've been trying to figure out is whether BlueSky is a 'white' space; I would argue that it is a 'male' space"
> RaveMage says "i'd say totally male, ya; I mean, look at all the sexist banter"
> RaveMage says "but then again all the males are caucasian or move well in caucasian spaces"

While perhaps stopping short of agreeing with my implied identification of BlueSky as a white space, RaveMage, a Filipino American, recognizes the possibility that social spaces can be racially categorized. He also suggests that those who are not members of the dominant racial group in a particular social space must learn to "move well" in that type of space. This implies a recognition of racial identities as performed within particular social contexts.

Similarly, Anguish, a Korean American, reveals a view of both online and offline social interaction steeped in a racial context and suggests the potential for racial identities to be performed:

Anguish whispers "I think most people assume most everyone else is white
  [online], and for the most part, they'd be right. When people find out
  I'm Asian, there is a little surprise, but not much"
Copperhead whispers "hmm."
Copperhead whispers "do you think people 'act white' here in some way?"
Anguish whispers "is there a way of acting otherwise? irl and online, I think
  people act white mostly."
Anguish whispers "I've acted 'not-white', but only among other not-whites."
Copperhead whispers "huh, that's interesting; can you tell me how that differs
  for you?"
Anguish whispers "well, I act in the ways I was taught to by my parents, i.e.,
  Korean customs. An intrinsic part of that is language. The language here is
  English."

Much as Tempest opposes his Filipino heritage to his fit within the
"American" context of BlueSky and Jet discusses "whiteness" versus
American identity, Anguish opposes the racial category of "white" to a
cultural category of "Korean." While identifying herself as Asian, she says
that she nevertheless "acts" white most of the time. As with Alisa's jux-
taposition of physical characteristics and cultural background, Anguish's
suggestion that she *is* Korean American but can *act* either white or Korean
again blends references to ethnicity and race and represents race as something both physical and cultural.

These examples demonstrate that nonwhites perform their identities
often within contexts dominated by whites. With race tied to both physical
and cultural factors, nonwhites thus can "act white" but not "be white."
No wonder, then, that many see cyberspace as a place where race "doesn't
matter" and where the effects of racism can be escaped. The absence of
bodies and access to physical markers of race online leads some to hope
that "acting" is "being." However, this fails to recognize that, as Omi and
Winant point out, "race is a matter of both social structure and cultural
representation" (1994: 56). In our racially charged culture, all performed
identities contain and convey racial meanings. As the statements by
BlueSky participants indicate, race continues to matter online, even if all
participants can act white and even pass for white.

However, the online absence of physical cues that people use to distinguish racial identities makes a difference in *how* race matters online. Indeed, some nonwhite participants find the online presumption of whiteness
advantageous.

Spontaneity whispers "I've noticed a lack of harassment on line in general."
Copperhead whispers "that's interesting; less harassment online than off?"
Spontaneity whispers "Yah. Now, it may just be that people are able to be
    more subtle on-line, but I don't think so. For example, it's fairly common for
    me to get shouted at on the streets."

As Spontaneity, a Chinese American, indicates, the lack of physical markers can result in freedom from harassment. If, as Anguish indicates, everybody acts white most of the time, those white acts online can float free of their ties to physical markers of race. However, because the space this opens up for speech from nonwhites remains white in some sense, this advantage constitutes a form of "passing" for white rather than a true dissolution of racial difference and hierarchy. All BlueSky participants, to some extent or another, perform a white masculine identity. Passing for white is also more feasible online than off. While this may constitute some degree of "leveling the playing field," the type of game and its rules remain unquestioned.

RACE AND SPEECH

As in other U.S. social spaces, current events provide context for discussions about identity. The following conversation occurred on October 3, 1995, the day the verdict was announced in the criminal trial of O. J. Simpson. On BlueSky, the O. J. Simpson trial occasioned many more discussions regarding race than usually occur. McKenzie reacts to Mender's discussion of a news report by engaging in the kind of associative wordplay commonly enjoyed on BlueSky. He associates the phrase "race card," which figured in media discussions of the trial, with a heavy metal song entitled "Ace of Spades." The combination results in more meanings than he intends.

Mender says "Shapiro said Cochran 'played the race card from the bottom of
    the deck'"
McKenzie says "RACE OF SPADES"
Copperhead reshuffles
henri eyes McKenzie
Mender HOWLS at McKenzie
McKenzie winces at that not-all-intentional pun
Barbie says "good thing there aren't too many black mudders"
Jet headbangs
Jet says "THE RACE OF SPADES ! THE RACE OF SPADES"

> Mender . o O (it's a wonder McKenzie hasn't been beat up more)
> Jet | McKenzie says "RACE OF SPADES"
> McKenzie says "honest, I didn't mean all the ugly implications, I was just
>   thinking Motorhead"
> Mender says "MCKENZIE'S A BAD COP"
> henri says "EXCEPT FOR THE COP PART"
> McKenzie says "EGREGIOUS RACISM"

Jet understands McKenzie's reference to heavy metal, as indicated by his pose "Jet headbangs." Other reactions to McKenzie's unintended meaning demonstrate the knowledge of participants that racial slurs violate the social norm. (Jet continued for days afterward to torment McKenzie by quoting his slip back to him.)

The suggestion that McKenzie's comment risks a beating, when combined with Barbie's comment that it's a "good thing there aren't too many black mudders," serves to naturalize racial conflict. The BlueSky participants present here an understanding of a world in which racial groups (in this case, blacks) can be expected to react violently to racial slurs targeted at them, but violence need not be feared from one's own group, even when members of that group object to the racist meanings.

The question of the presence or absence of black mudders in the above conversation highlights again the question of audience online. While on BlueSky people generally know the composition of their audience, they are aware of the potential for audience ambiguity online and the questions this raises with regard to racial speech.

> henri whispers "I think the race issue is very similar to RL, except that when
>   someone says something off-color I don't know in which direction to
>   wince"
> Copperhead whispers "hmmm, how do you mean?"
> henri whispers "well in general I don't like hearing racist jokes, for example,
>   and it makes me uncomfortable, but whenever I hear one on here (which is
>   very seldom, although I can remember some cases in the past) I expect
>   someone I've never met in RL to say 'but I'M black' (or whatever, but
>   clearly african-american is the most loaded situation)"

henri indicates that racist jokes might be told online by people who assume their audience is white. But henri's expectation that at that moment someone might protest the joke by revealing his or her nonwhite racial identity points out the ambiguity of audience online. To the extent that people are less likely to tell racist (or sexist, or homophobic) jokes when members of the targeted group are present, online forums might provide space for interactions among different groups of people. However, in Goffman's terms, this mainly transforms the stigma of race from a discredited identity to a discreditable identity. People with stigmatized identities possess a greater ability to manage information about themselves online, but this ability does not necessarily change the stigmatized nature of the identity once revealed (Goffman 1963).

Racialized meanings are not limited to jokes specifically targeted at racial groups. Whites' ability to "not think" about race allows racism embedded in patterns of speech and assumptions about "normal" interactions to go unnoticed. The following example demonstrates a way of thinking and type of speech that naturalize and take for granted the history of racism in the United States. Thomas talked to me about Boontit, a programmed object on the mud that acts something like a robot and that Thomas regularly loms. I asked him whether Boontit annoyed him and why he so consistently vented hostility on an object.

> Thomas whispers "Boontit meets a useful need I think that actually Jeff and Florin provided. That's an angst sink."
> Copperhead whispers "That's interesting. Tell me what you mean by that. For other people's angst?"
> Thomas whispers "Well, if you're frustrated with work or something. You can also think of it as sort of a punching bag or a target that can be universally reviled and everybody can sort of egg you on without fear."
> Thomas whispers "Unfortunately, what used to be in the past with some racial interactions, where the KKK would 'let's go find ourselves a nigger to go beat up' you know. Just sort of release. Boontit can be one of those. If you're frustrated you can take it out on Boontit."

Thomas talks about KKK actions "in the past," and his analysis of Boontit's usefulness essentially deletes the racism from racist organizations. By implying that KKK violence has been motivated by the kinds of frustrations that everybody experiences ("with work or something"), he denies the specifically racial character and motivation of racist violence.

Thomas's statement demonstrates some of the ways in which racism remains embedded in white speech at the level of fundamental assumptions about human behavior. BlueSky participants consider themselves to be tolerant and inclusive. Although they acknowledge that, as Peg says, "we don't really have a real cross-section of all society here," many of my interviewees pointed to the wide variety of people in terms of such variables as political opinions, religious affiliations, and so forth. My aim here is not simply to belie the claims of this relatively privileged group that their online forum provides a space for inclusive interactions. Rather, I want to point out the socially constructed nature of race and racism and the ways in which racism remains embedded in speech despite good intentions. Merely providing a forum where physical differences can be hidden does not eliminate racism. Such forums can, however, provide people with class and race privilege a place in which they can pretend that their privilege doesn't matter.

Omi and Winant point out that "one of the first things we notice about people when we meet them (along with their sex) is their race" (1994: 59) and that, on the basis of our cultural knowledge of racial differences, we make assumptions based upon those appearances. "We expect differences in skin color, or other racially coded characteristics, to explain social differences" (60). One might expect then that, in a social environment in which people encounter and interact with others without being able to see them, online participants would not make gendered, raced, and classed assumptions about each other. Certainly many online participants, in keeping with the predominance of the ideal of "color blindness" in our society, claim that this is the case.

Yet gender and race are concepts that "signif[y] and symboliz[e] social conflicts and interests by *referring* to different types of human bodies" (Omi and Winant 1994: 55, emphasis added). The importance of such signification and symbolization continues in online interaction. The bodies of others may remain hidden and inaccessible, but this if anything gives *references* to such bodies even more social importance. As Omi and Winant explain, "Despite its uncertainties and contradictions, the concept of race continues to play a fundamental role in structuring and representing the social world" (55). This remains true about race as well as about gender, class, sexuality, and age, *especially* when that "uncertainty" is compounded by the lack of physical presence in online encounters. Online participants assume that other participants do have bodies and that those bodies, if seen, would reveal important information. The assumed congruence between certain types of bodies and certain psychological, behavioral, and social characteristics results in the expectation by online participants that aspects of the hidden bodies—of, in effect, other participants' "true" identities—can be deduced (if imperfectly) from what is revealed online.

On the other hand, the inability to discern physical cues and the concomitant ambiguities of identity and potential for anonymity do have some effects on online interactions. Participants whose identity offline disadvantages them in some situations may be able to "pass" in the online environment: Spontaneity escapes the harassment he experiences offline because his looks identify him as Asian American. Also, the inability to be certain of one's audience may inhibit the use of hostile or insensitive language. If other changes occur that facilitate greater participation by people of color, they may find these advantages significant. Thus class and race issues permeate online environments. Class status affects people's ability to acquire the physical equipment and skills in its use that are prerequisite to online participation. Online forums such as BlueSky may also provide resources through which already privileged groups can bolster their earning power and social position.

The culture of BlueSky and those of similar online spaces have been constructed by people from particular (relatively homogeneous) backgrounds. As such, these cultural contexts continue to appeal to people from those backgrounds and to re-create particular meanings and understandings. Increases in online diversity will not necessarily change these existing norms.

8 Hungover in the Virtual Pub
Power and Identity Online

> This, right here, and places like it are the real laboratories for the
> future—the place where we find out what interaction will be
> like when it's all through a computer and you're judged on what
> you say and how you say it, and not on who or what you are.
> In RL, if I'm black, or handicapped, or don't have a college degree
> (or even a high school degree), that will affect how I'm treated.
> That matters for nothing here, really.
>
> Carets

On April 12, 1995, I log on to BlueSky and join the crowd in the Falcon.
My year's experience has familiarized me with most of the tools I need to
understand interactions on BlueSky, but tonight's interaction will challenge those skills. As soon as I enter, a couple of participants practically
pounce on me with requests that I "say 'antidisestablishmentarianism' fast
three times" and similar demands. Several participants have temporarily
changed their character names to common punctuation symbols, and at
first I have trouble sorting out who's who. I send a command to the mrd,
causing a hundred lines of text to scroll down my screen so that, desper-
ately, I can try to get the context of the confusing conversation. Of course,
while the mrd text is scrolling, I miss even more of the current conversation. But at least now I know that on this otherwise slow evening, the
people on BlueSky have decided to have some fun with mud features.

Using a command that shows me information for named characters—
including their aliases (often previously used character names), e-mail addresses, or whatever other pieces of information they have selected to
display—I start sorting out the identities of the punctuation symbols surrounding me. Jet renamed himself ".", BJ renamed himself "," and other
participants are currently running through the list of punctuation, determining which symbols the mud server will allow them to adopt as a character name. (Like many computer programs, the server reserves the use
of some punctuation marks to denote particular types of commands.) In
addition to playing with character names, BJ and McKenzie are in the
process of setting up an elaborate chain of triggers. Since any object, including a character, can be preprogrammed to respond to a set phrase with

another text phrase, it is possible to set up long chains of interacting objects, such that one object's textual reaction sets off another object, in a longer version of exchanges such as that between Xena and Xavier that McKenzie provoked, quoted in chapter 5. Tonight, McKenzie and BJ have cooperated in setting up an elaborate Rube Goldberg-esque spam producer, which explains McKenzie's request that I say "antidisestablishmentarianism" three times fast. I at first took this request to be either a test of typing speed or an attempt to determine if I could (or would) use mud client and server commands to speed my response, but in fact, because the request was so outlandish, McKenzie expected me to demand, "Why?"—the magic trigger word needed to start off his and BJ's long chain of nonsense.

For the next hour or so, they continue perfecting and elaborating their contrivance, linking in more and more of the objects in the Falcon. They incorporate several *kill* and *lom* commands into their string, so that when it really gets going, BJ, Florin, and Boontit keep bouncing in and out of the room. (Florin is not currently logged on but apparently was participating in the project earlier and allowed BJ to assume control of his character after he logged off in order to keep his triggers in the set. He later logs back on and rejoins the efforts. Boontit, as described in the previous chapter, is an object, but it has roaming capabilities in addition to text-response capabilities and can be made both to leave and to return to the Falcon.) This leads to several miscues, since sometimes an element in the chain will produce text for an object currently out of the room. So BJ and McKenzie continue to fix problems and figure out where each item needs to be at the beginning of the chain.

Although it never works perfectly, the result is hysterically funny. Most BlueSky participants don't envision the Falcon spatially in any detail, nor do they generally picture each other's faces while they converse online. Yet the social copresence does result in a feeling of space, of being in a "room" with several other people. Thus, the extremely fast automatic phrases generated by several different objects, accompanied by objects "flying" back and forth and characters killing each other and jumping in and out of the room, produce an insane, cartoonlike impression, like a dozen clowns on speed or Saturday morning cartoons played too fast.

Meanwhile, those of us not involved in the intricate debugging process of BJ and McKenzie's spam machine actually attempt to conduct normal conversations. Spontaneity wants to know if I'll be in Berkeley in July, because he's thinking of resuming his frequent travels, this time planning an Amtrak trip around the country. Lenny and Neko discuss a volleyball game in which Lenny accidentally broke another player's glasses while spiking the ball. But these conversations are necessarily brief. The text generated by BJ and McKenzie's play scrolls by so quickly that it is impossible to read as it occurs, making it difficult to sort out the "real" text of characters from the "fake" text of spam. Each time someone new enters the room, McKenzie and BJ badger him or her with bizarre requests, attempting to elicit the opening trigger of "why?" most likely because having someone else set off the chain makes it seem more spontaneous. At one point, McKenzie himself accidentally sets off the chain by asking "why?" during an argument with Locutus about whether or not shorthop's character should be allowed to remain in the room, even though shorthop is not currently logged on.

Finally I tire of the endless repetitions of misfiring triggers and give up on conversation. However, I'm not ready to log off for the night. Several things from school have frustrated me today, and I'm hoping later I can have a serious conversation with somebody. So I retreat to "limbo," BlueSky's entrance room, to wait out the spam fest. Meanwhile I open up a word processing window to take some notes about the evening and another window to my online account to check my e-mail. Periodically, BJ drops into limbo and bounces immediately back out, signaling that back in the Falcon the trigger play continues.

Several minutes later Carets logs on. Although at that point he is a rare BlueSky participant, I recognize Carets from other people's conversations and from his own posts to mud-related newsgroups. I start a conversation with him, addressing him by his offline name, which surprises him, since he doesn't recognize me. I explain my research project, which sparks a long conversation about the social realities of muds, from which I culled the epigraph at the beginning of this chapter (as well as the one at the beginning of chapter 4). Carets opines that I should investigate other muds, where people actually attempt to use mud features to create a new kind of society, rather than just sit around and chat, as happens on BlueSky. He says: "Why do people want to study BlueSky, anyway? It's pretty static and . . . not very cutting edge? To me, it's always seemed like a little bastion of people who don't really care about much else as long as they can still talk to the people they've been talking to for the last 4 years." Carets suggests that the male-dominated, computer-oriented bunch on BlueSky skews my perspective, and he claims that other muds have a far greater diversity of participants.

At that point, we're joined by a character I've never seen before, white.weasel. As if to demonstrate how BlueSky has indeed warped my perspective, I exclaim, "Jeez, who the heck is white.weasel!" With this unconscionably rude expression of the usual BlueSky suspicion toward strangers (perhaps exacerbated by the appearance earlier in the evening of shorthop and a new female character suspected by others to be shorthop), I "welcome" to the conversation a person who turns out to be Carets's wife. We continue (somewhat rockily now) to discuss various aspects of muds, with Carets and white.weasel generally arguing that I'm wrong in my evaluation of the homogeneity of participants on muds, the level of expertise necessary to participate on muds, and many of the other points I make in the previous chapters.

We're gradually joined by more and more people fleeing the spam in the Falcon, marveling at how long BJ and company can keep themselves amused with their trigger chains. As both Kay and BJ drop in and out of the room spouting misfired trigger text, Carets asks, "I'm curious how much of this is just the medium for communication, and how much that differs from other forms that we'd consider more traditional—what's different between this and letter-writing, besides the speed? are there forms of interaction that are *unique* to muds, that you can't find other places? are there things that can only be done on a mud (or related media)?" Carets and others online wonder whether their activities constitute something socially unique and new or just the same old stuff conveyed through a new medium. I present my view that people engage in many of the same types of relationships and identity performances online that they do offline. However, I acknowledge some differences that online participation can make.

Most people on BlueSky would scoff at Carets's statement that mud interactions constitute "laboratories for the future." (Even Carets, who is somewhat given to hyperbole, may not actually believe that in the future interaction will all be through a computer.) However, many would agree with his statements regarding the meaninglessness of race and other aspects of offline identity online. This belief in the liberatory power of cyberspace (expressed by John Perry Barlow in chapter 1) relies on a prejudice model of inequality. In this model, problems such as racism and sexism are based on prejudices, which in turn stem from mere misunderstandings about actual differences between people. Barlow's and Carets's statements represent the belief that when differences such as skin color and gender (as evidenced by physical characteristics) are hidden, as occurs in text-based online forums, prejudice can no longer operate. This stance fails to consider the structural aspects of racism and sexism in the United States as well as the socially structured nature of racialized and gendered identities.

The implication that prejudice disappears in cyberspace also naturalizes its occurrence offline. Neither Barlow nor Carets uses the term "racism," but by saying that race (among other identity attributes) does not matter online, they essentialize the importance of such differences offline. Their stance suggests that it is only natural that people react negatively to people who "look different" from themselves. In other words, text-based interactions online make information about participants' bodies and the clues those provide to gender and race identity unavailable. The view that this allows online interactions to leave behind the problems of racism and sexism implies that such problems must derive entirely from differences in the way people look and the reactions of others to these differences. This bypasses any understanding of race and gender as socially constructed, reduces racism and sexism to (almost automatic) reactions to physical cues, and implies that such reactions cannot be changed except through the removal of those physical cues.

Researchers need to critically evaluate claims that online interaction is more egalitarian or even that it subverts offline hierarchies, noting in particular the source of such claims. As demonstrated by available demographics of online participants, cyberspace remains a realm populated mostly by the white and middle class and is still largely dominated by men. Members of these groups benefit both from the current social structures and, in greater numbers, from online participation and the advantages thereof. Claims regarding the liberatory effects of online participation benefit such participants in a number of ways. If, as claimed, the Internet provides a haven from prejudice and social disadvantage, this relieves the more powerful of the responsibility either to change social structures in the offline world or to change their own behavior and beliefs. This stance toward the online world enacts the U.S. practice of "color blindness" to an even more literal degree. Online participants can "see no evil, hear no evil" and claim to "speak no evil" without making any attempts to create a more inclusive environment, either offline or online. Online forums such as BlueSky potentially become just more exclusive enclaves to which the privileged can retreat.

Researchers who assert that online interaction creates greater identity fluidity or gives participants a new sense of a more fluid or constructed self contribute to this extension and reification of privilege in cyberspace. The representation of online identity performances as qualitatively different from and more fluid than offline performances reproduces an understanding of offline identities as incrementally changing, integrated wholes. In such accounts, the technological mediation of online performance changes identity to something more fluid and exchangeable, suggesting that participants' previously stable identities have been disrupted solely by the capabilities inherent in online interaction. Another version of this account suggests that online performance at least disrupts people's *understandings* of their online performances and, by extension, of their offline identities as well.

In either case, these interpretations suggest that online interaction exerts powerful effects not accomplished by previously existing conditions such as multiple different audiences (Gergen 1991; Goffman 1959); the effects of other mediating technologies such as the telephone (Fischer 1992; Martin 1991) and the television (Meyrowitz 1985); inherent contradictions involved in the accomplishment of identity performances (Butler 1990, 1993); or the experience or observation of drag or similar offline "gender masquerades" (Garber 1992). Such accounts also imply that a participant online can convincingly enact an identity that offline he or she would not be able to manage and suggest that the experience of doing so is profound enough to transform that participant's sense of self both online and off.

Yet existing research regarding online performances does not provide adequate evidence to support assertions that online identity performances subvert hierarchies or disrupt power based on gender, race, and class. In particular, insufficient attention to the power differences inherent in gender, class, and racial identities leads researchers to overestimate the ability of online interactions to displace power hierarchies. Bruckman (1993), Dickel (1995), and Turkle (1995), for instance, confuse limited gender *exchangeability* (the ability to *represent* oneself, with variable success, as a different gender identity from one's offline identity) with gender *malleability* (an understanding of gender as constructed, fluid, and changeable). As Bornstein (1994) and others have pointed out, changing one's gender identity, even offline, can still perpetuate a rigidly binary understanding of the gender system. Bornstein, a radical feminist transsexual, indicates that "most transsexuals opt for the theory that there are men and women and no in-between ground: the agreed-upon gender system.... In my world view, I saw myself as ... something that needed to be ... placed neatly into one of the categories" (64). Bornstein later came to a more fluid understanding of gender identities. But the experience of changing identities, whether through behavioral change or through surgical body modifications, remains for most insufficient in and of itself to bring about this understanding.

The ability to switch representations online may affect people's understandings of the fixity of identity; however, the degree to which it does so depends greatly on their view of their online representations and the value they place on those representations to their self-identity. The ability of male actors to play female parts did not necessarily disrupt the fixed binary gender system of Renaissance England for either the actors or their audience. Other historical examples of gender switching or cross-dressing demonstrate that context and participant understandings need to be carefully considered in the analysis of such actions.

Garber proposes that instances of cross-dressing do "challenge . . . easy notions of binarity" (1992: 10). She suggests that the gender binary has always been fluid and disruptible, with cross-dressing frequently highlighting crises of gender representation. Much as Turkle sees online interactions, Garber views transvestism as "putting into question the very notion of the 'original' and of stable identity" (16). She thus portrays gender hierarchies as inherently unstable and fluid, a useful perspective in that it highlights the intrinsic contradictions contained in our notions of gender. Yet, as Butler points out, "parody by itself is not subversive" (1990: 139). Despite gender's apparent fluidity, hierarchies based on gender (and other aspects of identity, such as race) continue to organize social life. Power continues to be unevenly distributed along axes of identity. If cross-dressing—whether online or off—indeed disrupts identity, pointing to fissures in these very structures of power, then it usually does so only temporarily. Somehow, existing power structures survive the critique, often by reincorporating the liberatory possibilities into new sources of power for those who already had it.

Gender identities may be changed at will more readily online than off. However, regardless of their connection or lack of connection to offline identities, online identities can continue to carry rigidly defined expectations. As Cheris Kramarae states in reference to virtual reality programs, although "as in other kinds of play-acting, women and men can temporarily change their gender, there is little to suggest major overhauls of those so-called sex roles in VR programming" (1995: 40). Stone also finds it "significant that almost without exception a binary gender system is ontologized in virtual space" (1992: 618).

The act of "switching" genders online, although it crosses a gender boundary, need not blur that boundary. As Thorne (1993) indicates in her discussion of the concept of "borderwork," crossing gender boundaries can strengthen those boundaries rather than dissolve them. Differences between these two types of action can be subtle. Offline, the availability of information on a variety of verbal and nonverbal levels allows for more nuance in gender performances. But bodies and the gender identity cues they enact are unavailable in most online interactions. Also, particularly on interactive forums such as chatlines or muds, online interactions often involve short bursts of text. These factors can result in gender identity enactments online that rely to an even greater degree on stereotypical notions of identity than offline enactments do. Under these circumstances, as in Thorne's study of children's play, gender enactments online become "stylized moments [that] evoke recurring themes that are deeply rooted in our cultural conceptions of gender, and they suppress awareness of patterns that contradict and qualify them" (1994: 66).

While some participants may experience changes in their perceptions of identity, my research on BlueSky demonstrates that the experience of online communication does not in and of itself produce this type of change. Furthermore, perceiving identity as constructed *online* need not lead an online participant to an understanding of identity as constructed generally. To the extent that mudders bracket their mud performances as separate from the rest of their lives, such performances are unlikely to change understandings of identity greatly. Despite theorists such as Goffman, Gergen, and Butler having pointed out that identity in general is fluid and continually constructed, few people view their offline identities in these terms. Thus they may not view their online identities as inherently fluid either, or they may cordon off online identity performances from their sense of self in such a way that online identity fluidity does not affect offline identity perceptions. The fact that participants such as Fred/Amnesia and Toni/Phillipe can and do make such a separation between their online and offline personae suggests that the mere experience of online identity fluidity does not necessarily disrupt or subvert offline understandings of identity.

Whatever disruptions do occur for online participants cannot then be attributed to the technological mediation alone or to particular aspects of online culture(s). I argue against the technologically determinist view, expressed by both participants and researchers, that online interaction significantly changes either participants' experiences and understandings of identity or the power structures based on identities such as race, gender, and class. While the conditions of online communication do change some aspects of people's experience of identities, people continue to view their identities as whole and consistent and in some cases do specific interactional work to maintain this view. Forums such as BlueSky provide a new kind of meeting place, but far from solving some of the problems of the offline world, they may in fact intensify those problems by providing a forum in which the relatively privileged can escape to an arena where their privilege remains relatively hidden (to themselves as well as others).

Online relations do not occur in a cultural vacuum. However much people may desire to leave behind the constraints of their offline cultural backgrounds and social identities, their social interactions online remain grounded in understandings and contexts that intersect with offline realities. This is not to say that there are no differences between online and offline interactions or that the ambiguities of identity that obtain online might not present some possibilities for challenging identity expectations. However, ambiguities deriving from the communication of identity through text and the enhanced ability to hide identity characteristics in such communications do not nullify expectations concerning "real" offline identities and their online counterparts.

The various online forums available to an elite few do constitute a different form of social arena and provide opportunities for new types of identity performances as well as tangible and intangible benefits for participants. Turkle (1995) details various potential psychological benefits (and harm) for participants using muds and similar forums to work through identity issues. The experiences of BlueSky participants certainly point to a variety of benefits unique to online participation, including a degree of continuity in friendships sometimes difficult to obtain for the mobile young of the middle classes; courtship opportunities (although not as many as some participants might wish); various work-related benefits, including a network that provides powerful employment and continued job assistance; and, finally, more closely related to identity performance, the ability to escape harassment based on gender (a benefit Lisa indicated that BlueSky in particular provides) or race (as Spontaneity pointed out). These benefits demonstrate the potential utility of online participation but also highlight the connections between such participation and a young, mobile, middle-class population such as that found on BlueSky. Not only does this segment of the population disproportionately enjoy such benefits now, but also the connection of online participation to particular types of work and family situations as well as to particular gendered, raced, and classed subcultures suggests that online participation of the style practiced on BlueSky is never likely to benefit as large a segment of the population as many pundits, politicians, and scholars currently hope.

Most BlueSky participants offer no opinion about the future of online participation. They do recognize the benefits they obtain from their current online interaction, and their analogy of the space to offline spaces such as clubs or bars also implicitly recognizes the limited nature of those benefits. Despite privileging offline contact, BlueSky participants experience BlueSky as a place where they hang out with friends. The character of the social space of BlueSky and people's understanding of that space reflect existing offline identity understandings and social patterns. I close with Ulysses' interpretation of BlueSky:

> I think the main point that I would like to make is that it's hard for me to tell how different it is from people socializing in person. I think to myself how different would it be from . . . do we really do a lot of stuff that fundamentally couldn't take place in a neighborhood bar— maybe a neighborhood bar in a college neighborhood or on campus somewhere? There's all this wacky posing and stuff, but you can partially do that [offline]. I really wonder whether or not there's anything fundamentally different. Sometimes I think there is, and sometimes I think there isn't. Usually I think it's not all that different. It's fun to play with it as a medium, you know, interactive text is a great medium. But I don't know whether the *content* is all that different.

Epilogue
The "Where Are They Now?" FAQ

As I write this in the late summer of 2001, BlueSky, strictly speaking, no longer exists. However, most of the participants described herein still hang out together on a mud run primarily by Carets. Whenever I speak about my work on BlueSky, people have many questions about the current status of the mud and its participants, so I have provided this epilogue in a form commonly used online—as answers to frequently asked questions (FAQ):

Q: Do the BlueSky participants still mud as frequently?

A: For the most part, no. Many are still very active online, but overall, the mud participation has decreased somewhat. The patterns of activity remain similar, with most participants logging on from work during their normal work day.

Q: Do you still hang out with the BlueSky participants?

A: Yes, although not nearly as much. On the one hand, I made many friends during my research, and I like to keep up with them. On the other hand, without the motivation of my research, I am less likely to stick around when people are abusive. Furthermore, unlike most other BlueSky participants, my work can only rarely be done while socializing online.

Q: Didn't the BlueSky participants suffer during the recent economic downturn in the technological sector?

A: No, not really. Although the failure of many Internet start-ups and other "dot.coms" received considerable press in 2001, most BlueSky participants work for more established companies. Those who have changed jobs have generally had no problem finding work. Some BlueSky participants own quite a bit of stock in computer technology companies, and some have seen their holdings decrease considerably in value. However, this has had little effect on their day-to-day lives.

Q: Are the "heterosexual dropouts" still celibate?

A: As far as I know, most of the people who identified themselves as having given up on heterosexual relationships still do not participate in such relationships. BJ is the exception. He has a steady relationship with a woman who was also a participant on BlueSky.

Q: What other kinds of life changes have the BlueSky participants experienced?

A: Since I finished with most of the writing of this book, several more participants have gotten married and some have had children. Even more have bought houses. About a dozen participants now own their own homes, with some now owning a second home after selling the first. One participant owns and lives in a small apartment building.

Q: Did your participation on BlueSky have any effect on the participants' views of women or of feminism?

A: Some participants were sympathetic to feminism prior to my research and remain so. The others also maintain their previous convictions and opinions. So far as I can tell my effect on them has been negligible. Although I remain committed to feminism, if anything, their influence on me, my attitudes and behaviors, has been greater than my influence on them.

Appendix A
Basic Mud Commands

The following commands are formatted slightly differently on different muds, depending on the particular mud server being used. My examples are from one particular format, just to give a feel for how the programs work.

Say: Generates text that begins with the character name followed by the word "says." On most muds, this command can be accomplished by merely typing a double quotation mark (") before the text one wishes to "say." For example:
I type: *"hi everybody!*
The program displays to me: *You say, "hi everybody!"*
Everybody else sees: *Copperhead says, "hi everybody!"*

Pose: Eliminates the word "says" after the character name, enabling participants to portray themselves as performing other types of actions. It is usually abbreviated with a colon (:). Example:
I type: *:is feeling really tired tonight.*
Everybody (including me) sees: *Copperhead is feeling really tired tonight.*

Page: Sends a message to someone in another room. Example:
I type: *p Formosa = What's happening with you?*
The program displays to me: *You paged Formosa with "What's happening with you?"*
Formosa sees: *Copperhead pages: What's happening with you?*
Or, for a "paged pose," I type: *p Formosa = :nods.*
I see: *Long distance to Formosa: Copperhead nods.*
Formosa sees: *From afar, Copperhead nods.*

Whisper: Sends a message to a specific person in the same room. No other participants on the mud are able to see this message. (However, it and all communications are theoretically available to a wizard with high enough "clearance" on the mud.)

I type: *w Misty = How do I change my &info?*

The program displays to me: *You whispered, "How do I change my &info?" to Misty.*

Misty sees: *Copperhead whispers "How do I change my &info?"* For clarity's sake and to avoid the potentially discomforting feeling for readers of having words put in their mouths, in all cases where I've included logs of my own whispers to other participants, I've edited the above format to look like what the other participant saw, rather than what I saw (as it appears in my logs).

Mutter: Sends a message to everybody in the same room except a single designated person, who does not see the message.

I type: *mutter Abigail = I think she's a bit cranky tonight.*

Everybody, including me but excepting Abigail, sees: *Copperhead mutters "I think she's a bit cranky tonight." to everybody but Abigail.*

Look: When just "look" is typed, the description for the room one is in is displayed. One can also type "look" followed by the name of a character or object in order to view objects and other people's descriptions.

In addition to these commands, there are a variety of basic commands that allow the user to see who is logged on to the mud and how long since they've been active; to locate where people are on the mud; to set various automatic messages; to send e-mail type messages to others on the mud; and so forth. There are also commands that allow one to build rooms, create objects, and so forth. The particulars of these commands are not necessary to understand the examples I give of mud events. Some commands, particularly more sophisticated programming commands, are preceded by the symbol @, which therefore also appears frequently in mud conversation.

Mud participants use many abbreviations that are also in common use in other online forums. Very few people can type as fast as they can speak, so devices and abbreviations that save keystrokes are common (although BlueSky participants actually use these much less often than people on many other forums do). All mud abbreviations and their definitions are contained in the glossary. The following is just a short list of frequently used abbreviations: imo, imho, imnho, lol, ltns, oic, re, and rotfl (see the glossary for their definitions).

Character names may also be abbreviated. My character name "Copperhead" is usually shortened to CH. Most names are abbreviated to no more than four letters, regardless of how many they started with.

Another cultural term on BlueSky, "mav," describes mistakes in command use that result in text intended for one person being sent to many or in text formatted for a pose being represented using "say." Following are several examples of mavs. In the first example, I intended to use the *pose* command to transmit the text "Copperhead waves" but accidentally used the *say* command instead:

Copperhead says, "waves."

Here, I intended to whisper something to henri but instead sent it to Scrounge:

My command: *w Scrounge = so who's this woman Scrounge is bringing to the party?*

Scrounge sees: *Copperhead whispers "so who's this woman Scrounge is bringing to the party?"*

henri, the intended recipient, sees nothing.

Another type of whisper mav can result from people's practice of leaving a colon up on the screen with the intent of transmitting something to the group at large through *pose.* Then, overlooking the colon, they send a whisper to someone in the room, which results in everyone in the room seeing something like the following:

Misty w Abigail = well, I think you're pretty cute too! :)

The term "mav" refers to these and any similar slips, which can cause considerable embarrassment.

Appendix B
"Mudders in the Mist"

ETHNOGRAPHY IN A "PARTLY COMPATIBLE" SETTING

TEXTUAL CONGRUENCIES: MUDS AND ETHNOGRAPHY

Muds have been termed a type of "textual virtual reality" (Stone 1991). As in the graphic two- and three-dimensional immersive environments more commonly understood to fit the term "virtual reality,"[1] people on muds, through both technological and social means, create a feeling of place and presence. On muds, they do so in part through textual descriptions of locations, objects, bodies, and actions. This creates an odd congruence between my topic of study and my means of studying it, for ethnographies also can be seen as forms of textual virtual reality. Ethnographers too attempt to create a feeling of "being there" by providing "thick descriptions" (Geertz 1973) of places, objects, bodies, and interactions.

Mudding and ethnography also intersect in the practice of writing, which Clifford describes as "central to what anthropologists do both in the field and thereafter" (1986: 2). In the study of people's online interactions, both the ethnographer and participants write "in the field." An online ethnography, such as this one, is in part writing about writing. However, on social muds, participants do not necessarily perceive themselves as creating a written work. (Role players more often specifically view their activity as a form of interactive literature.) While the interactive written dialogues of mudders thus resemble conversation more than epistolary communication, when read after the fact as logs, these dialogues become flat. The reader has no investment in their direction or continuation and does not share participants' knowledge of the dense history of associations attached to particular phrases and habits of speech. For long-term mudders, such associations build up a continually expanding accretion of nuance and meaning that compensates in part for the loss of cues available in face-to-

233

face interactions. Readers of logs, on the other hand, cannot share participants' understandings of the interactions represented in the logs I quote herein.[2] One of my tasks as ethnographer, then, is to bridge the gap between participant and reader understandings. I do this in part by explaining some of the cultural history of BlueSky. I also attempt to reattach online interactions to the offline world by providing information about the offline contexts of these interactions.

Ethnographies routinely provide brief physical descriptions when introducing new "characters." Because I met my interviewees face-to-face, I am able to provide physical descriptions of them, despite the fact that most of my interactions with them occurred online. (Character descriptions also exist on muds but do not necessarily reflect the physical description of a participant's offline appearance.) The very fact that physical descriptions of people help to give the reader of an ethnography a sense of the people written about reveals something about identity, perhaps *especially* in virtual environments. We need something to help us cognitively organize our knowledge about each new person. For people online who have not met each other, character names can serve this function, although imperfectly. (As I discuss in chapter 6, people tend to forget details about others with whom they interact only online.) Having a face to associate with the name helps in remembering that person and his or her identity.

Online participants reflect this preference for face-to-face contact. BlueSky participants, like participants in many other long-term online groups, make great efforts to meet each other, even if only very briefly. Thus, in describing my interviewees, I duplicate to some extent a process they themselves engage in as they get to know each other over time, "fleshing out" the information provided by their online interactions or, in the case here, the information presented in my log and interview excerpts.

However, my descriptions and their emphasis on physical characteristics of identity risk reifying the very hierarchies I seek to critique in my examination of the importance of race, class, age, gender, and sexualities in online interaction. By describing people's race and gender as I introduce them in the ethnography, I potentially reassert the belief that such aspects of identity are inherent in the physical body and as such exist as presocial facts. I wish to argue against this belief, illuminating instead the myriad practices that socially construct identity and demonstrating how identity markers such as class and age are performed. Because I do make arguments here about identity, I feel the need to give readers a sense of how people define themselves and are defined (or are potentially definable) by others, both online and off. While race, class, and gender are socially constructed, they are nevertheless "real" in their effects.

In face-to-face encounters most people usually assign such categories very quickly, although not always permanently. Online, the process of "figuring out" others' identities can take longer. In the meantime, people make assumptions, however temporary. As I demonstrate throughout these chapters, the default assumption that everybody online is male, white, heterosexual, under forty, and works with computers has consequences for online participants.

PERSONAL CONGRUENCIES

Several aspects of my own identity facilitated both my ability to participate in the group and the progress of my research. For instance, my family background is similar to that of most of the group members. My father worked for many years as a computer programmer, and, as for many other BlueSky participants, this meant that I was exposed to computers at an early age. Further, although most participants are younger than I and most are male whereas I am female, I, like most of the others, am white.

Cultural factors within the BlueSky group also facilitated my research. My fears about the social character of the space and my desire as a re- searcher to understand the culture before participating actively assisted my entrance into BlueSky's culture, since starting out quietly observing is precisely the behavior regulars expect of a "newbie." In addition, BlueSky participants place a high value on education and the furtherance of knowledge. Corwin, one of the wizards responsible for running BlueSky, stated during his interview: "I've never been interviewed about [muds]. I wouldn't say I actively avoid it, but if I had to I might. This [interview] is obviously different, because I respect academic pursuits. I have very little respect for reporters." BlueSky participants in general hold education in high regard and tend therefore to give me the benefit of the doubt even when they disagree with my interpretations.

Other BlueSky cultural features dovetailed amazingly well with my research aims. The value attached to the exchange of personal information and cultural practices such as roll calls, which institutionalize the exchange of personal information, often made it unnecessary for me to ask for such information as salary ranges and ages. The desire of BlueSky participants to meet up with people whenever possible also set a precedent that made it easy for me to make interview contacts in various cities. Like other

BlueSky people, I arranged my "tour" through the e-mail list medmenham, soliciting both places to stay and people to interview.

ETHNOGRAPHIC STRATEGIES

In keeping with standards promulgated by professional organizations such as the American Sociological Association (although also aware of difficulties in implementing standards of informed consent in the process of fieldwork, as discussed by Thorne [1980]), I began my research with the intention of openly declaring my research activities.[3] However, as other online researchers have reported (see, for instance, Cherny 1999), keeping online participants aware of a research project can prove difficult. With no visual presence, I could not enact the role of an obvious researcher. For instance, people could not see me taking notes. Nor could they tell, without my informing them, that I was recording all text on my screen. My attempts to alert people to my role as a researcher through textual descriptions of my character met with very limited success, since BlueSky participants, unlike participants on some other muds, pay little attention to character descriptions. I tried instead to bring the topic of my research into the conversation periodically and to inform people as I met them. During sensitive conversations, I sometimes reminded people that I was "logging" (i.e., recording and saving) all text.

After I had been on BlueSky for over a year, I began to take for granted that people knew what I was doing there. Occasionally, this assumption proved unwarranted, but most regulars knew of my research. "Copperhead's thesis" became an occasional topic of conversation on BlueSky, further spreading the word to participants as well as providing me with feedback regarding interpretations I discussed with them. Such discussions also sometimes served as a reminder that the online space of BlueSky is not completely private, as in the following exchange, quoted in chapter 6:

> Locutus says "Xena, quote PAL"
> Xena says "I once heard PAL say 'I wish to erase all traces of my existence
>   here. Am I being unclear or what?'"
> henri says "erase all trace of his existence? TOO LATE BUDDY YOU'RE IN CH'S
>   THESIS NOW"

henri's mention of my thesis in a conversation completely unrelated to research illustrates the general awareness people had of being observed. It also signals an understanding that this could potentially change participant relationships. PAL was attempting to leave BlueSky completely, but henri notes that his presence would remain recorded in my research record. Of course, this excerpt also demonstrates that participants' ability to store quotes similarly thwarts the wishes of those desiring to disappear completely from the group. PAL was not present during this conversation and was unable to "erase all traces" of his BlueSky existence, not only because of my thesis, but also because of the robot Xena's quoting feature and others' memories of him.

BUT NOT LIKE BUGS!

Several regulars attempted to make sure that others knew they were being observed. henri, a long-term participant and one of the most active regulars, supported my project from early on. Highly respected on BlueSky for his wit and intelligence, henri contributes more to the mud environment than most other BlueSky participants. The hangout room he built is one of the group's favorites. His high status in the group and the early interest he took in me and my research were instrumental both to my being accepted as a newcomer on BlueSky and to the acceptance of my research project. In addition, as Traweek notes, "key informants are crucial; they are people with whom one can try out tentative interpretations and hypotheses" (1988: 13). henri's introspective disposition, his long history of very active mudding with the BlueSky group, and his place at the emotional center of the social group made him particularly useful in this regard.[4]

No participant indicated that he or she cooperated with my research because of henri's approval. However, his sometimes subtle influence undoubtedly had a great influence on several aspects of the research project. One of two participants who refused face-to-face interviews changed her mind after henri discussed the issue with her (albeit too late for me to schedule the interview). Another participant commented on my success in acquiring interview subjects (including himself), saying, "I myself am wondering how you pulled it off—that you've actually gotten so many people to talk to you . . . Basically I think the trick was that you just sort of hung around and didn't piss anybody off . . . And the fact that you can converse in an easy way with the regulars, with some of the social leaders like henri."

henri's high status thus made his support particularly important to me. His concerns about the research project also influenced the conduct of research, in part because of his intercession on my behalf with other participants and in part just through his own mention of research issues during general interaction. For instance, henri's concern for privacy issues led him to assist me in making sure that others knew of my role as a researcher.

> Locutus says "wait, is copperhead the latest nom de plume of pez?"
> henri says "not that I know of"
> Locutus says "so who are you, ch"
> henri says "CH is some sociologist that is studying us like bugs in ether bottles"
> Locutus says "excellent!"
> henri wiggles his antennae
> Copperhead says "Not like Bugs!"
> henri tried to tell CH we're the most atypical of mudders, but she doesn't care

As the "bugs" metaphor signifies, participants had concerns about being research subjects and about the connotations of this for their status as human beings. Wary of sociological generalizations, they assert their uniqueness, as when henri suggests BlueSky people are the most atypical of mudders. People continued to tease me with bug and other animal metaphors at various points during my research on BlueSky. On another occasion, after I objected to being characterized as an entomologist, henri altered his introduction somewhat.

> henri says "Copperhead"
> Copperhead says "hi"
> Locutus feels strangely like a bug in a bottle
> Copperhead looks strangely bug-eyed.
> henri says "Barbie, Ch is our sociologist studying us, but not like bugs"
> Florin says "studying?"
> Florin killed Copperhead!

Florin's initial reaction to hearing of my research was to "kill" my character, expressing (probably jokingly) the suspicion many BlueSky participants feel toward journalists and researchers.

As more people became aware of my research, my attempts to explain what I was doing sometimes resulted in humorous interpretations by BlueSky participants. In the following conversation (three months after my entrance to BlueSky), I tell Beryl, a BlueSky regular, about my research. Two other regulars, Florin and Roger Pollack, who already know about the research project, chime in with their interpretation of my activities, comparing them to those of Dr. Dian Fossey, the famous gorilla researcher.

Copperhead is doing research here on BlueSky and other MUDs, Beryl.
Florin says "we're like FLIES in BOTTLES"
Florin says "RATS in CAGES"
Copperhead gives Florin some ether.
Florin says "she's like that chick with the apes."
Florin says "mudders in the mist"
Copperhead laughs at Florin
Roger Pollack goes wuh wuh wuh wooooo eeeeh eeeh eeh and scratches his
   head.
Florin WE'VE ACCEPTED HER LIKE SHE'S ONE OF US
Florin GROOM ME

Here BlueSky participants characterize me as a primate researcher and themselves as again less than human, although perhaps the shift from bugs to primates indicates a more positive evaluation of my endeavors! This makes light of potential uneasiness regarding being studied but still expresses the potential imbalance of power between researcher and researched.

As Stanley and Wise point out, "The researched are vulnerable in the sense that their lives, feelings, understandings, become grist to the research mill and may appear, in goodness knows what mangled form, at the end of the research process" (1993: 177). They suggest, as partial amelioration, that researchers share the vulnerability of their subjects by "[locating themselves] within research and writing . . . placing 'us' in the research as well as 'them.' . . . If *they* are vulnerable, then *we* must be prepared to show ourselves as vulnerable too" (177, emphasis in original). Similarly, Rosaldo suggests that "because researchers are necessarily both somewhat impartial and somewhat partisan, somewhat innocent and somewhat complicit, their readers should be as informed as possible about what the observer was in a position to know and not know" (1989: 69).

I intend both this appendix and the descriptions of my own reactions and experiences sprinkled throughout the main chapters to go some way toward providing such information as well as balancing the vulnerability of my "subjects." These, along with the discussions and disagreements with participants concerning my interpretations of their culture also appearing herein (see especially chapter 4), allow the reader to consider my perspective and vantage point and evaluate the view I provide of BlueSky's social world.

I also solicited comments from participants and mailed out thirty copies of the dissertation to participants who requested it. Most of their subsequent corrections concerned minor errors and matters of history, although two participants sent me long and detailed critiques. henri provided several valuable points of historical and technical clarification. In addition, in keeping with his tendency to look out always for other members of the group, he took issue with a few of my personal characterizations. Bilerific-Sid took me to task for not seeking interviews with more participants from working-class backgrounds and knowledgeably critiqued my theoretical conceptions of race.[5]

The power imbalance between me as researcher and the BlueSky participants as researched is complicated by our mostly similar, but somewhat different, social locations and by the BlueSky participants' understandings and evaluations of social research. For instance, some of the reactions to my research project stem from the status of BlueSky participants as members of a computer-literate, net-savvy subculture. Many mudders, and net participants in general, have a negative attitude toward social research. BlueSky participants are perhaps more suspicious than most. Mudders view survey research, the type of research they most often associate with sociology, with particular suspicion. This reflects a connection between the mudding subculture and computer culture in general. For instance, the *Hacker's Dictionary*, a book compiling a large body of net jargon and culture, defines "social science number" as "A statistic that is content-free, or nearly so. A measure derived via methods of questionable validity from data of a dubious and vague nature" (Raymond 1991: 327). This suspicion of survey research was compounded during the course of my research by the increasing appearance on the mudding newsgroups of poorly thought out and badly executed surveys that mudding college students inflicted on their fellow mudders, hoping to glean a term paper from their favorite pastime. I frequently had to describe my research as "similar to anthropology" in order to distance it from such fly-by-night research projects and from an understanding of sociological research as solely quantitative.

Ethnography, although sometimes characterized pejoratively as "anecdotal" by members of computer cultures, nevertheless garners more respect than other forms of social research. In part this may be because attention paid by anthropologists to online social groups gives such groups autonomous status analogous to that of the (presumed discrete) cultures that anthropologists traditionally study. This status fits well with many online participants' view of cyberspace as a separate reality or sovereign "country" (as expressed by John Perry Barlow and quoted in chapter 1). Also, use of anthropological researchers in the computer industry has increased in recent years. Managers and programmers within that industry have recognized that to cash in on the increasing popularity of online socializing, they need an understanding of social processes and factors affecting success and failure of online groups and social spaces.[6]

ETHICS IN ONLINE RESEARCH

The conditions of online participation create new problems for the ethical conduct of research. Researchers are beginning to take stock of these problems, with little agreement among them as yet, as illustrated in a recent special issue of the *Information Society* on "the ethics of fair practices for collecting social science data in cyberspace" (Thomas 1996). King (1996), for instance, points out that putatively public online forums may be experienced and understood as private by participants, who intend messages posted therein for the benefit of other group members and do not expect their words to travel to other arenas. He recommends stripping all identifying information from list and newsgroup postings. Boehlefeld (1996), while agreeing with King's suggestions for protection of research subjects, disagrees with King (as well as with Waskul and Douglas 1996) that computer-mediated communication necessarily blurs boundaries between public and private. She adds the concept of "obscurity," noting that few personal messages sent in "public" forums catch the notice of those other than for whom they are intended.

Gurak (1997), on the other hand, differentiates between interactive chat environments and bulletin board postings, suggesting that the latter constitute copyrighted material that should be credited to individual authors. However, she recognizes the conflict between this principle and concerns of privacy and therefore adopts a compromise strategy in which she cites all information *except* the last name of the poster.

I based my decision to change BlueSky participants' online pseudonyms in part on the conclusion, based on my research, that such pseudonyms are important "identity pegs" that enter into real and important online interactions and relationships. In my experience, objections to the provision of "pseudo-pseudonyms" in research reports often come from people who do not view online forums such as muds as "real" social spaces. But as discussed in a recent publication by the American Association for the Advance of Science, "Ethical and Legal Aspects of Human Subjects Research on the Internet": "Researchers have traditionally disregarded pseudonyms as real identities and have quoted them directly along with the names of the newsgroups in their published research. Yet, one workshop participant observed that online, people invest in their pseudonyms the way they invest in their real identities within a physical community" (Frankel and Siang 1999: 5–6). Similarly, Cherny argues that although a pseudonym "might seem to be sufficient in itself to protect MUD players from an invasion of privacy," this is in practice not the case. "Use of real character names can affect the MUDders' experiences in their community" (1999: 311). She cites the well-known example of a case of "netrape" on LambdaMOO, in which one participant used mud commands to simulate the rape of several characters. A newspaper publication of the account of that incident (Dibbell 1993) included actual pseudonyms of participants and resulted in a significant amount of unwanted attention from outsiders and newcomers toward these participants.

Changing online pseudonyms does not provide perfect protection and remains a controversial strategy, despite its similarity to long-standing ethnographic practices in protecting research subjects. Allen, for instance, adopts a quite different stance toward online participant subjects of social science research, suggesting that the technological capabilities of search and retrieval of online information negate such strategies as replacing pseudonyms. She points out that any participant on the social mud she studied can search for key words in the texts she reproduced in her dissertation, thereby discovering the identity of her interviewees. She argues that replacing the pseudonyms of research subjects on muds and similar forums "constitute[s] a facile protection, rather than a real protection" (1996b: 181).

Allen's argument illustrates how online communication can blur distinctions between ephemeral speech and persistent text. However, the problem she identifies of the "insider" knowledge of some potential readers is not new to studies of online forums. Researchers can rarely protect the identities of the researched so thoroughly that even their own mothers (or, more to the point, fellow participants) won't know them. My discussion of some of the unique features of the BlueSky group will probably result in the ability of other experienced "dinos" to guess some of the identities of my respondents, and I realize that most BlueSky participants would be able to recognize each other. Yet I disagree with Allen that changing the names of the forum and its participants thereby constitutes merely a facile protection. Like Gurak's strategy of providing everything except the last name of posters to online forums, replacing forum and participant online names provides at least an initial barrier to the idly curious.[7] I provide this barrier in accord also with the wishes of people on BlueSky. During discussions of my efforts to protect their identities, most participants indicated a much stronger interest in keeping these identities hidden from offline acquaintances and the idly curious and professed not to care if other mudders might discern their identities.

Indeed, one difficulty that arose with the pseudonyms involved respondents themselves defeating the protections I extended to them, not only for themselves, but also for other participants. For instance, on several occasions Jet issued roll calls on the topic of "your name in Copperhead's thesis." As soon as they received copies of the dissertation, Jet and Carets created an object on BlueSky that provided a key to almost all the pseudonyms I used. (I objected to this, pointing out that it could potentially reveal identities to outsiders as well as regulars, and after much discussion, the object was removed.)[8]

In addition to protection of individual privacy, groups also need protection from harmful effects of research. As demonstrated in chapter 5, online groups have special vulnerabilities, and BlueSky participants value their group's privacy. Reid (1996) found that even the most careful consultation with research subjects and compliance with their wishes could result in harm to the group. When the online publication of her research resulted in interest by other researchers in a mud she had studied for survivors of sexual abuse, she consulted with members of the mud, who agreed to allow additional researchers access to the group. The increased scrutiny caused problems for the feel of the mud's social space, making it all but useless for its original purposes. As Reid argues, these problems are never completely solvable but require researchers to continue to struggle with attempts both to present good social research and to protect the subjects thereof.

VIOLATING THE "PRIME DIRECTIVE": FEMINIST INTERVENTIONS

Star Trek viewers will recognize the above subtitle as referring to the Federation's restriction against interference in other cultures, a requirement usually honored in the breach by the *Enterprise* crew (especially in the original *Star Trek* television series). Like the *Enterprise*'s exploratory mission, ethnographic practice has roots in colonialist projects. As Sarah Projansky states:

> The Federation's Prime Directive outlaws interference in the internal affairs of other (read: less-evolved) species and cultures. This paternalistic isolationism, however, creates a paradox that the Enterprise's ethnographic mission "to go where no one has gone before" heightens. The socially evolved Federation tries to avoid influencing other cultures

directly, even while it must have some form of contact with them in order to amass as much knowledge about those other cultures as possible, affirming its own superiority over them in the process. This paradox often leads to (only sometimes) thinly veiled rescue missions that test the boundaries of the Prime Directive. (1996: 33)

Projansky's description of the Federation's interests echoes critiques of traditional anthropological ethnographies. Anthropologists in the nineteenth and early twentieth centuries, like the crew members of the *Enterprise*, were enjoined to preserve the "authenticity" of their studied cultures, collecting and preserving portraits of "endangered" cultures. Rosaldo points out that "the context of imperialism and colonial rule shaped both the monumentalism of timeless accounts of homogeneous cultures and the objectivism of a strict division of labor between the 'detached' ethnographer and 'his native' " (1989: 31). Accounts that attempt either to authenticate (or present "authentic" views of) a culture or to save it from encroaching technological change risk falling into this trap of condescending imperialism.

My own rescue mission, not exactly colonizing, although perhaps similarly compromised, has focused on addressing and critiquing problems shared within the various overlapping subcultures both I and the BlueSky participants inhabit. This has created tension for both myself and those I'm researching concerning the theory and experience of doing research as a feminist researcher in a group made up mostly of people who do not consider themselves feminists and who are in some cases hostile to feminism. BlueSky participants' awareness of my feminism, my critiques of various BlueSky practices, and the implicit charge of sexism that these critiques sometimes carried have brought these issues into conversation.

Schacht (1997) found himself in a somewhat similar situation during his study of a rugby team. He found many of the cultural practices of the team extremely offensive. For this reason, he termed his research site an "incompatible setting." During his research he remained open with subjects about his research project but not about his feminism. One of Schacht's most important insights involves his discussion of the correspondence between his own feelings and behavior and that of the rugby jocks. He points out the importance of doing research that exposes the complicity of all men in masculinist hierarchies. Given this complicity, the term "incompatible setting" ironically fails to acknowledge the implication of participant-observers in the activities in which they both participate and observe.

I suggest that most (if not all) research sites can be termed "partly compatible" rather than "incompatible" settings. In Schacht's case, his subjects could assume his agreement with them because of their perception of his masculinity and his silence concerning his feminism. While more open about my feminism, I, like Schacht, tend to "go along to get along" with the other participants on BlueSky. While I sometimes openly criticize sexist expressions and behaviors, I often let such aspects of BlueSky's culture go by without comment and even participate in some of them. In a previous account (Kendall 1996), for instance, I describe a form of sexist joking along with my discovery that I'm one of only two women on BlueSky who participate in that form of joke. Like many participant-observers, I have found myself caught between my own cultural allegiances to feminism and my attempts to join and respect the culture of BlueSky.

When I did attempt to offer critiques of sexism or racism on BlueSky, such critiques generally had little effect. As demonstrated by the discussion of the term "spike 'er" in chapter 4, some participants disputed my interpretation, and others agreed or partly agreed. Yet, over time little changed overall, nor did participants appear to behave any differently in my presence. Jet recently commented to me that he was surprised it was possible to do participant observation without changing the group studied, yet in his estimation, that had indeed been the situation in this case. During that same conversation, McKenzie asked whether the reverse had occurred, that is, whether BlueSky had changed me, and I acknowledged that I have been changed more by BlueSky than it has been changed by me. While I certainly already possessed a love of wordplay and a somewhat raunchy sense of humor, BlueSky provided a forum for the exercise of those, which has affected my behavior offline as well.

The importance of the example of my partial cooptation into BlueSky culture is that it exposes two crucial aspects of that culture. First, there are real advantages to "being one of the boys." Second, as I argue in several chapters herein, online cultures can be even more resistant to change than those offline. This suggests that, far from providing an escape from offline cultural problems such as racism and sexism, online forums can provide an arena for retrenchment of these attitudes.

If this ethnography is itself a textual virtual reality, it is not the same kind of textual virtual reality as a mud, nor does it derive from the same cultural understandings as those of mudders. As Karen McCarthy Brown has recounted, ethnography is "an exercise in bridge building" (1991: 14). The ethnographer builds bridges between her own academic world and the people she studies. She also bridges her own interpretation of the studied culture and the presumed culture of her readers. As Brown points out, the ethnographer therefore remains between cultures and not fully of the world studied.

The stories I tell here are not the stories the people of BlueSky would tell. My concerns, as a feminist sociologist, mostly do not match the concerns of the younger, male computer professionals who form most of the group hanging out on BlueSky. Some of the differences between their concerns and mine are apparent in my descriptions of their lives. I also include examples of discussions in which participants disagree with my interpretations of their online world. My hope is that such disagreements reflect the distance between our worldviews rather than the imperfection of my translation.

Appendix C

A Grand Am comes squealing around the corner and stops.

Itchy[1] says "It's equal to only .6 USAs"

Corwin climbs out of the Grand Am.

Corwin has arrived.

henri says "Michael J./A. Fox was whinign about how hard it is for canadians to get work permits in the US"

henri says "Corwin"

Corwin says "henri"

login: On: fnord

Levon says "Corwin"

henri says "MA"

Itchy says "Corwin"

Levon says "It's a lot harder the other way around"

Levon says "Well, to get permanent work it is, not contract crap"

Nightcrawler says "Corwin? get the machines back working?"

Nightcrawler says "Alisa was here telling on you."

Corwin says "yeah. it sucked."

Locutus says "SHOW ME: IT SUCKED"

Corwin says "SUUUUUURVEY SAYS!"

Corwin I X I I X I I X I

Rostopovich says "SHOW ME: I SUCK"

Corwin says "SURVEY SAYS!"

Corwin I X I

Locutus' day has been a three-X day as well

Rostopovich says "uh, wait a minute"

fnord says ". . . there I was, naked and exhausted, miles from shore. Dolphins taunted me for hours" fnord has arrived.

Itchy says "SHOW ME: GREAT MUD MOMENTS"

Corwin says "SURVEY SAYS!"

Rostopovich says "that CAN'T be right"

Corwin I X I

fnord says "evening"

Rachel has disconnected.

Ulysses says "augh I don't wanna go to Washington tomorrow"

henri says "AIE SHOW ME: SPAM"

Itchy says "I sincerely love that, Corwin"

Rostopovich says "maybe that answer is for the purity test sense of 'suck'"

fnord heh Rosty

Locutus says "SHOW ME: PURITY TEST SENSE OF 'SUCK'"

Corwin says "SURVEY SAYS!"

Corwin I X I

henri LAUGHS at 'walter and stern'

Rostopovich says "SHOW ME: GAMMA-RAY BOMBARDMENT"

Corwin says "SURVEY SAYS!"

Corwin I X I

Locutus says "answer unclear, try again later"

Mender says "It's our nation's capital, you know, Uly"

login: Off: Rachel

Ulysses says "Indeed"

Nightcrawler says "answer unclear, bombard later"

Locutus says "bomb the living bejeezus out of those forces"

Ulysses says "but OSSW is there"

Ulysses presses the HAIL button on the intercom and says "YOU WILL NOT
    KILL" into it.

Rostopovich says "SHOW ME: TEN THOUSAND CURIES"

Corwin says "AAAND SURVEY SAYS!"

Corwin I X I I X I

Mender says "SHOW ME: TEN THOUSAND CURRIES"

Corwin says "SUUUUURVEEEEY SAYS!"

<DING>

[5. TEN THOUSAND CURRIES—19]

henri says "YES"

Ulysses says "I found out she's doing maintenance on our production SQL
    Server database via Q+E"

Locutus says "finally!"

Rostopovich laughs.

Nightcrawler says "fuck. fuckfuckfuck. I was all set to screw around for HOURS
and set up an anmiation to drop to video and the fucking MAC DIES!"

Mender bleah Uly

Ulysses nods

Locutus+E

Jet shinnies up the pole and out of the bar.

Jet has left.

henri says "SHOE ME: BOONTIT VINDALOO"

henri says "SHOW ME: BOONTIT VINDALOO"

Corwin says "SUUUUUURVEY SAYS!"

Corwin I X I I X I I X I

Nightcrawler says "IT DIED, I TELL YOU! DIED!"

Jet's voice comes over the radio: says "SHOW ME: A DIDGERIDOO"

Corwin says "SURVEY SAYS!"

Corwin I X I

Jet comes sliding down the pole and into the room.

Jet has arrived.

RaveMage whispers "new ones going up now . . . can you view? :)"

Locutus says "SHOW ME: SUSHI"

Corwin says "AAAND SURVEY SAYS!"

Corwin I X I I X I

Locutus says "we suck"

RaveMage says "SHOW ME: THE HUNGER"

Nightcrawler says "Ooh.. sushi. that sounds good."

Corwin says "SUUUUUURVEY SAYS!"

Corwin I X I I X I I X I

Corwin says "I AM TRYING TO HAVE A CONVERSATION IDIOTS"

fnord says "the Big X is topless in mrd"

You whisper "yup! whaddyou do, scan 'em right there?" to RaveMage.

Corwin flies back into the past and gives Rostopovich's parents pamphlets on
contraception.

Rostopovich has left.

Corwin killed Mender!

Mender has left.

Corwin killed RaveMage!

RaveMage has left.

Itchy quickly types u

Ulysses says "She calls me up with questions like 'okay, so I want to add those
rows to the database, so it's insert tableFoo where . . . ?' and I say 'uh
well no' "

henri says "we ARE conversation idiots"

Locutus laughs

Rostopovich has arrived.

The bartender strikes a dramatic pose and points at Rostopovich, "THIS
   PERSON HAS NO CUSTOM GR—oh, you do, sorry."

henri says "did she fly off the handle again"

Ulysses says "No"

henri laughs at Rost's ncbgreet

Rostopovich says "Twist in the wind, Corwin"

Mender has arrived.

Mender barges in, exclaiming, "Out of my way, little monkey ass."

henri says "very surreal"

RaveMage has arrived.

RaveMage says "EXPIRING FOR LOVE IS BEAUTIFUL BUT STUPID"

Rostopovich says "or go somewhere else"

RaveMage says "heh"

henri says "as the little alien living in rosty's chest pokes its head out"

Locutus says "hey the new taurus SHO is out"

RaveMage whispers "the base dir is http://www.[provider].net/[user]/"

Copperhead buh

RaveMage whispers "color-cat.jpg"

Ulysses says "hey the new issue of 'From Hell' is out"

Rostopovich says "where's Peg"

Locutus says "3.4L V8, can you believe it"

RaveMage whispers "cat-morning.jpb"

Levon says "3.4L buh"

RaveMage whispers "cat-morning.jpg that is"

henri says "Ann Arbor"

WHO

Player Name On For Idle Futuristic replacement for elevators

fnord 00:05 1m

Jan 00:07 2m

Rostopovich 00:09 8s

Ulysses 00:24 12s Uncle Fester pull-chains

Bilerific-Sid 00:27 22m teams of spoon-benders levitate you up

Stick 00:33 25m Go! Go! Gadget Legs!

Corwin 00:41 1m

Quickrick 00:50 5m Stairs

Levon 00:56 5s

Itchy 01:18 1m Nuclear holocaust levels everything

Locutus 01:34 10s catapults

RaveMage 01:35 4s

Perry 01:56 12m Fountain of Florin launches you skyward

Copperhead 01:54 0s

Greygate 02:49 2m rocket jump w/pentagram of protection

henri 03:05 3s guy goes BWAAH, you leap to right floor

Mender 03:59 37s helium-filled pants

Nightcrawler 04:10 1m

Jet 05:15 1m Stilts

dozer 09:35 3m

devnull 09:48 18m You step onto a level teleport trap!—M

Xena 14:42 53s flying suit

Conductor 14:45 48s

Xavier 14:45 15s robotic litter bearers

24 Players logged in.

Levon says "The Accord is once again the #1 car in the US"

RaveMage whispers "grin-morning.jpg"

henri says "in sales?"

Locutus says "235 hp, haha ahem"

Levon nods

RaveMage whispers "cat-prim.jpg"

Rostopovich says "what % does it have"

henri says "the TAURUS has 235hp?"

Levon says "That's despite the fact that honda doesn't do fleet sales and ford
    does"

Levon does not know that rosty

henri says "3.4L V EIGHT?"

RaveMage whispers "rug.jpg"

henri's neck widens in bogglement

Corwin says "GO SOMEWHERE ELSE?"

Corwin flies back into the past and gives Rostopovich's parents pamphlets on
    contraception.

Rostopovich has left.

Itchy says "spooky"

Rostopovich has arrived.

Corwin says "no I did NOT hear you tell me go somewhere else on my mud"

The bartender . o O (oh, GREAT)

Rostopovich says "or turn it OFF or something."

Rostopovich says "boy"

Nightcrawler l The engineers of the electric vehicle charging system had a benchmark. They wanted to make it EV1 so safe you could stand barefoot in the rain, up to your ankles in water and lick the charger paddle.

Quickrick says "what about a 1978 BMW!"

henri laughs at nightcrawler

Levon chortles at nightcrawlerquote

Rostopovich says "you'd think there was an electric machine attached to your back which forced you to leave that 'survey says' trigger on."

Nightcrawler says "What a great quote."

Itchy chants "@toad, @toad"

Mender pauses with a charger paddle at his mouth "WHAT?"

Quickrick says "man, my car has this awful oily smell to it"

Quickrick says "I don't know what to do abot it"

Itchy chants "@toad, @toad"

Rostopovich says ""

henri says "try licking it clean"

henri says ""

Rostopovich says "yes you did hear me tell you to go somewhere else on your mud"

Levon says ""

Quickrick took the fan apart, cleaned the grit off, cleaned the carpeting

Corwin turned it off, then killed you. then killed you again.

Corwin says "and will kill you again, if you don't get over it soon"

Quickrick says "I think I need to look in A/C ducts for spilled oil or something"

Itchy jeers, "BOOT HIM!!"

henri runs over and SHOVES Itchy onto the green circle, then DIVES for the lever! Ka-CHOING!

Itchy has left.

Rostopovich says "and it felt good."

Itchy has arrived.

Itchy yells, "RELEASE THE KRAKEN!"

Mender presses the HAIL button on the intercom and says "I remember Rosty, he was always quiet and kept to himself." into it.

Itchy loves being Corwin's toady.

You whisper "what no 'normal?' AHAHAHA BRAAAP" to RaveMage.

henri @toady

Levon laughs at Mender

Itchy FITS THE QUIET AND KEPT TO HIMSELF PROFILE POLL

Itchy

Mender yes

fnord I Corwin says "not in your lifetime, which is about one more line"

Nightcrawler QUIET? ARE YOU MAD?

Copperhead no: LOUD AND GREGARIOUS

Levon only around women

Itchy HOWLS at fnord's quote

henri is quiet and keeps to himself except he's also an intrusive jerk

Mender says "augh after 6"

Levon buh no yankee game tonight WHAT TO DO

Nightcrawler says "My wife and I have a deal. If it involves a human, she has to take care of it. Otherwise, it is my job."

henri walks down the hall, hears someone suggest a ludicrous plan, and steps into the office to explain why it shouldn't be done that way

Mender says "Masturbate frantically, Levon"

Itchy says "What? I thought it was tonight"

henri says "or more often to make 'are you KIDDING' faces until they ask me"

Levon says "It was"

Copperhead *used* to be quiet, etc. "Sometimes it still shocks me that I'm not anymore."

Levon says "But it got ppd because of rain"

Rostopovich says "I'm just bored crosseyed, and being gratuitously rude to Corwin keeps me from keeling over insensate."

fnord used to be not quiet, long ago

Itchy says "F the rotting skull of rain"

Copperhead laughs 'are you KIDDING' faces

henri is forced to root for the yankees

Itchy says "forced"

Mender says "The longer the Yankees are in it, the more Dave wackiness we can expect"

Levon is forced to root for the yankees because he's been a fan since 1977

Itchy says "Dave's twisting your arm"

Itchy and Levon cry for Thurman Munson

Mender says "Do you think he'll have PEE WEE on again"

fnord says "Beryl wants everyone to root against Dallas so she can start using their parking lot sooner"

Levon and Itchy cry.

Corwin will pay doubloons for a better resume style file

Itchy actually did cry.

Levon says "I was too young to really grasp it"

Mender says "Wuss"

Nightcrawler gets a handout packet from a meeting he didn't go to, and finds view-graphs he made in it. "what the hell is this?"

Levon says "I did cry when Len Bias died though"

Ulysses is more the quiet loner type

Itchy says "I sort of cried, I just sat in a big chair and didn't talk"

RaveMage whispers "are they coming across okie? :) i took the pictures and
kept them in a Now Scrapbook, then i paste them into graphicconverter and
save them, and then upload the dir using fetch :) "

Ulysses says "quiet loners fit in at Postal"

Notes

1. I have changed all names throughout this book (except for real names referenced in published works), including those of online spaces, characters, participants, offline institutions (such as universities), and geographical locations. I have changed some identifying data of participants to disguise their identities further. In addition, in a few cases, I have used more than one name to refer to the same participant. Following their own practice, I generally refer to BlueSky participants using character names. I have attempted to retain some of the original tone and essential nature of these names by using similar source material or by using character pseudonyms that participants themselves supplied. Bilerific-Sid, for instance, insisted on that pseudonym, asked that I indicate as much herein, and further opined that the use of pseudonyms was silly. For a further discussion of ethical considerations in changing online pseudonyms, see appendix B.

2. The *Hacker's Dictionary* defines "flame" as: "1. vi. To post an email message intended to insult and provoke. 2. vi. To speak incessantly and/or rabidly on some relatively uninteresting subject or with a patently ridiculous attitude. 3. vt. Either of senses 1 or 2, directed with hostility at a particular person or people. 4. n. An instance of flaming" (Raymond 1991: 158). A flame war consists of several flames sent back and forth by e-mail, newsgroup posting, or similar means.

3. I owe my understanding of the latter point to Doug Orleans, a programmer and participant on a variety of online forums.

4. See esp. his chapter 4.

5. Personal communication with T. L. Taylor, based on her research with people participating in graphical online forums.

6. Sterling states that "cyberspace is the 'place' where a telephone conversation appears to occur" (1993: 1). This comparison between the experience of being on the telephone and being online has proved popular among computer

developers and analysts. I have heard several speakers at computer-related conferences use this analogy (not always with attribution to Sterling), including Sterling himself, John Perry Barlow, and Maclen Marvit.

7. The use of the term "multitasking" to describe the ability to switch rapidly back and forth among several tasks, media, or demands on attention provides an interesting example of the increasing use of metaphors derived from computers to describe human activities. The *Hacker's Dictionary* states that "multitask" is "often used of humans in the same meaning it has for computers, to describe a person doing several things at once" (Raymond 1991: 250). See also Turkle 1984 for a discussion of people's use of computer terminology to describe human beings.

8. Goffman's chapter 13, "The Frame Analysis of Talk," is particularly relevant to my discussion here.

9. Benedickt describes cyberspace as "a globally networked, computer-sustained, computer-accessed, and computer-generated, multidimensional, artificial, or 'virtual' reality. In this reality, to which every computer is a window, seen or heard objects are neither physical nor, necessarily, representations of physical objects but are, rather, in form, character and action, made up of data, of pure information" (1991: 122–23). Cyberspace is also sometimes used interchangeably with the term "Internet" (inaccurately, some argue). BlueSky participants abhor the term as silly and unrealistic, in part because of perceived hype surrounding online participation.

10. The Communications Decency Act, passed by the U.S. Senate in 1996, was in part an attempt to restrict the dissemination of sexually explicit content over the Internet. It provoked widespread protest on (and off) the Internet. A good source of information about this legislation, its potential impact, and the various protests and measures against it is the website of the Center for Democracy and Technology, at http://www.cdt.org.

CHAPTER 2

1. One person in the group legally changed her name a few years ago to the name she uses online, eliminating this potential confusion, and possibly indicating the degree of importance to her of her online identity and relationships.

2. Information regarding EFF can be found at http://www.eff.org, where they describe themselves as "a non-profit civil liberties organization working in the public interest to protect privacy, free expression, and access to public resources and information online, as well as to promote responsibility in new media." John Perry Barlow is among the founders of this organization. His presentation of himself as a plain-spoken, down-to-earth "Montana rancher" has contributed to his popularity as a commentator about online life.

3. "Copperhead" is not, of course, my real character name on BlueSky. Since my name there is unique, it would provide a clue to the BlueSky group's

location and identity. However, "Copperhead" resembles my BlueSky name, particularly in its implication of a poisonous entity. My name choice (arrived at partly by a serendipitous flip through the dictionary) turned out to be a good one; after getting to know me, several people commented that they liked the name and suggested that its connotations, both colorful and poisonous, fit in well with BlueSky's atmosphere.

4. To the extent that participants build objects on muds, muds also supply some programming experience. Object building consists of writing small programs (sometimes quite elaborate), which become part of the mud server and interact with characters and other objects. (See Bruckman 1994 on using muds to teach programming skills.)

5. Some academic institutions bar computer account holders from mudding and other activities classified as "games."

6. To protect BlueSky's privacy, the screen examples I use in this chapter are composites derived from various different muds.

7. Although I've participated in muds for well over three years, I still do not know even the most basic building commands and have never built my own room or objects. Earlier in mudding history, and on some other current muds, this would probably have decreased my status considerably. Even on BlueSky, being able to build interesting or useful objects gives participants greater status among the group. However, since most participants do not engage in much building activity, my lack of facility did not impair my social position.

8. Role-playing muds sometimes require participants to set several different character parameters, including things such as strength and intelligence. These character aspects derive from similar choices made in the initial stages of offline role-playing games. "Race" in such cases usually refers to distinctions such as "elf," "human," "troll," and the like. However, see Kolko 2000 for a description of a mud in which the operators attempted specifically to address questions of racial identity.

9. In some cases, they are referred to as gods, although this term is also sometimes reserved for people who own the host computers. On some muds, there are both gods and wizards, neither of whom necessarily own the computer but who are differentiated by levels of access to the program.

10. The *Hacker's Dictionary* provides the following definition of crash: "1. n. A sudden, usually drastic failure. Most often said of the system, sometimes of magnetic disk drives. . . . 2. v. To fail suddenly. . . . Also used transitively to indicate the cause of the crash (usually a person or a program, or both)" (Raymond 1991: 110).

11. This quote comes from the BlueSky help file, accessed while on BlueSky by typing "help."

12. Because this mud command fills the screen with a list of the people currently logged on, I can use it to remove potentially offensive statements from the screen.

13. "tf" refers to Tinyfugue, a popular mud client.

CHAPTER 3

1. Role-playing games such as Dungeons & Dragons (from TSR Hobbies) originated in the 1970s (derived in part from earlier war strategy games). Many such games take place in a conceptual universe owing much to Tolkien's *Lord of the Rings* series of fantasy books (Tolkien 1966), in which vaguely medieval human characters coexist with elves, dwarves, orcs, and other mythological creatures. Players take on roles of characters in this universe (fighters, magicians, etc.) and traverse a terrain (such as a dungeon) laid out for them by the dungeon master. The dungeon master plans the play session by developing a locale and populating it with treasures and monsters. Most play occurs through verbal description, with dice rolls to determine the outcomes of various encounters. In early online versions of adventure games for single players, the computer played the role of dungeon master, posing various puzzles for players to solve. (For a more detailed look at the social world of gaming, see Fine 1983.)

2. Most themes relate to science fiction, fantasy, or comic book literature, demonstrating the strong overlap between the science fiction fan community and muds in general. This connection in turn reflects and helps perpetuate particular demographics among mud participants, who are predominantly white and middle class. Even many standard mud commands reflect this alliance with science fiction. For instance, many muds, like BlueSky, include a *teleport* command, which allows people to "jump" directly to a chosen room rather than follow a "realistic" path through other linked rooms. (On some muds, people object that teleportation violates the experience of the mud as a place, so they require that mud rooms connect to each other in a logical fashion and that participants move through those rooms sequentially. However, in recognition of the possible tediousness of this requirement when many of those rooms are empty, some muds include commands that move the character through the rooms automatically, pausing just long enough to allow the participant to read each room description.)

3. With regard to e-mail and newsgroups, spamming refers to sending unsolicited messages indiscriminately to multiple addresses or lists without regard for the usual purpose or content of those newsgroups or e-mail lists. A few recent media reports have used spam to refer to *any* unwanted e-mail, but most experienced net participants do not use the term as broadly.

4. In the early months of my research, participants sometimes expressed surprise at my level of participation and joked that I was in danger of "going native." This reflects participant uncertainty about how ethnographic research is conducted and, to some extent, fears that I would "experiment" on them by doing things solely to observe particular reactions. For further discussion of BlueSky participants' ideas about ethnography and reactions to my research, see appendix B.

5. For instance, I have a T-shirt, produced for the group by henri and Peg, that identifies me as a member of the BlueSky "lomming team."

6. The term "CowOrker" is a typo for "coworker," which participants found humorous enough to continue. The derogatory sound of "cow orker" suits the mostly negative talk about coworkers that occurs on BlueSky.

7. One of the most famous muds, LambdaMOO, has been referenced in several articles in both academic and popular media. Among the features most interesting to researchers are LambdaMOO's attempts to set up democratic methods of making decisions about organization and maintenance of the mud as well as problem solving and dispute mediation.

8. This ambiguity has received considerable discussion with regard to several cases of sexual harassment on muds taking the form of "virtual rapes." In a well-known account of one of these, Dibbell (1993) reports on discussions among LambdaMOO participants concerning whether mud representations of violent sexual assault constitute sexual harassment or would be better characterized as virtual rape.

9. Changes in the administration or ownership of the computer on which a mud runs can force a mud to move to a new site or cease operation. If it is run without permission, a mud may be shut down when the illicit use of computer equipment is discovered. Usenet mud-related newsgroups frequently feature requests from someone with a mud program or an idea for a mud who seeks a site from which to operate it. Most of these solicitations appear to be unsuccessful.

10. As with most logs included herein, I have edited the following excerpts to clarify the interaction and remove other conversations. This incident occurred at a particularly busy time on the mud and has thus been heavily edited. The full log segment from which I selected this excerpt appears in appendix C as an example of an unedited mud log.

11. Many mud commands include the @ symbol before the command.

12. Here, henri uses the *lom* command for this room.

13. In labeling himself a toady, Itchy plays off both his suggestion to toad Rostopovich and his support of Corwin's position as wizard.

14. Ironically, many early muds, and some that still exist, have as their main gathering place a room described as a town square. Discussions of LambdaMOO's Living Room, which used to be the first "hangout" room encountered on LambdaMOO, have similarly suggested that, rather than a private person's living room (its textual description), the room more closely resembles a town square. However, these descriptions are misleading in that they promote an expectation of the right of free speech. The policies of various private online service providers, such as GEnie and AOL, limiting types of acceptable speech amply demonstrate this. Several years ago, AOL attempted to censor the word "breast" in its chat areas and on topical message boards. This policy had to be dropped when members of various groups, including recipe exchange groups and a women's breast cancer support group, complained that they were no longer able to discuss their topics of interest.

CHAPTER 4

1. As discussed in chapter 2, gender choices on BlueSky include neuter and plural, and participants use the gender setting mainly for joke purposes or ignore it entirely. Other muds include more gender choices. Many MOOs (a type of mud server: Mud, Object Oriented) offer ten different choices, including several that attempt to bypass gender-specific pronouns through invented pronouns (at least one set of which is borrowed from Marge Piercy's 1983 novel *Woman on the Edge of Time*). Clearly these gender designations attempt to play with gender possibilities online, and some people no doubt use them to disrupt gender assumptions. The success or failure of these disruptive strategies would be an interesting topic for future study.

2. Ullman (1995) describes a hierarchy of types of programming, in which programmers who work on "user-friendly" application software have lower status than programmers who work on programs understandable only by machines or other programmers (1995: see p. 135). henri works on this latter type of program.

3. The concept of "male answer syndrome" appeared in a 1986 issue of a relatively obscure comic strip called "Eyebeam," written by Sam Hurt and read by several BlueSky participants in their youth. Hurt saw the term used in a 1983 column by David Stansbury in the Texas magazine *Third Coast*.

4. The "Nerdity Test" is available on the World Wide Web at, among other places, http://165.91.72.200/nerd-backwards.html.

5. "hsm" is a deliberate typo for "hms," which is a coined verb form for "says hmm." Mender's use of "hsm" with "says" would actually be considered incorrect, because it would be interpreted to read: "Mender says 'says hmm.'" The usual usage would be "Mender hsm," which BlueSky participants would interpret as "Mender says hmm."

6. I have gleaned information concerning participants' sexual identities from their own statements about their identities and sexual practices and from more general conversations concerning romantic and sexual relationships. Given the acceptance on BlueSky of a wide range of sexual identities and sexual practices (or at least discussion of sexual practices), and given also that the group culture encourages self-disclosure, I believe these figures accurately represent participants' own understanding of their sexual identities.

7. "Slamp" is an abbreviation for the term "slampiece," used on BlueSky (mainly by BJ) to refer to sexual partners.

8. Since *pose* commands are generally written in third person, participants have far more occasion to use third-person pronouns in reference to themselves than they would in face-to-face encounters.

CHAPTER 5

1. Although the distinction rarely appears in reports of online research, online names that differ from offline names should be designated as pseudo-

nyms when they are used by people who consistently portray an online identity similar to their offline presentation of self. Online spaces where participants expect this type of identity enactment cannot be characterized as anonymous, since people generally know quite a bit about each other. In fact, I would argue that as people make more and more connections offline, their online names cease to function even as pseudonyms but instead become more like nicknames used by a particular group of friends and acquaintances, as part of the idioculture of their group (Fine 1987b).

2. My thanks to Brad Elmore for providing me with this succinct definition.

3. Julia, perhaps the most famous mud robot, has been entered into a contest for artificial intelligence programs, as a few other mud robots have. See http://www.vperson.com/mlm/julia.html for a description and discussion by Michael Mauldin, Julia's creator.

4. henri wrote this second verse (beginning with "Julia, Julia, she's our spy").

5. One mud known to BlueSky participants functions as a social "backstage" area for participants from several different role-playing muds. People gather there to discuss plot developments, plan dramatic strategies, and converse socially, often while simultaneously role-playing their fictional characters on the role-playing muds.

6. The message in this last line was visible only to me.

7. Meyrowitz points out that the people most likely to watch "special interest" television programs are not people with those special interests but rather people who watch a lot of television (1985: 84, citing Goodhart, Ehrenberg, and Collins 1975).

8. Accounts of this incident can be found at: http://infoweb.internetx.net/axcess/Issue5/UsenetWars/holy.wars.html, http://www.cs.ruu.nl/wais/html/na-dir/bigfoot/part2.html, http://www.phys.uts.edu.au/len/tasteless.html, and, from a slightly different point of view, in Brail 1996.

9. I accessed Quittner's article at http://www.phys.uts.au/len/tasteless.html.

10. See Stone 1995 for a similar account of disruptive invasive behaviors of newcomers destroying an existing online social space. In her example, the invaders were also young males.

11. I had just discovered the group, and I too was driven off.

12. Gag commands on muds prevent only the targeted (or offended) person from seeing text from his or her harasser. Other participants can still see the harassment and may interpret the target's ongoing nonresponse as acquiescence or agreement. Additionally, if other participants continue to converse with the gagged participant, the person using the gag command sees a chopped-up, partial conversation.

13. LambdaMOO, a large and well-known mud, has been written up in several articles about muds, with each article sparking an influx of new people to that mud. LambdaMOO participants periodically discuss possible ways to limit population growth and to improve integration of newbies into the culture

of the mud. Reid (1996) also describes the negative effect that online publication of her research had on one of the muds she studied.

14. In addition, typing skills, once associated with femininity and female jobs, are now also valued and boasted of by computer programmers, a group still predominately male. Several BlueSky participants, male and female, pride themselves on their high typing speeds.

CHAPTER 6

1. "ltns" is an abbreviation commonly used on the Internet, meaning "long time, no see."

2. All the people I discussed these issues with are sighted. The issues for those with vision impairment might be different; however, even for the visually impaired, face-to-face encounters would provide a greater variety of information sources about the other person than text online affords.

3. "IMO" stands for "in my opinion."

4. "@dest" refers to the command that destroys objects on the mud. Although a participant controls his or her own character, on a registration mud that character was created by a wizard. In order for PAL to make his "suicide" complete through the destruction of his online character, he needed the assistance of one of BlueSky's wizards.

5. "Ohe" means "oh he." On BlueSky, when participants begin a sentence with "Oh," they frequently drop the *h* and combine the remaining *o* with the next word. "Oit" for "oh it" and "oiam" for "oh I am" are also common.

CHAPTER 7

1. I obtained these and the following figures about Internet demographics from an online search that I conducted on November 28, 1997. Since conditions of online survey administration may exacerbate self-select and self-report biases, I do not consider these statistics particularly reliable. So far as I know, only the Nielsen study purports to have taken a probability sample. However, the percentages are relatively consistent from report to report and fit expectations based on Internet history and attitudes toward computers in the United States. My aim is to give an idea of the range of responses reported in these studies and to suggest likely patterns of Internet participation. Because different surveys asked their questions differently, my figures in the text are approximations only. Although an earlier search turned up a few studies that looked at race, in this search I was unable to find *any* statistics on race, ethnicity, or nationality. Following is a partial list of sites I reviewed:

http://www2.chaicenter.org/otn/aboutinternet/Demographics-
Nielsen.html

http://www3.mids.org/ids/index.html

http://www2000.ogsm.vanderbilt.edu/surveys/cn.questions.html (this site provides a detailed critique of the Nielsen study)

http://thehost.com/demo.htm

http://www.scruznet.com/%7Eplugin01/Demo.html

http://www.cyberatlas.com/demographics.html

http://www.cc.gatech.edu/gvu/user_surveys/survey-1997–04

http://www.ora.com/research/users/results.html

APPENDIX B

1. See Benedikt 1991; Heim 1993; Rheingold 1991; and Schroeder 1996 for discussions of virtual reality technology, theory, and social ramifications.

2. Readers of prior drafts of these chapters commented that they happily read long interview excerpts and felt these provided a good feel for the interviewees. However, they could not follow and were bored by long log excerpts. Increasing my interpretive comments and analysis assuaged some of the confusion and boredom, but some of these problems stem from the nature of mud logs. I kept log excerpts as short as possible, editing out comments from other ongoing conversations as well as comments that do not significantly contribute to the dialogue. (For an example of an unedited log, see appendix C.)

3. The ASA Code of Ethics can be obtained at http://www.asanet.org/ecoderev.htm.

4. Several participants also provided me with a variety of technical assistance. During an upgrade of her login object, Beryl willingly accepted my requests for particular types of information to be gathered by the object and helped me better learn its use. Faust also wrote a program that allowed me to gather statistics about characters on GammaMOO, another mud he frequented in addition to BlueSky. My thanks also to BJ, elflord, and fnord, who supplied me with useful programs or similar assistance. Numerous other BlueSky participants also helped me with mud commands. Like many other BlueSky participants, I benefited from the ability to log on and ask computer-related questions of anybody present.

5. Participants also had a great deal of fun with the conventional academic nature of my titles and subtitles. Proving the formulaic traits of such titles, henri was able to create a mud object that automatically generated dissertation titles by combining random phrases in standard formats (For instance, the following constitutes the form of my dissertation title, slightly altered in this work: ["ing" verb form] [noun phrase]: [noun], [noun], and [noun]; alternatively, [noun] vs. [noun]: ["ing" verb form] [noun phrase].) Bits and pieces of my own titles were included in the stock of phrases, mixed with miscellaneous academic concepts, ironic versions of postmodernist phrases, vulgar and sexual expressions, and so forth, resulting in humorous and sometimes plausible alternative titles.

6. During a presentation at the American Anthropological Association

meetings in November 1996, a representative of a virtual reality development company suggested that computer programmers and other computer industry personnel need to become ethnographers themselves in order to understand better the online needs of customers and potential customers. While this certainly expresses an appreciation of the utility of ethnographic methods, it also tends to represent them as something other than a complex, learned specialization. I and several other colleagues in attendance expressed doubt that he would similarly suggest that all ethnographers could or should as easily become computer programmers.

7. An additional problem with Allen's strategy stems from the difficulties involved in obtaining "informed consent" when studying groups. While Allen's interviewees consented to the use of their real online pseudonyms, those interviewees mentioned other mud participants, sometimes revealing very personal information about people not directly involved with the research. Many of those participants did not consent to interviews with Allen and would likely have welcomed the "facile" protection of changed pseudonyms.

8. In a few cases of dealing with sensitive information, I created duplicate pseudonyms for participants, in effect representing a single person as two people. Those pseudonyms successfully hid identities from even the determined sleuthing of Jet and Carets.

APPENDIX C

1. All names have been changed, as in the text. An edited section of this log appears in chapter 3, in the discussion of wizards.

Glossary

Italic type designates words defined in this glossary.

@	Symbol preceding many mud commands, especially those used in the creation of *objects*. (See *dest; toad*.)
:) or :-)	Basic smileys (recognized by tilting your head to the left).
artificial intelligence (AI)	Programs that mimic human reasoning are referred to as artificial intelligence programs. Some mud *robots* can be considered rudimentary AI programs.
asynchronous	A mode of communication in which participants send and receive messages at different, sometimes widely separate, times. Letters, *e-mail*, and *bulletin board systems*, such as *Usenet*, are all asynchronous. (Compare *real-time chat; synchronous*.)
attributes	Aspects of a mud object that can be "set" to different values. For instance, the "@sex" attribute on many muds allows participants to set their gender designation to one of several choices. Character attributes can be used to automatically generate text triggered by certain events, words, or phrases. Some attributes affect interaction among different objects. They can also be used to transmit information to other participants. (See *gender, character, objects*.)
BBS	See *bulletin board system*.
boot	A command used by mud *wizards* to disconnect a participant from the mud.
btw	Abbreviation for "by the way."

buh — Expression used on BlueSky to convey disbelief or startlement.

building — On muds, the creation of *objects*. This can range from very simple projects, such as *rooms* (which require only a few commands, a description, and specifications of how and where the room connects to other mud rooms, spaces, or objects), to extremely elaborate multiroom puzzles (which may involve various different exits, command responses, etc., in each room).

bulletin board system — "A message database where people can log in and leave broadcast messages for others grouped (typically) into topic groups. Thousands of local BBS systems are in operation throughout the U.S." (Raymond 1991: 52). While some bulletin board systems allow for *real-time chat*, most generally involve *asynchronous* communications in which each message is accessible by all other subscribers. (See *Usenet; newsgroup*.)

character — A type of mud *object* that usually represents a participant online. Characters generally have unique names and passwords, making them available to only one participant, although these protections can sometimes be defeated. (See *spoof*.)

character registration — Some muds require participants to apply to the *wizards* of the mud for a character, often by submitting information such as an e-mail address. Nonregistration muds allow participants to create a character instantly (with a password) at the entrance screen to the mud.

crash — Catastrophic failure of computer hardware or software. Computer programs or processes (subparts of programs) that cease functioning unexpectedly and cannot recover without human intervention are said to have crashed.

cyberspace — Coined by William Gibson (1984) in his influential novel *Neuromancer*, this term is used by some participants, journalists, and commentators to describe the "space" in which online interaction occurs.

description — Each *object* on a mud has a description written by the participant who created that object (or, in the case of characters, by the participant using that *character*). Descriptions give clues to participants concerning the capabilities of particular objects, possible *exits* from *rooms*, and information about their fellow participants (depending on the norms of character use on each particular mud). Descriptions are accessed by using the *look* command. Participants often refer to these (especially character descriptions) as descs, from the description creation command, @desc.

dest, @dest

From "destroy." Command that deletes items from the mud server database. Participants can generally apply this command only to *objects* they have created (through their *character*). *Wizards* and other administrator characters have broader deletion capabilities and can dest characters as well as other types of objects. (Participants cannot dest their own character, since technically it was created by a wizard, not by the participant.) (See *toad.*)

dino

People who can trace their mudding experience back to Classic or the other earliest muds are called dinos (from "dinosaur"). (More recently, some people also apply the term to anyone who has been mudding for three to four years or more.)

Dungeons & Dragons

One of a class of role-playing games; also sometimes used generically to refer to all such games. The earliest muds originated as online versions of these games, and many muds still include role playing, puzzle solving, and other aspects derived from role-playing and adventure games.

e-mail

Computer function, available through a variety of different programs and commands, that enables *asynchronous* one-to-one communication (or, in the case of e-mail listservers or multiple addressees, one-to-many communication).

emote

See *pose.*

ew

Expression used on BlueSky to convey disgust.

exit

In simple terms, exits take one's character from one *room* to another on muds. Clues to the existence of exits are usually included in room descriptions. Exits are programmed by the person who "builds," or creates, the room *object*. Technically, all sorts of mud objects can have exits, and mud programmers make creative use of them and of the messages triggered by them to create various useful and playful objects.

gag

Available on most *mud servers* and *mud clients*, this command enables a participant to suppress text generated by a particular *character* or to suppress all text containing particular words or phrases. You can, for instance, suppress any text containing profanity (although it takes some creative programming to defeat alternate spellings such as "f*ck").

gender

A character *attribute*. The gender setting of a *character* allows, among other things, the mud server to insert appropriate pronouns into text produced (either by the server itself or by other mud *objects*) in reference to that character. Basic character creation usually includes setting both a *description* and the gender attribute. Upon creation, characters have a default gender setting of "neutral," which most muds include as a gender option. At a minimum, muds also include "male," "female," and sometimes "plural" (using the pronouns "we," "they," etc.). Some muds also include a wide variety of other options, many of which participants use to attempt to escape the restrictions of binary gender assumptions.

guest characters

Generic non-password-protected characters available to temporary mud visitors (or others seeking anonymity). Guest characters usually have limited command capabilities. (Interestingly, while some muds do not allow guests to set their own *description*, all muds I have seen allow guests to set their *gender*.) (See *character registration*.)

heh

Expression used on BlueSky to convey mild amusement.

highlight

Mud client command that enables the user to highlight particular text with different screen colors or through other similar differences in appearance. Participants can use this to call attention to text that includes their name, text from particular people, or text containing key words or phrases.

home

As part of the organizational structure of the *mud server* program, each *object* on the mud has a home—a *room* or other object within which it resides by default. An object's home may be set by the creator of that object. Characters generally start with a default home setting, usually a designated room on the mud (often called limbo). On most social muds, participants can also create their own home and change their character's home setting to that location. When a participant types the command "home," it sends his or her character back to this designated location. On some muds, including BlueSky, the *kill* command also sends someone else's character back to its home.

hsm   Traditional and deliberate mistyping of "hms," a coined verb form meaning "says hmm."

idle   Participants on a mud are said to be idle if they have gone for several minutes or more without participating in conversation or responding to text directed at them.

imo   Abbreviation for "in my opinion."

imho   Abbreviation for "in my humble opinion."

imnsho   Abbreviation for "in my not so humble opinion."

irl   Abbreviation for "in real life."

kill   Available on many (but not all) muds, kill commands vary in their effect. On some (usually combat- or adventure-oriented) muds, they destroy the killed character. In other cases, the killed character is disconnected from the mud and can subsequently log back on. On BlueSky and many other social muds, the kill command merely sends a character back to its *home*.

lag   Technically, any command-processing delay resulting from various causes, including competition for computing time on a single computer, program inefficiencies, and transmission delay between different computers. Mudders also use this term to describe delay in communication brought about by the same causes. Mud participants periodically complain about "net lag" or say that a particular mud is "laggy." They may explain a pause or missed conversational cue by complaining that they were "lagged," suggesting that either the conversational cue was delayed in getting to them or their response was delayed in return.

lol   Abbreviation for "laughing out loud."

lom   Command on BlueSky that expels a character from one of the hangout rooms to the room "just outside" that hangout. Use of this command is controlled by the person who built the particular hangout. (See *kill*.)

look   Command that displays the text description of whatever is "looked" at. See appendix A for examples.

ltns   Abbreviation for "long time, no see."

mav   Any utterance formatted for use with one type of command (such as *whisper*) but unintentionally transmitted using a different command (such as *say*). The quintessential, and most embarrassing, mav is to attempt to whisper something intimate to another character and then accidentally transmit that text to everyone in the room. However, on some muds, including BlueSky, participants also use "mav" to refer to any similar error. (See appendix A for examples.) The term, known across a wide variety of muds, comes from the name of a character, "mav," known to make such blunders frequently. Used as a noun or a verb.

MOO   Acronym for mud, object-oriented. Although MOOs are merely a particular type of *mud server*, they tend to be referred to by MOO participants as if they were a separate type of environment from other muds. Most MOOs contain several minor stylistic differences from other TinyMUD derivatives.

mrd   Acronym for magic recording device. This programmed object in the Falcon on BlueSky stores several hundred lines of recently generated text, which participants can access. Many participants use it to get the context of the ongoing conversation when they first enter the mud.

mud   Originally from the acronym MUD, for multiuser dungeon (also multiuser dimension or domain). A computer program that enables many people in different locations (and using different computers) to connect to the same computer, manipulate aspects of the program, and communicate with each other. It creates a text-based, quasi-physical social space that can be used for various communicative purposes, including gaming, role playing, meetings, socializing, exchange of information, etc. (See *mud server.*)

mud client	A program running on the participant's local computer, enabling him or her to connect to a mud server. Clients also provide an easy-to-use interface to the mud, an "unmessy" screen, and several additional command capabilities that allow participants to tailor the way text appears on their screen. Clients can be used to connect to several different muds at the same time and include commands that allow the participant to switch from one mud to the other. They also usually include commands that allow certain types of text to be *highlighted* or suppressed (see *gag*).
mud server	The mud program itself, which processes all interactions on the mud and stores the mud database of *objects.*
mutter	A command that allows a participant to direct text to everyone in a mud room except a single (or group of) participant(s), effectively talking behind the target(s)' back. The person against whom muttering is directed is said to be "muttered around." (See appendix A for an example.)
newbie	Term used on the Internet to refer to those with little or no online experience. BlueSky participants use "newbie" in that sense and also to refer to people new to mudding or new just to BlueSky.
newpassword	A command used by mud *wizards* to change a *character's* password, which prevents a participant from using his or her character.
newsgroup	Part of a *bulletin board system,* such as *Usenet.* Each newsgroup generally covers a particular topic or set of topics (which are described broadly and cover such things as "messages related to migraine headaches," in the newsgroup alt.support. headaches.migraine; "messages related the administration of muds," in rec.games.muds.admin; and so on).
objects	On muds, discrete portions of the mud code with particular functions that often mimic offline objects. Each object usually has a description and various programmed functions that enable it to react to text

and to produce text in response. Objects can consist of little more than a description or can be quite complex, responding to many types of text, as the "bartender" object does on BlueSky.

oic   Abbreviation for "oh, I see."

ose   A coined verb form of "Oh" used on BlueSky to mean "says 'Oh,'" as in "Jet ose."

page   Command that allows text to be sent to someone connected on the same mud but not in the same mud room. (See appendix A for examples.)

pennies   Most muds have some system of accounting in which characters accrue wealth in the form of credits, pennies, or some other form of virtual currency. Pennies were the designated currency on TinyMUD Classic and on many other early social muds. On gaming muds, mud money constitutes a type of scorekeeping and also functions as part of the game; characters may "purchase" equipment and other objects with it.

port   Ports allow different computers to connect to one another. Each computer has several different ports, many of which are dedicated to particular types of connections, such as *telnet, e-mail,* etc. The system administrator of a particular computer can also designate ports for particular purposes, such as mud connections. The port number is a crucial part of the address used to connect to a mud.

pose   The action text command. It begins text with the name of the participant without including the word "say" or dialogue within quotation marks. Participants use this command to show their character performing an action or to switch to third person for variety in speech. The pose command (referred to as emote on some muds) generates text to all participants in a room and only in that room. (See appendix A for examples.)

re   Abbreviation for "hello again"; for example, re-Copperhead = hello again, Copperhead (said when Copperhead has logged off or idled for a while and then returned).

real-time chat   Online communication between two or more participants in which responses back and forth occur nearly immediately, providing a feeling similar to that of simultaneous offline communication (such as face-to-face or voice-to-voice communication). Online chat is technically near-synchronous, because messages cannot overlap and participants cannot interrupt each other. Each "utterance" is first composed and then sent as a single unit. (See *synchronous*; compare *asynchronous*.)

RL   Abbreviation for "real life."

robots   Robots are *characters* that are controlled by programs rather than by human participants. Some robots function as rudimentary *artificial intelligence* programs, while others differ little from complex *objects* with multiple *triggers*.

room   A mud *object* that designates a discrete space on a mud. *Characters* can enter and *exit* rooms (sometimes with limitations to specific characters only), and rooms can also contain other objects. (Technically any mud object can be built to contain other objects; rooms are thus distinguished primarily through their descriptions and uses.) Muds usually include several different rooms that may be within buildings or described as outdoor or other types of spaces.

rotfl   Abbreviation for "rolling on the floor laughing."

RSI   Acronym for repetitive stress injury; that is, an injury incurred through repetitive motions.

say   The standard speech command on muds. Broadcasts text to all other participants in the same room and only in that room of the mud. (See appendix A for examples.)

spam, spamming   Large amounts of text inappropriately transmitted. On muds, this usually refers to text produced very rapidly through the use of automatic *triggers*, the quoting of large chunks of text (especially from an off-mud source), or practices such as quote fests, which also quickly generate large amounts of text. The term derives from the canned meat of the same name.

spoof   A practice in which participants hide their identity by suppressing the appearance of their name before their text or pretend to be another participant by inserting that person's name instead.

synchronous

Communication in which participants can simultaneously send and receive messages. Face-to-face and some voice-to-voice communication (telephone calls, for instance) are synchronous. (See *real-time chat;* compare *asynchronous.*)

teleport

Many muds include various commands that allow characters to transcend (or perhaps transgress) the mud's logical, usually geographical, layout of *rooms* or spaces by "jumping" immediately to another location of choice rather than by using the more conventional means of entering and exiting. On some muds, this command is still called teleport, revealing the concept's science fiction origins. On others, more prosaic terms have been substituted, such as "@go," which is used on many MOOs. (See *exit.*)

telnet

Unix command that allows a user to connect to a remote computer from his or her local computer account. The telnet command can be used to connect to a mud. Mudders use the term "raw telnet" to refer to the connection made through this command, because it results in a "raw," messy interface with no capability for customization, compared with the interface provided by a *mud client* program.

toad, @toad

On BlueSky, a command that *wizards* can use to destroy a designated *character.* In other cases, the toad command merely changes the character's description to that of a toad and cause any text typed by the character's typist to come out as a croak, rendering the character useless.

triggers

Triggers are code functions that can be set on *objects* (including *characters*) to "listen" for particular text and then cause the object to provide an automatic textual response to that text.

Unix

A type of computer operating system. (Other operating systems include Windows, DOS, MacOS, etc.)

Usenet

"A distributed bulletin board system . . . [that] is now probably the largest decentralized information utility in existence" (Raymond 1991: 364). Although Raymond's definition predates the World Wide Web (through which Usenet newsgroups can now be accessed), it captures the two main features of Usenet: (1) it is a bulletin board–type system, that is, people post messages in various topically divided "newsgroups" and can read other people's posts; and (2) it is extremely large and well-distributed and continues to grow. (See *newsgroup; bulletin board system.*)

whisper — Command that allows text to be sent only to a particular individual in the same mud room. Whispered text is not seen by other participants in the same room. (See appendix A for examples.)

WHO — The who command ("WHO" on many muds, "@who" on many MOOs) displays the list of *characters* currently connected to the mud.

wizard — A *character* or a person responsible for administrative duties on the mud. In reference to a character, the term "wizard" indicates the possession of particular abilities usually not available to generic characters (such as the ability to view *whispers* of other characters or to disconnect another character from the mud). "Wizard" is also used to describe the person operating such a character.

References

Adams, P. C. 1992. "Television as Gathering Place." *Annals of the Association of American Geographers* 82(1): 117–35.

Addelston, Judi, and Michael Stirratt. 1996. "The Last Bastion of Masculinity: Gender Politics at the Citadel." In C. Cheng, ed., *Masculinities in Organizations*, 54–76. Thousand Oaks, Calif.: Sage.

Allan, Graham. 1989. *Friendship: Developing a Sociological Perspective.* New York: Harvester.

Allen, Christina Lee. 1996a. "Virtual Identities: The Social Construction of Cybered Selves." Ph.D. dissertation, Communication Studies, Northwestern University.

———. 1996b. "What's Wrong with the 'Golden Rule'? Conundrums of Conducting Ethical Research in Cyberspace." *Information Society* 12(2): 175–88.

Anderson, Benedict. 1991. *Imagined Communities: Reflections on the Origin and Spread of Nationalism.* London: Verso.

Anderson, Elijah. 1978. *A Place on the Corner.* Chicago: University of Chicago Press.

Barlow, John Perry. 1996. "A Declaration of the Independence of Cyberspace." Paper available on the World Wide Web at http://www.eff.org/pub/Publications/John_Perry_Barlow/barlow_0296.declaration. (May 11, 1998.)

Bartle, Richard. 1990. "Interactive Multi-User Computer Games." Paper available on the World Wide Web at http://www.mud.co.uk/richard/imucgo.htm. (May 11, 1998.)

Baym, Nancy K. 1993. "Interpreting Soap-Operas and Creating Community—inside a Computer-Mediated Fan Culture." *Journal of Folklore Research* 30(2–3):143–76.

———. 1995. "The Emergence of Community in Computer-Mediated Communication." In S. G. Jones, ed., *Cybersociety: Computer-Mediated Communication and Community,* 138–63. Thousand Oaks, Calif.: Sage.

277

———. 1996. "Agreements and Disagreements in a Computer-Mediated Discussion." *Research on Language and Social Interaction* 29(4): 315–34.

———. 2000. *Tune in, Log on: Soaps, Fandom, and Online Community.* Thousand Oaks, Calif.: Sage.

Benedikt, Michael. 1991. "Cyberspace: Some Proposals." In Michael Benedikt, ed., *Cyberspace: First Steps,* 119–224. Cambridge, Mass.: MIT Press.

Berger, Peter, and Thomas Luckmann. 1966. *The Social Construction of Reality.* New York: Anchor Books.

Bernardi, Daniel Leonard. 1998. *Star Trek and History: Race-ing toward a White Future.* New Brunswick, N.J.: Rutgers University Press.

Bettie, Julie. 1995. "Class Dismissed? *Roseanne* and the Changing Face of Working-Class Iconography." *Social Text* 45(winter): 125–50.

Boehlefeld, Sharon Polancic. 1996. "Doing the Right Thing: Ethical Cyberspace Research." *Information Society* 12(2): 141–52.

Bornstein, Kate. 1994. *Gender Outlaw: On Men, Women, and the Rest of Us.* New York: Vintage Books.

Brail, Stephanie. 1996. "The Price of Admission: Harassment and Free Speech in the Wild, Wild West." In L. Cherny and E. R. Weise, eds., *Wired_Women,* 141–57. Seattle, Wash.: Seal Press.

Brown, Karen McCarthy. 1991. *Mama Lola: A Vodou Priestess in Brooklyn.* Berkeley: University of California Press.

Bruckman, Amy S. 1992. "Identity Workshop." Paper available on the World Wide Web at http://www.cc.gatech.edu/fac/Amy.Bruckman/papers/index.html. (August 3, 2001.)

———. 1993. "Gender Swapping on the Internet." Proceedings of INET '93. Reston, Va.: The Internet Society. Available on the World Wide Web at http://www.cc.gatech.edu/fac/Amy.Bruckman/papers/index.html. (August 3, 2001.)

———. 1994. "Programming for Fun: MUDs as a Context for Collaborative Learning." Paper presented at the National Educational Computing Conference in Boston, Mass., June 1994. Available on the World Wide Web at http://www.cc.gatech.edu/fac/Amy.Bruckman/papers/index.html. (August 3, 2001.)

Burkhalter, Byron. 1996. "Race in Cyberspace: The Culture of Costless Communities." Paper presented at the annual meetings of the Pacific Sociological Association, March 22, Seattle, Wash.

Burris, Beverly, and Andrea Hoplight. 1996. "Theoretical Perspectives on the Internet and CMC." Paper presented at the annual meetings of the American Sociology Association, August 17, New York.

Butler, Judith. 1990. *Gender Trouble: Feminism and the Subversion of Identity.* New York: Routledge.

———. 1993. *Bodies That Matter: On the Discursive Limits of "Sex."* New York: Routledge.

Byrne, Noel. 1978. "Sociotemporal Considerations of Everyday Life Suggested by an Empirical Study of the Bar Milieu." *Urban Life* 6(4): 417–38.

Calagione, John, and Daniel Nugent. 1992. "Workers' Expressions: Beyond Accommodation and Resistance on the Margins of Capitalism." In John Calagione, Doris Francis, and Daniel Nugent, eds., *Workers' Expressions: Beyond Accommodation and Resistance*, 1–11. Albany, N.Y.: State University of New York Press.

Camp, L. Jean. 1996. "We Are Geeks, and We Are Not Guys: The Systers Mailing List." In L. Cherny and E. R. Weise, eds., *Wired_Women*, 114–25. Seattle, Wash.: Seal Press.

Cavan, Sherri. 1966. *Liquor License: An Ethnography of Bar Behavior.* Chicago: Aldine.

Cheng, Cliff. 1996. "We Choose Not to Compete: The 'Merit' Discourse in the Selection Process, and Asian and Asian-American Men and Their Masculinity." In C. Cheng, ed., *Masculinities in Organizations*, 177–200. Thousand Oaks, Calif.: Sage.

Cherny, Lynn. 1994. "Gender Differences in Text-Based Virtual Reality." In Mary Bucholtz et al., eds., *Cultural Performances: Proceedings of the Third Berkeley Women and Language Conference*, 102–15. Berkeley: Berkeley Women and Language Group, University of California.

———. 1995. "The Mud Register: Conversational Modes of Action in a Text-Based Virtual Reality." Ph.D. dissertation, Stanford University.

———. 1999. *Conversation and Community: Chat in a Virtual World.* Stanford: CSLI Publications.

Clerc, Susan. 1995. "Estrogen Brigades and 'Big Tits' Threads: Media Fandom Online and Off." In L. Cherny and E. R. Weise, eds., *Wired_Women*, 73–97. Seattle, Wash.: Seal Press.

Clifford, James. 1986. "Introduction: Partial Truths." In James Clifford and George E. Marcus, eds., *Writing Culture: The Poetics and Politics of Ethnography*, 1–26. Berkeley: University of California Press.

Cockburn, Cynthia. 1985. *Machinery of Dominance: Women, Men and Technical Know-How.* London: Pluto Press.

Collins, Patricia Hill, et al. 1995. "Symposium on West and Fenstermaker's 'Doing Difference.'" *Gender and Society* 9(4): 491–513.

Communication Studies 298. 1997. "Fragments of Self at the Postmodern Bar." *Journal of Contemporary Ethnography* 26(3): 251–92.

Connell, R. W. 1995. *Masculinities.* Berkeley: University of California Press.

Correll, S. 1995. "The Ethnography of an Electronic Bar: The Lesbian Cafe." *Journal of Contemporary Ethnography* 24(3): 270–98.

Coupland, Douglas. 1995. *Microserfs.* New York: ReganBooks.

Deuel, Nancy. 1995. "Our Passionate Response to Virtual Reality." In Susan C. Herring, ed., *Computer-Mediated Communication: Linguistic, Social and Cross-Cultural Perspectives*, 129–46. Amsterdam: John Benjamins.

Dibbell, Julian. 1993. "Rape in Cyberspace, or How an Evil Clown, a Haitian Trickster Spirit, Two Wizards, and a Cast of Dozens Turned a Database into a Society." Paper available on the World Wide Web at http://www.levity.com/Julian/bungle_vv.html. (August 3, 2001.)

Dickel, M. H. 1995. "Bent Gender: Virtual Disruptions of Gender and Sexual Identity." *Electronic Journal of Communication* 5: 95–117.

Duneier, Mitchell. 1992. *Slim's Table: Race, Respectability, and Masculinity.* Chicago: University of Chicago Press.

Ehrenreich, Barbara. 1989. *Fear of Falling: The Inner Life of the Middle Class.* New York: Pantheon Books.

Faderman, Lillian. 1989. "A History of Romantic Friendship and Lesbian Love." In Barbara Risman and Pepper Schwartz, eds., *Gender in Intimate Relationships: A Microstructural Approach,* 26–31. Belmont, Calif.: Wadsworth.

Feagin, Joe R., and Hernan Vera. 1995. *White Racism.* New York: Routledge.

Fine, Gary Alan. 1983. *Shared Fantasy: Role-Playing Games as Social Worlds.* Chicago: University of Chicago Press.

———. 1987a. "One of the Boys: Women in Male-Dominated Settings." In M. S. Kimmel, ed., *Changing Men: New Directions in Research on Men and Masculinity.* Newbury Park, Calif.: Sage.

———. 1987b. *With the Boys.* Chicago: University of Chicago Press.

Fischer, Claude S. 1992. *America Calling: A Social History of the Telephone to 1940.* Berkeley: University of California Press.

Fitzgerald, Frances. 1986. *Cities on a Hill: A Journey through Contemporary American Cultures.* New York: Simon & Schuster.

Foner, Leonard N. 1993. "What's an Agent Anyway?" Paper available on the World Wide Web at http://foner.www.media.mit.edu/people/foner/Julia/Julia.html. (September 7, 2001.)

Frankel, Mark S., and Sanyin Siang. 1999. "Ethical and Legal Aspects of Human Subjects Research on the Internet: A Report of a Workshop." Washington, D.C.: American Association for the Advancement of Science. Paper available on the World Wide Web at www.aaas.org/spp/dspp/sfrl/projects/intres/main.htm. (September 7, 2001.)

Frankenberg, Ruth. 1993. *The Social Construction of Whiteness: White Women, Race Matters.* Minneapolis: University of Minnesota Press.

Fuller, Mary, and Henry Jenkins. 1995. "Nintendo® and New World Travel Writing: A Dialogue." In Steven G. Jones, ed., *Cybersociety,* 57–72. Thousand Oaks, Calif.: Sage.

Fuss, Diana. 1989. *Essentially Speaking: Feminism, Nature and Difference.* New York: Routledge.

Garber, Marjorie. 1992. *Vested Interests: Cross-Dressing and Cultural Anxiety.* New York: HarperCollins.

Geertz, Clifford. 1973. *The Interpretation of Cultures.* New York: Basic Books.

Gergen, Kenneth J. 1991. *The Saturated Self: Dilemmas of Identity in Contemporary Life.* New York: Basic Books.

Gibson, William. 1984. *Neuromancer.* New York: Ace Science Fiction Books.

Gilroy, P. 1987. *"There Ain't No Black in the Union Jack": The Cultural Politics of Race and Nation.* Chicago: University of Chicago Press.

Goffman, Erving. 1959. *The Presentation of Self in Everyday Life*. New York: Anchor Books.

———. 1963. *Stigma: Notes on the Management of Spoiled Identity*. New York: Simon & Schuster.

———. 1974. *Frame Analysis: An Essay on the Organization of Experience*. Cambridge, Mass.: Harvard University Press.

———. 1981. *Forms of Talk*. Philadelphia: University of Pennsylvania Press.

Goodhart, G. J., A. S. C. Ehrenberg, and M. A. Collins. 1975. *The Television Audience: Patterns of Viewing*. Farnborough, England: Saxon House.

Gray, Herman. 1995. *Watching Race: Television and the Struggle for "Blackness."* Minneapolis: University of Minnesota Press.

Gurak, L. J. 1997. *Persuasion and Privacy in Cyberspace: The Online Protests over Lotus Marketplace and the Clipper Chip*. New Haven, Conn.: Yale University Press.

Hacker, S. 1989. *Pleasure, Power, and Technology: Some Tales of Gender, Engineering, and the Cooperative Workplace*. Boston: Unwin Hyman.

Haddon, L. 1992. "Explaining ICT Consumption: The Case of the Home Computer." In R. Silverstone and E. Hirsch, eds., *Consuming Technologies: Media and Information in Domestic Spaces*, 82–96. London: Routledge.

Hall, Kyra. 1996. "Cyberfeminism." In S. C. Herring, ed., *Computer-Mediated Communication: Linguistic, Social and Cross-Cultural Perspectives*, 147–72). Amsterdam: John Benjamins.

Hansen, Karen. 1992. "'Our Eyes Behold Each Other': Masculinity and Intimate Friendship in Antebellum New England." In Peter M. Nardi, ed., *Men's Friendships*. Newbury Park, Calif.: Sage.

Haraway, Donna. 1991. "A Cyborg Manifesto: Science, Technology, and Socialist-Feminism in the Late Twentieth Century." In Donna Haraway, *Simians, Cyborgs, and Women: The Reinvention of Nature*. New York: Routledge.

Heim, Michael. 1993. *The Metaphysics of Virtual Reality*. New York: Oxford University Press.

Herek, G. M. 1987. "On Heterosexual Masculinity: Some Psychical Consequences of the Social Construction of Gender and Sexuality." In Michael S. Kimmel, ed., *Changing Men: New Directions in Research on Men and Masculinity*, 68–82. Newbury Park, Calif.: Sage.

Herring, Susan C. 1992. "Gender and Participation in Computer-Mediated Linguistic Discourse." Washington, D.C.: ERIC Clearinghouse on Languages and Linguistics, document no. ED345552.

———. 1994. "Politeness in Computer Culture: Why Women Thank and Men Flame." In Mary Bucholtz et al., eds., *Cultural Performances: Proceedings of the Third Berkeley Women and Language Conference*, 278–94. Berkeley: Berkeley Women and Language Group, University of California.

———. 1996a. "Gender and Democracy in Computer-Mediated Communication." In Rob Kling, ed., *Computerization and Controversy*, 476–89. 2d ed. San Diego: Academic Press.

———. 1996b. "Posting in a Different Voice: Gender and Ethics in Computer-Mediated Communication." In Charles Ess, ed., *Philosophical Perspectives on Computer-Mediated Communication*, 115–45. Albany, N.Y.: State University of New York Press.

Hochschild, Arlie Russell. 1997. *The Time Bind: When Work Becomes Home and Home Becomes Work*. New York: Metropolitan Books.

hooks, bell. 1990. *Yearning: Race, Gender, and Cultural Politics*. Boston: South End Press.

Jenkins, Henry. 1992. *Textual Poachers: Television Fans and Participatory Culture*. New York: Routledge.

Katovich, Michael A., and William A. Reese. 1987. "The Regular: Full-Time Identities and Memberships in an Urban Bar." *Journal of Contemporary Ethnography* 16(3): 308–43.

Kendall, Lori. 1996. "MUDder? I hardly know 'er! Adventures of a feminist MUDder." In L. Cherny and E. R. Weise, eds., *Wired_Women*, 207–23. Seattle, Wash.: Seal Press.

———. 1998. "Meaning and Identity in 'Cyberspace': The Performance of Gender, Class and Race Online." *Symbolic Interaction* 21(2): 129–53.

———. 1998. "Are You Male or Female? The Performance of Gender on Muds." In J. Howard and J. O'Brien, eds., *Everyday Inequalities: Critical Inquiries*, 131–54 . London: Basil Blackwell.

Kiesler, S., and L. Sproull. 1986. "Reducing Social Context Cues: Electronic Mail in Organizational Communication." *Management Science* 32(11): 1492–512.

Kiesler, S., J. Siegal, and T. W. McGuire. 1984. "Social Psychological Aspects of Computer-Mediated Communication." *American Psychologist* 39(10): 1123–34.

Kiesler, S., D. Zubrow, A. M. Moses, and V. Geller. 1985. "Affect in Computer-Mediated Communication: An Experiment in Synchronous Terminal-to-Terminal Discussion." *Human-Computer Interaction* 1: 77–104.

King, Storm. 1996. "Research Internet Communities: Proposed Ethical Guidelines for the Reporting of Results." *Information Society* 12(2): 119–28.

Kolko, Beth E. 2000. "Erasing @Race: Going White in the (Inter)Face." In B. Kolko, L. Nakamura, and G. Redman, eds., *Race in Cyberspace*. New York: Routledge.

Kondo, D. K. 1990. *Crafting Selves: Power, Gender, and Discourses of Identity in a Japanese Workplace*. Chicago: University of Chicago Press.

Kramarae, Cheris. 1995. "A Backstage Critique of Virtual Reality." In Steven G. Jones, ed., *Cybersociety*, 36–56. Thousand Oaks, Calif.: Sage.

———, ed. 1988. *Technology and Women's Voices: Keeping in Touch*. New York: Routledge.

Kramarae, Cheris, and H. Jeanie Taylor, eds. 1993. "Women and Men on Electronic Networks: A Conversation or a Monologue?" In H. J. Taylor, C. Kramarae, and M. Ebben, eds., *Women, Information Technology, and Scholarship*, 52–61. Urbana, Ill.: Center for Advanced Studies.

Lea, Martin, T. O'Shea, P. Fung, and R. Spears. 1992. "'Flaming' in Computer-Mediated Communication." In Martin Lea, ed., *Contexts of Computer-Mediated Communication,* 89–112. New York: Harvester Wheatsheaf.

Leiner, B. M., V. G. Cerf, D. D. Clark, R. E. Kahn, L. Kleinrock, D. C. Lynch, J. Postel, L. G. Roberts, and S. Wolff. 1997. "The Past and Future History of the Internet." *Communications of the ACM* 40(2): 102–8.

LeMasters, E. E. 1975. *Blue-Collar Aristocrats.* Madison: University of Wisconsin Press.

Liebow, Elliot. 1967. *Tally's Corner.* Boston: Little, Brown.

Livingstone, Sonia. 1992. "The Meaning of Domestic Technologies: A Personal Construct Analysis of Familial Gender Relations." In R. Silverstone and E. Hirsch, eds., *Consuming Technologies: Media and Information in Domestic Spaces,* 113–30. London: Routledge.

Lyman, Peter. 1998. "The Fraternal Bond as a Joking Relationship: A Case Study of the Role of Sexist Jokes in Male Group Bonding." In Michael S. Kimmel and Michael A. Messner, eds., *Men's Lives,* 171–81. 4th ed. Boston: Allyn and Bacon.

McClintock, Anne. 1995. *Imperial Leather: Race, Gender and Sexuality in the Colonial Contest.* New York: Routledge.

McRae, Shannon. 1997. "Flesh Made Word: Sex, Text and the Virtual Body." In D. Porter, ed., *Internet Culture,* 73–86. New York: Routledge.

Martin, Michele. 1991. *Hello Central? Gender, Technology, and Culture in the Formation of Telephone Systems.* Montreal: McGill-Queen's University Press.

Mercer, Kobena. 1991. "Skin Head Sex Thing: Racial Difference and the Homoerotic Imaginary." In Bad Object-Choices, eds., *How Do I Look? Queer Film and Video,* 169–210. Seattle, Wash.: Bay Press.

Messerschmidt, James W. 1993. *Masculinities and Crime: Critique and Reconceptualization of Theory.* Lanham, Md.: Rowman & Littlefield.

Meyrowitz, Joshua. 1985. *No Sense of Place: The Impact of Electronic Media on Social Behavior.* New York: Oxford University Press.

Miller, Laura. 1995. "Women and Children First: Gender and the Settling of the Electronic Frontier." In James Brook and Iain A. Boal, eds., *Resisting the Virtual Life: The Culture and Politics of Information,* 49–58. San Francisco: City Lights.

Myers, David. 1987. "A New Environment for Communication Play: On-line Play." In Gary Alan Fine, ed. *Meaningful Play, Playful Meaning,* 231–45. Champaign, Ill.: Human Kinetics Publishers.

Nippert-Eng, Christena E. 1996. *Home and Work: Negotiating Boundaries through Everyday Life.* Chicago: University of Chicago Press.

Oldenburg, Ray. 1997. *The Great Good Place: Cafes, Coffee Shops, Community Centers, Beauty Parlors, General Stores, Bars, Hangouts, and How They Get You through the Day.* 2d ed. New York: Marlowe & Co.

Omi, Michael, and Howard Winant. 1994. *Racial Formation in the United States from the 1960s to the 1990s.* 2d ed. New York: Routledge.

Ortner, Sherry B. 1993. "Ethnography among the Newark: The Class of '58 of Weequahic High School." *Michigan Quarterly Review* 32: 410–29.

Penley, Constance. 1991, "Brownian Motion: Women, Tactics, and Technology." In Constance Penley and Andrew Ross, eds., *Technoculture*, 135–62. Minneapolis: University of Minnesota Press.

Pfeil, Fred. 1995. *White Guys*. Verso: London.

Piercy, Marge. 1983. *Woman on the Edge of Time*. New York: Fawcett Crest.

Porter, David. 1997. "Introduction." In David Porter, ed., *Internet Culture*, xi–xviii. New York: Routledge.

Poster, Mark. 1995. *The Second Media Age*. Cambridge, Mass.: Polity Press.

Pratt, Mary Louise. 1986. "Fieldwork in Common Places." In James Clifford and George E. Marcus, eds., *Writing Culture: The Poetics and Politics of Ethnography*, 27–50. Berkeley: University of California Press.

Pred, A. 1996. "Interfusions—Consumption, Identity and the Practices and Power Relations of Everyday Life." *Environment and Planning A* 28(1): 11–24.

Projansky, Sarah. 1996. "When the Body Speaks: Deanna Troi's Tenuous Authority and the Rationalization of Federation Superiority in *Star Trek: The Next Generation* Rape Narratives." In Taylor Harrison, Sarah Projansky, Kent A. Ono, and Elyce Rae Helford, eds., *Enterprise Zones: Critical Positions on Star Trek*, 33–50. Boulder, Colo.: Westview Press.

Radway, Janice. 1991. *Reading the Romance: Women, Patriarchy, and Popular Literature*. Chapel Hill: University of North Carolina Press.

Raymond, E. S. 1991. *The New Hacker's Dictionary*. Cambridge, Mass.: MIT Press.

Reid, Elizabeth. 1994. "Cultural Formations in Text-Based Virtual Realities." M.A. thesis, Department of English, University of Melbourne, Australia.

———. 1996. "Informed Consent in the Study of On-line Communities: A Reflection on the Effects of Computer-Mediated Social Research." *Information Society* 12(2): 169–74.

Reid, Helen, and Gary Alan Fine. 1992. "Self-Disclosure in Men's Friendships: Variations Associated with Intimate Relations." In Peter M. Nardi, ed., *Men's Friendships*. Newbury Park, Calif.: Sage.

Rheingold, Howard. 1991. *Virtual Reality*. New York: Summit Books.

———. 1993. *The Virtual Community: Homesteading on the Electronic Frontier*. Reading, Mass.: Addison-Wesley.

Rosaldo, Renato. 1989. *Culture and Truth: The Remaking of Social Analysis*. Boston: Beacon Press.

Rubin, Lillian. 1985. *Just Friends: The Role of Friendship in Our Lives*. New York: Harper & Row.

Schacht, Steven P. 1997. "Feminist Fieldwork in the Misogynist Setting of the Rugby Pitch: Temporarily Becoming a Sylph to Survive and Personally Grow." *Journal of Contemporary Ethnography* 26(3): 338–63.

Schroeder, Ralph. 1996. *Possible Worlds: The Social Dynamic of Virtual Reality Technology*. Boulder, Colo.: Westview Press.

Schutz, Alfred. 1967. *The Phenomenology of the Social World*. Evanston, Ill.: Northwestern University Press.

Segal, Lynne. 1990. *Slow Motion: Changing Masculinities, Changing Men*. New Brunswick: Rutgers University Press.

———. 1994. *Straight Sex: Rethinking the Politics of Pleasure*. Berkeley: University of California Press.

Sheehan, E. 1993. "The Student of Culture and the Ethnography of Irish Intellectuals." In Caroline B. Brettell, ed., *When They Read What We Write: The Politics of Ethnography*, 75–90. Westport, Conn.: Bergin and Garvey.

Sleeter, Christine E. 1996. "White Silence, White Solidarity." In Noel Ignatiev and John Garvey, eds., *Race Traitor*, 257–65. New York: Routledge.

Smith, Jennifer. 1998. "FAQ #1/3: MUDs and MUDding." Posted periodically to the Usenet newsgroups, rec.games.mud.announce, rec.games.mud.misc, as well as several other newsgroups. Obtained on April 16, 1998, through an Alta Vista search.

Smith, Marc. 1997. "Measuring and Mapping the Social Structure of Usenet." Paper presented at the 17th Annual International Sunbelt Social Network Conference, San Diego, California, February 13–16. Available on the World Wide Web at http://www.sscnet.ucla.edu/soc/csoc/papers/sunbelt97. (September 7, 2001.)

Smith, Michael A. 1985. "A Participant Observer Study of a 'Rough' Working-Class Pub." *Leisure Studies* 4: 293–306.

Smith, Paul. 1993. *Clint Eastwood: A Cultural Production*. Minneapolis: University of Minnesota Press.

Spelman, Elizabeth V. 1988. *Inessential Woman: Problems of Exclusion in Feminist Thought*. Boston: Beacon Press.

Spertus, E. 1991. "Why Are There So Few Female Computer Scientists?" AI Lab Technical Report. Available on the World Wide Web at http://www.ai.mit.edu/people/ellens/Gender/why.html. (September 7, 2001.)

Stacey, Judy. 1996. *In the Name of the Family: Rethinking Family Values in the Postmodern Age*. Boston: Beacon Press.

Stanley, Liz, and Sue Wise. 1993. *Breaking Out Again: Feminist Ontology and Epistemology*. London: Routledge.

Steiner, Peter. 1993. "On the Internet, nobody knows you're a dog." Cartoon from the *New Yorker*, July 5, p. 61.

Sterling, Bruce. 1993. *The Hacker Crackdown*. New York: Bantam Books.

Stone, Allucquere Rosanne. 1991. "Will the Real Body Please Stand Up? Boundary Stories about Virtual Cultures." In Michael Benedikt, ed., *Cyberspace: First Steps*, 81–118. Cambridge, Mass.: MIT Press.

———. 1992. "Virtual Systems." In Jonathan Crary and Sanford Kwinter, eds., *Incorporations*, 608–25. New York: Zone, distributed by MIT Press.

———. 1995. *The War of Desire and Technology at the Close of the Mechanical Age*. Cambridge, Mass.: MIT Press.

Sutton, Laurel. 1994. "Using Usenet: Gender, Power, and Silence in Electronic

Discourse." *Proceedings of the 20th Annual Meeting of the Berkeley Linguistics Society.* Berkeley, Calif.: Berkeley Linguistics Society.

Swain, Scott. 1989. "Covert Intimacy: Closeness in Men's Friendships." In Barbara Risman and Pepper Schwartz, eds., *Gender in Intimate Relationships: A Microstructural Approach,* 71–86. Belmont, Calif.: Wadsworth.

Thomas, Jim, ed. 1996. "The Ethics of Fair Practices for Collecting Social Science Data in Cyberspace." Special issue of *Information Society* 12(2).

Thorne, Barrie. 1980. "You Still Takin' Notes?" *Social Problems* 27(3).

———. 1993. *Gender Play: Girls and Boys in School.* New Brunswick, N.J.: Rutgers University Press.

Tolkien, J. R. R. 1966. *The Lord of the Rings.* 2d ed. London: Allen and Unwin.

Traweek, Sharon. 1988. *Beamtimes and Lifetimes: The World of High Energy Physicists.* Cambridge, Mass.: Harvard University Press.

Turkle, Sherry. 1984. *The Second Self: Computers and the Human Spirit.* New York: Simon & Schuster.

———. 1988. "Computational Reticence: Why Women Fear the Intimate Machine." In C. Kramarae, ed., *Technology and Women's Voices: Keeping in Touch,* 41–61. New York: Routledge.

———. 1990. "Epistemological Pluralism—Styles and Voices within the Computer Culture." *Signs* 16(1): 128–57.

———. 1995. *Life on the Screen: Identity in the Age of the Internet.* New York: Simon & Schuster.

Ullman, E. 1995. "Out of Time: Reflections on the Programming Life." In J. Brook and I. A. Boal, eds., *Resisting the Virtual Life: The Culture and Politics of Information,* 131–44. San Francisco: City Lights.

Virnoche, Mary E. 1997. "When a Stranger Calls: Strange Making Technologies and the Transformation of the Stranger." Paper presented at the Pacific Sociological Association Meetings, San Diego, California.

Wajcman, J. 1991. *Feminism Confronts Technology.* University Park, Pa.: Pennsylvania State University Press.

Wakeford, N. 1996. "Sexualised Bodies in Cyberspace." In S. Chernaik, M. Deegan, and A. Gibson, eds., *Beyond the Book: Theory, Culture, and the Politics of Cyberspace,* 93–104. Oxford: Office for the Humanities Communication, Humanities Computing Unit, Oxford University Computing Services.

Walker, Karen. 1994. "Men, Women, and Friendship: What They Say, What They Do." *Gender & Society* 8(2): 246–65.

Waskul, Dennis, and Mark Douglas. 1996. "Considering the Electronic Participant: Some Polemical Observations on the Ethics of On-line Research." *Information Society* 12(2): 129–40.

We, Gladys. 1994. "Cross-Gender Communication in Cyberspace." *Arachnet Electronic Journal on Virtual Culture* 2. Paper available on the World Wide Web at http://cpsr.org/cpsr/gender/we_cross_gender. (September 7, 2001.)

Wellman, Barry. 1997. Book review. *Contemporary Sociology* 26(4): 445–49.

West, Candace, and Sarah Fenstermaker. 1995. "Doing Difference." *Gender and Society* 9(1): 8–37.

West, Candace, and Don Zimmerman. 1987. "Doing Gender." *Gender and Society* 1 (2, June): 125–51.

Wheelock, Jane. 1992. "Personal Computers, Gender and an Institutional Model of the Household." In R. Silverstone and E. Hirsch, eds., *Consuming Technologies: Media and Information in Domestic Spaces*, 97–112. London: Routledge.

Whyte, William F. 1955. *Street Corner Society*. 2d ed. Chicago: University of Chicago Press.

Willis, Paul E. 1981. *Learning to Labor: How Working Class Kids Get Working Class Jobs*. New York: Columbia University Press.

Wright, R. 1996. "The Occupational Masculinity of Computing." In C. Cheng, ed., *Masculinities in Organizations*, 77–96. Thousand Oaks, Calif.: Sage.

Index

@, use of, 230, 259n11
@dest, meaning of, 176, 262n4

AberMUDs, 40, 41
Adams, P. C., 5
administration, of muds: changes in, 259n9; sanctions in, 64–67; social norms and, 62–63. *See also* wizards
African Americans, as mudders, 209–10, 213
age, 15, 20, 22, 90
AI (artificial intelligence) programs, 113, 261n3
Alien (film), 67
Alisa (pseud.), 34, 67, 117, 144, 147; on mud administration, 63–64; muds run by, 42; on newbies, 135–37; on race, 203–4, 211
Allen, Christina Lee, 157, 242, 264n7
allia (pseud.), 147, 172
American Anthropological Association, 263–64n6
American Association for the Advancement of Science, 241–42
American Sociological Association (ASA), 236
America Online (AOL), 259n14
Amnesia (pseud.), 101–3, 105, 120, 224
Anderson, Benedict, 5

Anguish (pseud.): on race, 210–11, 212; sexual relationships and, 92–93
AniMUCK, 18
anonymity, 111–12, 166; of guest characters, 129–30; limitations of, 221–26; online relationships and, 163–64; racial issues and, 215–16; uncomfortable topics and, 163
anthropomorphic animal–themed muds, 45–46
antifurries. *See* Surly Gang
AOL (America Online), 259n14
artificial intelligence (AI) programs, 113, 261n3
ASA (American Sociological Association), 236
Asian Americans, on race and ethnicity, 205–12
Aspnes, Jim, 40–42
Atticus (pseud.), 129, 156, 160, 198
audience: ambiguity of, 213–14, 216; eavesdropping and invasions by, 126–27; for special interest programs, 261n7
Aurora (pseud.), 139–41

babes, use of term, 82–84, 88
Barbie (pseud.): disappearances of, 148, 151–53; names and gender of, 61, 118–19, 120; on offline meet-

289

linked to, 182–83; stereotypes of, 91, 96–97, 101–3, 105
feminism, ethnographic practices and, 243–45
Fenstermaker, Sarah, 187
Fine, Gary Alan, 98, 167–68
Fitzgerald, Frances, 22
flames and flaming, 4, 11, 167, 255n2
Florin (pseud.): research supported by, 238–39; sanction against, 65, 66; triggers built by, 218–19
fnord (pseud.), 146, 203, 263n4
Foner, Leonard N., 116
Frankel, Mark S., 242
Frankenberg, Ruth, 201–2, 204
Fred (pseud.), gender switching of, 101–3, 105, 224
friendships (on- and offline), 141–42, 142–43, 146–48, 165–66, 166–67; gender and, 167–70, 170–79; geographic location and, 144–46
Fuller, Mary, 18
furries, 45–46

games and gaming, 37, 40–43, 50, 95, 257n5. *See also* role-playing muds
GammaMOO, 18, 19, 22, 104, 124–25, 263n4
Garber, Marjorie, 223
gays, 90, 105, 106–7
Geertz, Clifford, 233
gender: absence/presence of (online), 95–96, 220–26; assumptions about, 153–54; attitudes toward, 71–72; of BlueSky participants, 20, 90, 95; of characters and character names, 34, 35, 50–51, 72, 260n1; class identities and, 193–95; computer use and, 185–86; construction of, 170–79; as exchangeable or malleable, 222; friendship and, 169; invasions and, 127, 261n10; of nerds, 88; of participants, in real life, 124–25; performance of, 107–8; pronouns for, 101, 102, 104, 260n1; restroom object and, 50–51; sexuality linked

to, 84–90, 95–96, 172, 175, 177–79; as signifier, 215–16; social norms of, 10–11, 107. *See also* femininity; masculinities; men; sexuality; women
gender switching, 11, 100–101; dislike of, 124–25; examples of, 101–7; reification of roles through, 222–24; romantic online relationships and, 119–20; TinySex and, 120–21. *See also* masquerades
GEnie, 259n14
George (pseud.), 52–53
Gergen, Kenneth J., 9, 137, 224
Gilroy, P., 209
gods, use of term, 257n9. *See also* wizards
Goffman, Erving, 8, 9, 157, 214, 224
Gravity (pseud.), 48
group identity, 85–87, 170–79. *See also* BlueSky participants; mud culture
guest characters, 65 129–30, 130–32, 136; harassment of, 132–35, 138; hostility toward, 135–36. *See also* newbies
Gurak, L. J., 241, 242

Hacker, S., 98, 100
hackers, as nerds, 94
Haddon, L., 185
HalfLife (pseud.), 58, 203
HappyHour (mud), 18, 63
harassment: invasions as, 127; of newbies and guests, 132–36; racial, 212, 215–16. *See also* sexual harassment
Heisenbug Uncertainty Principle, 79–80
Hello Kitty, 52–53
henri (pseud.), 14, 20, 32, 51, 55–56, 57, 67–68, 74–78, 188; on combining mudding and work, 26, 27, 29, 38, 39; diving platform object and, 48–49; gender discussion and, 175–78; guest characters and, 130–32; nerd identity and, 82–83; object

Compositor:	Binghamton Valley Composition
Text:	10/13 Aldus
Display:	Aldus
Printer and Binder:	Maple-Vail Manufacturing Group

Apricot Press Order Form

Book Title	Quantity	x	Cost / Book	=	Total

All Cook Books are $9.95 US.   All other books are $6.95 US.

Do not send Cash. Mail check or money order to:
**Apricot Press   P.O. Box 1611
American Fork, Utah   84003**
Telephone 801-756-0456
Allow 3 weeks for delivery.

**Quantity discounts available.
Call us for more information.**
9 a.m. - 5 p.m. MST

Sub Total =

Shipping = $2.00

Tax 8.5% =

Total Amount
Enclosed =

Shipping Address

Name:

Street:

City: State:

Zip Code:

Telephone:

Email: